STIRLING
The Royal Burgh

CRAIG MAIR

JOHN DONALD PUBLISHERS LTD
in association with
STIRLING DISTRICT LIBRARIES

For my friend
Kenneth Gray

First published in hardback, 1990
First paperback edition, 1995

The colour photographs of Stirling Castle and Bridge on the
front and back covers are reproduced by permission of
Loch Lomond, Stirling & Trossachs Tourist Board.

ISBN 0 85976 420 6

Phototypeset by WestKey Ltd, Falmouth, Cornwall
Printed and bound in Great Britain by Bell & Bain Ltd, Glasgow

Preface

This is intended as a straightforward history of Stirling for general readers. It has not been easy to compress the story of many centuries into one volume, and in doing so I have made two compromises.

Firstly, in an effort to paint the wide sweep of Stirling's history I have sacrificed many details—those interesting stories and personal reminiscences which often colour in the bare story of a town. Many specialised topics, such as the story of local industries, or of Stirling's various churches, and especially of the town during this century, could have been books in themselves. Fortunately, while there has never been a suitable broad history of the town, numerous articles, such as those in the *Forth Naturalist and Historian* (particularly by John Harrison), or Stirling District Council's *Community Heritage Booklets,* or the various books written by Bob McCutcheon or Tom Lannon, do offer much on specific topics. The *Proceedings* of antiquarian groups such as the Stirling Natural History and Archaeological Society, while variable in quality, are also well worth delving into. I have certainly not tried to repeat everything which these publications already contain; I see them as adding details to the broader picture which I have tried to paint.

Secondly, I have compromised on the old Scots language; the burgh council, guildry, trades, court and kirk records contain a wonderfully rich vein of dialect and spelling which throws light on how our forefathers spoke. I have reluctantly translated most extracts into more modern English but I accept that, in doing so, much of the flavour of Stirling's history has been diluted. On the other hand, the original records are always waiting at the Regional Archives department for those who wish to read them.

There are no references or footnotes, but I have indicated in passing some of my most obvious sources of information. I am particularly indebted to Lorna Main the Regional Archaeologist, to Michael MacGuinness at the Smith Museum, to Alan Borthwick for help in deciphering old documents while he still worked at the Regional Archives and, quite exceptionally, to Regional Archivist George Dixon who unhesitatingly gave hours of his time and knowledge, and without whom this book would never have been completed. These people have all given unfailing and patient assistance on a host of varied topics. Their collective knowledge has added much which mere books or photographs could never have done.

Many other people have helped by providing access to books, maps or pictures. Illustrations have been acknowledged in captions but I thank the following for their particular help with pictures or information: Chris Walker, Librarian at Wallace High School; Malcolm Allan of the Dr W. H. Welsh Historical and Educational Trust; Andrew Muirhead of Stirling District Libraries; Alastair MacLaren at the Regional Archives department; Ken Gray and Margaret Sutherland of the Bridge of Allan Local History Group; Jack Sutherland of the Stirling Camera club; and David Angus, local historian and Burns enthusiast.

I also acknowledge notes made by myself at various lectures or talks: the Reverend Ian Davidson's series on the Church of the Holy Rude; Alan Brotchie on Stirling's trams; Betty Willsher on the Logie kirkyard; John Walker on flying pioneers in the Stirling area; Eric Simpson on Bridge of Allan as a spa; Dr Ewan Mackie on the Leckie Broch; and Dr Lawrence Keppie on the Romans in the Stirling area.

Finally, I thank my wife Anne, without whose patience and understanding this book might never have been written. Many meals have gone cold while I worked at the Archives, the Smith Museum or the University, or rushed off to photograph in suitable light. I apologise now, and thank her for her support.

Bridge of Allan C.M.

HEARTLAND

To this town I lately came,
A stranger from the southern country;
On a night of stars and rain
Crossed that long-disputed boundary.
Found a place and called it home
Here beside the flowing water,
And though this land was not my own
I heard it call so sharp and clear to me.

See the Forth from Flanders wind
Between the crag and castle turning;
Close below the highland line
Hills of gold in sunrise burning.
Here where north and south converge,
The course of history's pathway forging
A cradle for that fateful urge,
To fight for freedom's riches or to fall.

But the past is least of all
Amongst this wealth of new-found treasure.
Folk whose worth is seldom small
Gild the cup and fill the measure.
Friendship's hand extends to me,
Love and laughter intertwining;
Would that I might worthy be
Of all that I receive on every side.

Climbing to the western height,
Mist upon the carseland swirling;
Watch the dawn's revealing light
Advance across the plains of Stirling.
May my life its fullness run,
Here between the firth and mountain,
By this heartland fairly won,
No more to wander restless and alone.

—Song by Rob Griffith

Contents

Introduction

Every town has its own story, the chronicle of its people and their everyday lives. In that sense, Stirling's is little different from that of any other place—but Stirling has much more. From the dawn of recorded events the burgh has influenced the course of the Scottish nation's destiny. The very name *Stirling*, whether it is spelled Strivelin, Streueling, Stryveling, Strigh-lang or any of the other variations which occur in history, seems to mean 'the place of strife'—as well it might. Six battlefields, each crucial to the story of Scotland, can be seen from the top of the Wallace Monument—itself a memorial to one of Scotland's greatest warrior heroes.

Stirling stands at the heart of Scotland, geographically and historically. For centuries its bridge was the lowest road crossing-point on the River Forth, forcing every invading army, from the Romans to the English and the Jacobites, to pass that way. Stirling Castle, perched on an overlooking crag, protected the bridge and kept watch over the Highlands. As a palace the castle was also a place of safety for generations of Scottish kings and queens; many were either born, crowned or died within the security of its walls. Many Scottish Parliaments were also held at the Castle, or at nearby Cambuskenneth Abbey, and Stirling became a centre for Scotland's nobility and courtiers—some of their fine town-houses still survive, close to the palace.

The town was also important. The great medieval church of the Holy Rude ranks as one of the finest in Scotland. The town wall is the only good example still surviving in Scotland. Over the centuries its ancient streets have echoed to the words of Wallace, Bruce, Mary Queen of Scots, John Knox, Bonnie Prince Charlie and a host of other names from the pageant of Scotland's past. As a river port Stirling has seen centuries of bustle, a vital trading place and market burgh equally at home with Highland cattle drovers or Dutch merchants from the Continent.

Above all, the town has treasured its royal connections. Created by David I as one of the four oldest royal burghs in Scotland, it has for over eight centuries watched an endless cavalcade of kings and queens pass through its gates. It has welcomed monarchs who knew only Gaelic and others who spoke only French, and rung bells in salute to everyone from Robert the Bruce to Queen Victoria and beyond. It has witnessed royal christenings, coronations, marriages, births, kidnappings and executions. With the possible exception of Edinburgh, no other burgh in Scotland can truly claim to have such a royal pedigree as Stirling.

Today the community is a medium-small shopping town, not very industrial or modern, but with a university, a strong tourist trade, a magnificent scenic setting, and a wonderfully rich heritage. In spite of growth and changes over the years that colourful, human, unbreakable thread of its history is still perhaps Stirling's greatest asset. It is a history well worth telling.

CHAPTER 1

Life Before the Burgh

Stirling is a wonderful place to visit or come home to, for no matter which route you take, the view on arrival is superb. As you come from Edinburgh through Bannockburn, the town appears to descend elegantly from the castle on its commanding hilltop to a wider spread of houses on the flatter land around. Taking instead the motorway from Edinburgh or Glasgow, the view is largely obscured by undulations until, quite unexpectedly, the castle appears to the right perched on the very edge of precipitous cliffs—a stirring sight indeed, often heightened by a magnificent backdrop of snowy highland peaks in the distance.

If you approach from the west by Kippen and Gargunnock the castle on its high vantage point can be seen from some distance, but as it grows steadily larger, so a craggy skyline of rooftops, spires and towers, the details of an old historic town, also emerge to stir the interest of many a traveller. Coming instead from Dunblane, there is no hint of Stirling's presence until the road crests a rise at the Hill of Keir and offers a first distant view of the castle, standing high on guard over a huddle of rooftops. As you continue on through Bridge of Allan, the castle can again be glimpsed between nearer houses or trees until, as you pass by Stirling University, the town's sloping skyline stands out against the southern light in sharp-edged relief. This ridge, similar to the view of Edinburgh's royal mile from Princes Street, grows larger as the road leads on by an elegant Victorian bridge over the River Forth and so into the town. Some might choose to cross instead by Stirling's more famous sixteenth-century bridge but the effect is similar for, once across, the traveller is soon absorbed into the town. It is, quite simply, a place which excites the senses and invites discovery.

Today Stirling is a town of about forty thousand people, the current custodians of a heritage which goes back over eight hundred years to the twelfth century, when the town was first granted a burgh charter. The most obvious landmark is the castle, from which a long hill slopes down towards the modern town's main shopping area and railway station. The oldest part of Stirling survives on this hill; the Holy Rude kirk dates back to the 1450s and several houses were built during the sixteenth and seventeenth centuries. Parts of a sixteenth-century town wall surround this 'top of the town' area, conveniently marking for visitors and locals alike the limits of the original burgh.

As with Edinburgh, which developed on a very similar site, the 'old town' is now only the heart of a much larger community. Over the past two centuries especially, Stirling has gradually spread to include villages like Torbrex, St Ninians and Causewayhead—once quite separate communities which are now fully integrated into a growing patchwork of housing estates and zones for light industry. Today the spread has continued and threatens to engulf the neighbouring, but still fiercely independent, communities of Bannockburn, Cambusbarron, Bridge of Allan and Cambuskenneth. The burgh may be old, but it is still a living, growing place.

One of the best vantage points from which to view the modern town is the top of the Wallace Monument, a prominent Victorian tower which stands above the River Forth on a rocky crag and catches the eye for miles around. From here there is a magnificent view south across the fertile carseland of the Forth Valley towards the spires and smoking chimneys of Stirling. The land is very level, so flat that the river meanders about in a chain of great loops and bends known locally as the windings. All around, to east and west and directly below the monument itself, tidy farms and villages dot the landscape in a patchwork of fields and hints of local industries. Fine straight roads head off towards Alloa, Falkirk and Loch Lomond and a new bridge crosses the Forth at Manor Powis, for this is a busy place, the heart of central Scotland where roads and railways converge to head off again in all directions. But of course this scene was not always so, for in the not-so-distant past the now-peaceful carseland of the Forth was a long, shallow sea loch where oysters and fish, even whales, used to live.

At one time the entire Forth Valley area was covered by thick rivers of ice which ground and scraped their way across the Ochil Hills and Campsie Fells, smoothing and rounding those hills to something like the shape they have today. As the great tongues of ice pushed forward and sometimes partly retreated, they dumped beds of sand and gravel on what is now the carseland, especially around Doune where they still provide an income for sand and gravel merchants to this day. In the same way the ice crunched over an old volcano, pushing loose soil and glacial debris behind a mass of harder lava to create the 'crag and tail' where Stirling's castle and old town stand today.

Eventually, but only about 10,000 years ago, the ice melted and disappeared for ever. Enormous quantities of meltwater first caused a huge lake to form in the low, flattened valley where the ice had once lain, and then as still more ice melted, the level of the North Sea rose and it crept in to create a long sea loch stretching as far as modern Aberfoyle and the upper reaches of the River Forth. The skeletons of whales found at Thornhill, Causewayhead and Blairlogie are evidence of this. Later, with the huge weight of pressing ice now gone, the land began to rise slowly. The sea level fell again, leaving behind several raised beaches like tide marks along the edges of the Forth Valley. These are most obviously seen around Stirling at Annfield where the land drops sharply to the by-pass road below, and at the Craigs which rise from the bus station to Port Street. Another good example is at the university campus where the flat carseland steps up onto the A9 road and Airthrey estate, and then again in two more steps to the foot of the Ochil Hills. Beyond Stirling, the old coastline is easily seen at the Carse of Lecropt, where a back road at Old Keir ascends to the Hill of Row and passes a sandstone cliff well worn by prehistoric tides.

About 6–8,000 years ago the first people ventured into the Forth Valley, 'strandlooping' or camping along the shores of the sea loch in search of whatever food they could find. They were of a Baltic, perhaps Danish, culture and seem to have been heading west towards Loch Lomond. At that time the climate was warmer but wetter than today; much of the higher land was heavily forested while the valley floor was marshy and peaty—the easiest access into this area was therefore along the 25-foot raised beach where there was scope for hunting in the nearby forests or gathering shellfish on the tidal mudflats.

Prehistoric 'kitchen middens' excavated at Polmont, near Falkirk, suggest that the first visitors to this uninhabited, virgin district lived mainly on oysters, supplemented by cockles, mussels, whelks and periwinkles when available. Tools of bone and antler dating from the same period and found at Causewayhead indicate that these people may also have been hunters, eating stranded whales but also catching birds or small animals in the river marshes and hill forests all around. It must have been a bare and very fragile existence.

In due course, about 5,000 years ago, the first Stone Age or Neolithic farmers appeared. They kept cattle and cultivated crops of wheat and barley, and so with less need to keep moving in search of food they settled on the lower slopes of hills all around Stirling; bits of pottery, stone axes and hammers (the sort of objects most likely to survive) have been discovered at Cambusbarron, St Ninians, the Abbey Craig, Dumyat, Keir and so on. Perhaps some of these people were first to occupy the castle rock—as a prominent hill with a convenient slope on which to farm, yet surrounded by protective marshlands, it would have been an inviting place on which to settle. Sadly no evidence survives to offer any clues.

Around 4,000 years ago the first metal workers seem to have moved into the area, some from the Clyde Valley and others by the North Sea route first used much earlier by the strandloopers. These new arrivals, who brought with them the Bronze Age, are today known as the Beaker people because of the clay pots or beakers often associated with their burials. At least four beakers have been found around Stirling, at Cambusbarron and Bridge of Allan.

To begin with, the dead were buried in 'cists' or stone coffins, sometimes covered by a mound or cairn. Numerous cists and cairns have been found at Cambusbarron, Menstrie, Logie, Pendreich, Airthrey and especially Bridge of Allan where the Fairy Knowe is an excellent example. Later the custom changed to cremation and the ashes of the dead were then buried in funerary urns made of clay. Several have been found locally—indeed the site of an entire cremation cemetery was found at Cambusbarron. It suggests a very organised culture, including burial rites (perhaps even religion) and a social system which allowed craftsmen to make metal objects while others farmed. A 'cup and ring' stone found on the King's Park is believed to indicate a Bronze Age metalworking site. The mysterious standing stones at Airthrey must also have had some significance, but exactly what can only be guessed at today.

By about 1500 BC the climate was drier and warmer than before, which encouraged the expanding Bronze Age population to farm still higher on the slopes of hills around the Forth. One of their farm houses was excavated at West Plean and may be typical of others; it was circular with a 23-foot diameter, formed by building a ring of wooden posts, with a central post to support a roof of thatch or rushes. The walls were of wickerwork, with clay pressed into the gaps and skins probably hung up as an additional draught excluder. Animals were probably kept indoors during winter, if only because of their warmth, but there may also have been a fire hearth for cooking—the smoke would have gathered in the pointed roof, which was useful because it would have extinguished rising sparks and killed off bugs before filtering out through the thatch. The entire farm was surrounded by a circular ditch and mound, which can still be seen today.

And so these Bronze Age people came to settle and farm all around Stirling. Over the next thousand years they dropped, buried, threw away or simply lost an interesting assortment of possessions which now shed light on their way of life, including clay food jars, a bronze and metal plate, a stone armlet, several bronze axes and a range of stone or bronze weapons such as arrowheads, spearheads, sword blades, a macehead, a stone knife and a battle-axe (found at St Ninians).

Then came the Celts of the Iron Age. From about 500 BC these new people, famed today as fearsome warriors, began to move in from the south. Soon they dominated the local population, much as the invading Normans in England were later to rule the Anglo-Saxon population. Indeed, just as the Normans spoke French, so the new Celtic landowners also used a foreign language, which emphasised their power over the natives. Unfortunately, just as the local population was growing with this influx of Celtic people, the climate became colder and food production fell. This inevitably caused a struggle in which only the strongest and fittest groups survived.

The incoming Celts belonged to several tribes. One, known to the Romans as the Maeatae, lived mainly in Fife but also on Dumyat, from which the hill reputedly gets its name. The Damnonii lived more to the south-west in Strathclyde while the Votadini were to the south-east in the Lothians, but both tribes also spilled over into the Forth Valley where they fought each other for local supremacy. To make matters worse, the Caledonians of the north also spread down to the Forth—the Stirling area must have been quite a melting pot of rival warlike tribes jostling for power and land.

This is easily shown around Stirling, where almost every strategic hill or crag is crowned with some kind of defensive fort. The earliest type was made by interlacing stones and wooden posts, which were then burned so that the stones melted or fused to form a vitrified defensive wall; an example stands on the Abbey Craig, while even the Gowan Hill beside Stirling Castle is believed to have been a vitrified fort. Those who care to climb to the cannon which stand at the top of this hillock will perhaps notice the defensive ditch and rampart which still surround the summit.

Later the design of local forts improved and developed. They became much larger and more complex, protected by several banks of earth and ditches such as those seen at Dumyat, Gillies Hill, Mill of Keir and elsewhere. These forts were not just places of refuge during times of danger; they seem to have been in day-to-day use, acting as a focus or social centre for people all around. One at Bannockburn which was excavated in 1982 was dated to 495 BC, which indicates how quickly the Celts began to influence and change local life. There were, of course, no towns, roads or even villages as we think of them today in the Forth Valley.

There were some local metalworking craftsmen—metal slag was found near Cambusbarron, for example—but most folk were simply farmers. Signs of their homesteads have been found at Cambusbarron, Bannockburn, Plean, Logie and elsewhere and the area is littered with ditches, dykes, enclosures and hillside cultivation terraces, even on the King's Park in Stirling itself. Several quernstones have also been found to confirm that they grew grain as well as kept cattle.

These were the ordinary people of the Iron Age, but all around Stirling, especially on the Touch Hills where it was safer, there are also signs of the Celtic chiefs who lorded over them. They lived in duns—small but well fortified homesteads where a few huts, probably belonging to just one nobleman's extended family, were clustered inside a defensive stone rampart. An excellent example survives at Castlehill Wood; the stone wall, entrance gate and circular markings of huts can still be clearly seen, while the entire site gains additional protection from surrounding cliffs and steep slopes. It was a carefully chosen site with native farms still detectable nearby, perhaps to keep the Celts well fed. Trees obscure the view today, but when it was occupied the inhabitants of the Castlehill dun would have had a panoramic view in all directions—a vital consideration in those turbulent times.

For five hundred years the Celts had the run of the land, but in AD 80 their power was shaken by the invasion of 20,000 Romans under General Agricola. They came to the Forth Valley to drive the hostile tribes of Caledonia well back from the Roman province of Britannia to the south—in other words, to create a defensive military zone beyond the Roman Empire. No Roman towns were ever established in Scotland and, of course, the very name 'Scotland' was unknown to them since the invasion of the Scots from Ireland did not occur until much later.

Agricola established several forts across the narrow waist of Scotland between the firths of Forth and Clyde, and from there pushed north past modern Dunblane and Perth towards Aberdeen. Somewhere in the north he destroyed 30,000 Celts at the battle of Mons Graupius; Agricola's son-in-law, the historian Tacitus, later claimed that 10,000 were killed for the loss of only 360 Romans, but even allowing for his obvious bias, it is clear that the Celts were heavily defeated. The Romans then consolidated a chain of forts along the highland edge at Ardoch (Braco), Strageath (near Muthill), Bertha (Perth), Inchtuthil (near Dunkeld) and beyond, driving the Celts still further away from the south. Additional signal stations and marching camps were established all along the line, and forts at Callander, Comrie, the Sma' Glen and further on into the highlands bottled up most glens. The Stirling area was therefore within the Roman area of military occupation.

The men in these isolated northern forts were supplied and reinforced by a military road which can still be followed in places today, especially beyond Ardoch and Strageath. Part of it can be picked up in Stirling itself, coming from Torwood down towards St Ninians. From there it swings towards Stirling, cutting through the back gardens of several houses in Snowdon Place before curving round through the King's Park towards Raploch. The road then seems to cross the Forth around Kildean, and heads off across fields to Bridge of Allan.

Stirling is also surrounded by the possible sites of several Roman camps—one was recently found at Old Mills Farm near the Forth at Kildean, for example, and a signal station and camp may have existed at Airthrey. There may also have been something on the castle rock—it would be difficult to imagine the Romans *not* using such an obvious site—but the construction of later castle fortifications has obliterated any signs of them.

Nevertheless, Roman soldiers almost certainly stood on the castle rock. A coin from the reign of Nero was dug up on Lower Castlehill, and another from the time of Tiberius was found on the Upper Craigs. Other coins from this first period of occupation have been discovered at Bridge of Allan and Polmaise, so the Romans were certainly around. Less convincing evidence comes from much-worn inscriptions on a rock near the Ballengeich Road. which separates the Gowan Hill from the Castle rock. Antiquarians of the past used to believe that the lettering commemorated the Second Legion which supposedly kept watch from the crag, and a more recent interpretation suggests that the lettering is an abbreviated shorthand list of Roman army units. The fact is that no-one really knows what the stone records.

Soon after his victory at Mons Graupius, Agricola was recalled to Rome and part of the army was withdrawn to replace losses elsewhere in the empire. The military occupation continued but with less conviction than before; by around 100 AD the army had been withdrawn first from its forward positions north of Ardoch camp at Braco, then from north of the Forth, and eventually to the Cheviot Hills. In 122 AD, following the construction of Hadrian's Wall in northern England, the troops pulled out completely and abandoned all forts in Scotland. No doubt many a celebratory drink was consumed in duns and hillforts all around the Forth!

This withdrawal by the Romans only encouraged the Celts to mount raids on Britannia to the south, so in 142 AD the Romans returned, this time under General Lollius Urbicus. His men reconquered southern Scotland, repaired the earthworks of old abandoned forts, and finally built the Antonine Wall from Bo'ness to Old Kilpatrick on the Clyde. This earth and timber rampart was strengthened by a ditch, signal stations, milecastles and forts every two or three miles along its length, and was in effect a forward frontier line for the Roman empire itself. Much of it can still be seen today, especially around Falkirk. From here the Romans then ventured further north, reoccupying Ardoch and other important forts beyond the Forth so that they must also have returned to the Stirling area. Soon the local tribes were defeated; peace was made and there followed a period of about thirty years during which the

Romans had regular, well-developed contacts with the local population.

By the second century the 'Romans' were mostly not Roman at all. Much of the army was built around auxiliaries—non-Romans who did most of the 'cannon-fodder' fighting in battles in return for Roman citizenship after twenty-five years. It is known that tribesmen from Spain, Germany, Belgium, Syria and Bulgaria all did service in Scotland; by the second century they were being increasingly replaced by Celts from Britannia and even southern Scotland, so that the men who forged links and even friendships with the locals were themselves often Celts, but from tribes now friendly to the Romans.

Somewhere about this time new people may also have moved into the district. They lived in brochs—high, circular, windowless, stone towers otherwise found mainly in the far north and west of Scotland and unique to this country. The remains of four such brochs survive around Stirling, at Torwood near Larbert, Leckie near Gargunnock, Coldoch near Blair Drummond, and Buchlyvie—in other words on the fertile soils of the old raised beaches along the edges of the carseland. They have been compared to medieval manor-houses, built on good arable land and surrounded by the farms of local natives who presumably paid homage to their overlords.

As you stand on the walls of Coldoch broch today, the scene has completely changed; the land still drops to the flat carseland a stone's throw away and offers a clear view southwards to Leckie, but where desolate marshes once flanked the River Forth there is now a green and fertile valley dotted with small farms. In Roman times the people of Leckie would perhaps have seen the daily cooking smoke rise above Coldoch. Perhaps they used long-lost tracks across the marshes to visit each other.

Why these brochs should have existed so far from any others in Scotland is, however, a mystery. They may have been built by a new tribe moving in from the north, or perhaps invited there to form some kind of buffer-state under Roman protection. They may simply be the work of itinerant contractors or builders, moving wherever their broch-building skills were in demand—no-one knows. The broch people must have enjoyed friendly contacts with the Romans, however, for pottery, coins, jewellery and the like have been found in excavations to suggest trade between the two; the locals presumably provided grain or cattle, and perhaps wool. In addition, remains of food including garlic and frogs' legs have also been discovered.

A scattering of Roman glass, pottery, quernstones and coins has been found around Stirling, from Lecropt to Castlehill Wood and St Ninians, suggesting quite a widespread Roman presence beyond the safety of the Antonine Wall. Nevertheless there were risings against the Romans—around 155 AD, for example, the Antonine Wall was completely overrun and its forts were destroyed and burned down. Within a year or two they were rebuilt and the Romans were back, but in 170 AD the Antonine Wall was again abandoned, this time for good, and within ten more years the Romans had retreated to Hadrian's Wall.

In 209 AD the Romans marched north for the last time. In that year an army of about 40,000 men (which says much for the strength of the Celts in Roman eyes), accompanied by a fleet which followed along the eastern coast, set off on a campaign against the Maeatae in Stirlingshire and the Caledonians beyond in the north. It is clear that the Celts were again defeated, for most hillforts and duns around Stirling seem to have been wrecked (although this may have happened earlier, for the evidence is unclear). From excavations undertaken during the 1970s it seems that the Leckie broch was also destroyed, probably by besieging Roman catapults which set the tower on fire, following which it was deliberately pulled down. No bodies were discovered under the ruins, suggesting that the fleeing inhabitants were perhaps slaughtered outside or were taken into captivity and eventually slavery. By 211 AD, however, the Romans were gone from the Forth Valley for good, leaving only fragmentary signs that they were ever there at all.

The period from the end of the Romans to the twelfth century has often been called the Dark Ages—not because it saw a collapse of civilisation or was a time of barbarity, but because so little is known about those years. It seems that the various Celtic tribes may have blended into the race now called the Picts, but during this period new peoples also came to Scotland. The departure of the Romans from England around 400 AD left a power vacuum which was filled by incoming European tribes of Angles, Saxons and Danes; they soon occupied most of the English east coast and began moving up through Northumbria into Lothian, and so into the Forth Valley. These invasions pushed native Britons across the

Pennines to the west; Britonic kingdoms appeared in Cornwall, Wales, Cumbria and Strathclyde (where the name Dumbarton probably means 'dun of the Britons'); soon they also began to explore the upper Forth area. Around the year 500 AD the Scots migrated from Ireland to Argyll (which they called Dalriada), and from there began to move inland towards Loch Earn and so down towards the Forth. Once again, the Stirling area became a battle-ground for power between rival peoples who clashed in the central lowlands—the 'crossroads of four different cultural streams' as one writer has described it.

The areas occupied by these peoples can be indicated by a study of local place-names. Explained simply, Pictish place-names such as those beginning with *pit* or *aber* (as in Pitlochry or Abernethy) are plentiful north of the Ochils but then thin out around the River Forth. The name Manau, found at Clackmannan or Slamannan in the Forth Valley, derives from the Manau Goddodin tribe of Celtic Britons—perhaps the most powerful group to occupy the area following the Roman departure. Scots names such as *bal* (Balfron, Balmaha, Balquhidder etc), or *auch* (Auchterarder) or *kil* (Killearn, Kilmadock, Kilsyth) are commonly found in the west but also peter out towards Stirling. The Angle-ish or English area in Lothian can be traced by place-names ending with *ham, ton* and *ing* (though Stirling itself is probably not from the same root)—these dwindle in number around Falkirk, suggesting that this influence also barely stretched to Stirling. In other words, Stirling's castle rock and the river crossing which it dominated, lay at the extremity of several powerful kingdoms—a vital border defence for whichever people could hold it.

From the scant evidence which survives, it would seem that for much of the period the Picts held some sort of fortification on the rock. They were under frequent attack, however. Arthur (of the Round Table), probably a sixth-century king of the Welsh Britons, is supposed to have fought at least one battle in the Caledonian forest—a campaign perhaps intended to check the southern spread of the Picts. Since Stirling was then the lowest crossing point on the Forth, he may have marched, or more likely plundered, through the area. The idea that the King's Knot has anything to do with Arthur's round table is highly unlikely, however. Barbour, writing in the fourteenth century, makes reference to this, but it would seem that, if anything, a mound may have existed which, as elsewhere in Britain, became known later as Arthur's round table. In fact, the existing King's Knot is largely a Victorian recreation of whatever stood there previously.

A number of battles are also recorded against encroaching Angles, notably in 574 AD (when the Scots won), 634 AD (when the Scots lost), and 711 AD (when the Picts lost). These have been vaguely placed by historians anywhere between Stirling and Bo'ness. The Scots also fought the Picts, as in 736 AD when the Picts invaded Dalriada and then destroyed a counter-attack near Falkirk. Then around 843 AD came perhaps the most important contest of all, when the Scots king Kenneth MacAlpin defeated the Picts in a great battle and thereafter united both races under his leadership—at least, that is the story. It has been suggested that the Airthrey estate, now the campus of Stirling University, *may* be the site of that battle—a solitary standing stone near Airthrey Castle may therefore have some significance. At any rate, that battle finally established a Gaelic-speaking kingdom of Scots and Picts north of the Forth and so marked the birth of a distinctive highland culture, as opposed to that of the Britonic and Northumbrian 'sassenachs' who lived south of the river. Once in power, it appears that Kenneth MacAlpin then had Stirling's castle pulled down; any castle in that period would have been wooden, so demolition would have been easy.

This did not, of course, put an end to local warfare. Kenneth MacAlpin died in 858 AD and was succeeded by his brother Donald. Although plagued with mutinous Picts and Viking raids, he nevertheless decided to invade Northumbria and duly captured Berwick. It seems that he then relaxed his guard too much, for the Northumbrians, who were by now mostly Saxons, retaliated. Led by two princes called Osbrecht and Ella, and in alliance with Britons from Cumbria, they surprised and captured Donald and forced him to give them all his land south of the Forth. The poor folk of Stirling thus found themselves again with new masters, for the Northumbrians naturally re-fortified the castle rock as a precaution against the Scots to the north.

In fact a greater danger came from new invasions by the Danes. Worried by this threat, the Northumbrians placed sentries all round the castle, but (so the story goes) one fell asleep at night just when the Danes were sneaking up to attack. The story then goes on: 'The besieging foe was at hand, and was about to take the city, when a wolf, alarmed at the noise and din of the advancing hordes, crept for safety to the crag on which the sleeping soldier lay. But still he found no safety. He growled in terror. It was his wild cry that saved the city. It awoke the sleeping sentinel, who, seeing the position of matters, raised the alarm. He was not yet too late. The citizens arose, buckled on their armour, and drove the Danes from the district; thus the wolf saved the city.' Until 1975 when the town lost its burgh status with regionalisation, Stirling had on its coat of arms the picture of a wolf crouching on a crag.

Two small points should be made about the story. First, Stirling was *not* a city during the ninth century—indeed it barely existed even as a village around a wooden castle. Second, there certainly were wolves in the area at that time. Records from 1288 AD mention payment 'for two park-keepers and one hunter of wolves at Stirling', for example.

The two Northumbrian princes Osbrecht and Ella were later killed while trying to win York back from the Danes. This weakened the Saxons, so around the year 900 AD they apparently made an alliance with the Scots and returned Stirling to them. It does not seem to have been captured again until the time of Wallace and Bruce. Indeed when Kenneth III set off in 973 AD to defeat a Danish invasion at Luncarty in Angus, his army mustered at Stirling, where it is believed he was staying when he sent out the order.

If Kenneth III *was* living at Stirling when the Danes invaded, then it is very significant, for it establishes the castle as one of the Scots' royal strongholds long before the town became a burgh. By this time the king of Scots had organised his territory into a number of 'shires'; in the Forth Valley of the ninth and tenth centuries these certainly existed at Stirling, Falkirk and Clackmannan, and probably also at Dunblane and Doune. Each shire was administered for the king by a 'thane' or lord, with a ladder of social levels below this lord. First came the 'hiredmen', the equivalent of 'honourable servants' or knights. Then followed the 'bonders' and below them the 'gresmen' or ordinary peasant farmers—early documents refer to the gresmen of Airthrey, for example.

These shires (sometimes called 'sokes') have no link with the later shires of medieval or feudal Scotland. They were much smaller, being little more than a scatter of villages around the lord's hall. The shire boundary of Stirling extended north from

Cambusbarron to Cornton, then east to Airth and Bothkennar (Skinflats), then south to Larbert and Dunipace, and back across the Touch Hills to Cambusbarron.

Each village was surrounded by an area of 'fields' further divided into 'oxgangs' and 'ploughgates'—unfenced agricultural strips where the peasants grew oats and barley. The lord owned a mill where the farmers were obliged to have their crops ground—for a charge of course. Cattle were grazed further off on the 'common', usually an area of higher land unsuitable for cultivation; since the shire at Dunblane had the grazing on Sheriffmuir it is possible that Stirling's common was somewhere on the Touch Hills.

Unfortunately nothing visible survives from this time except in documents. Village buildings, indeed even the lord's hall, were made of wood (documents from as late as 1287 mention that stonemasons were actually *building* a castle at Stirling, because it was still such an exceptional thing). It is known, however, that the village locals grew grain, peas and beans. They had no root crops and cut very little hay, so it was difficult to keep animals over a long winter. As a result, although the plough oxen were stabled, most milk cattle were killed in November and their meat was then salted. For a people who also lived close to the Forth, meat and fish were therefore plentiful (for centuries the river was full of salmon). They also seem to have kept many hens, so the local diet included lots of oats, broth, cheese (one way of keeping milk), and barley ale—a way of life which was to last on the castle rock for centuries.

By the ninth century a church also existed at St Ninians (which was then called Eggles or Eccles, the Britonic word for church, suggesting that it was established before the local arrival of Gaelic-speaking Scots in the seventh century). St Ninian, based at Whithorn, was a fifth-century Britonic missionary who worked in the land of the southern Picts but there is no convincing evidence to prove that he, or any of his followers, definitely visited the Stirling area. It is more likely that the church there was simply named in his honour. Nevertheless, between the efforts of the Christian Britons and the later Scots (who brought St Columba's Celtic form of Christianity to Aberfoyle, Dunblane and elsewhere), a network of churches and parishes was established across the Forth Valley. No church is thought to have existed yet at Cambuskenneth or on the site of modern Stirling (except possibly within the castle); the parish was therefore centred on St Ninians from which any other outlying churches were administered.

By the tenth and eleventh centuries the basis of the modern town of Stirling was already in place. There was an important castle on the rock—a stronghold evidently used by Scottish kings as they travelled around the land. There was some sort of primitive wooden-hutted village on the castle hill, and a church community at St Ninians. Perhaps even more important, Stirling stood at the lowest crossing point on the River Forth—a geographical factor which was to force armies and common travellers alike to come by Stirling as they moved north into Scotland. (In the early 1980s, workmen digging on a sewage scheme project uncovered what were said to have been the remains of a ford or causeway just downstream from the present 'new' bridge at Stirling. It was not reported officially in case the work was suspended to allow investigation, so there is no way of knowing how old this alleged ford was.) In 1072 AD, for example, William the Conqueror and his Norman army are known to have crossed the Forth by one of the fords at Stirling, on their way to Abernethy where a peace was signed with Malcolm III. So even before it became a proper town, Stirling was on the Scottish map.

CHAPTER 2

The Making of the Burgh 1120–1290

During the eleventh century Scotland began to develop into the country we think of today. In 1018 Malcolm II defeated the Angles at the battle of Carham and so Lothian and Berwickshire were added to the kingdom of the Scots. When Duncan I came to the throne in 1034 he already ruled in Strathclyde (a kingdom which included Dumfries and Galloway), and so this area too came under Scottish rule. Viking lords still controlled the northern and western isles, but Scotland was otherwise complete. Stirling Castle was therefore no longer a border post on the Forth, but a vital fortification at the very crossroads of the country.

During this period Scotland also began to change. Power shifted south from the Gaelic-speaking Celts and the Irish church of St Columba to a country in which French or Lowland Scots (basically English) was mostly spoken, at least by those who mattered. At the same time the church moved away from the teachings of Iona to those of Rome. From then on, for example, no more Scottish kings were buried with the forty-eight (it is said) who already lay at Iona. It also led to much bitterness and hostility among the Celtic warlords of the north; Scottish kings now had to watch their backs and live in strong castles.

Much of this 'Englishing' of Scotland (it is nothing new!) stemmed from Queen Margaret, the English wife of Malcolm III (or Canmore). She brought Benedictine monks to found Dunfermline Abbey, where she now lies, and was followed by three sons who all became kings of Scotland, and who all continued this process of change. First came Edgar, who not only invited Saxon and Norman lords into Scotland with gifts of land, but further endowed Dunfermline Abbey and also the Roman churches at St Andrews and Coldingham.

When Alexander I came to the throne in 1107 he was immediately faced with a rebellion in the highlands which he subdued with such ferocity that he was thereafter nicknamed 'the

Fierce'. His greatest interest was the church, however; he completed the building of Dunfermline Abbey, made gifts to the church at St Andrews, founded a priory at Loch Tay, an Augustinian monastery at Inchcolm in the Firth of Forth and another at Scone. More interestingly, in the charter which he granted to the monks at Scone, he provided them with five houses in what appear to have been the main towns of the times—Edinburgh, Perth, Inverkeithing, Aberdeen and Stirling.

Alexander seems to have stayed at Stirling Castle quite often. In those days kings did not live mostly in one place but moved around the country, lodging at favoured royal castles until all available food was eaten and the place smelled too much. Then their servants packed up the royal furniture and the royal party moved on to somewhere else. Stirling Castle, with its excellent defensive position and reasonably fertile hinterland from which to feed the royal retinue, was very probably one of these stopping places.

A royal castle at Stirling would have encouraged the growth of a community nearby, with merchants and craftsmen to meet the king's desires, and markets from which to purchase food for the king's household. Almost certainly there was a straggle of wooden or wattle houses, probably where Broad Street is today, with farming strips sloping down the hillside to the marshy land beyond. Almost certainly there were merchants and some craftsmen—metalworkers, tanners, weavers, potters, brewers or bakers perhaps—and markets where the staple foodstuffs of everyday life were exchanged (but not for money, which did not come into circulation until the 1130s).

One of Alexander I's most significant acts was in 1119, when he created Berwick-on-Tweed (then still Scottish) a royal burgh. This was followed, probably in 1120, by the similar creation of Roxburgh. The desire to make these border towns into burghs actually came from Alexander's brother David, who was then Earl of southern Scotland, but the fact is that for the first time, existing Scottish towns were not only given official recognition, but important rights and privileges, by the crown.

A short explanation about burghs would be useful at this point. In France and Norman England the practice of granting royal privileges and freedoms to certain towns was already well established. These privileges usually permitted a town to govern itself with an elected town council, to protect itself with a defensive wall and gates, to form merchant guilds, to enjoy exclusive trade or market rights within a certain district, and to levy tolls on outsiders who came to sell at the burgh market. Further, they allowed the merchants of royal burghs to trade overseas, which gave them exclusive access to foreign luxury goods—for some, the profits from a few luxuries like wine, fine cloth, iron goods or exotic foodstuffs (such as peppers, spices, onions or rice) vastly outweighed the day-to-day income from market stalls.

Such privileges usually ensured undoubted wealth and power for burgh merchants and were certainly well worth having. In return the monarch expected loyalty and fighting men when required, the enforcement of proper law and order in his burgh domains, and a substantial proportion (called a cess) from any customs or tolls charged within a burgh. In early cases, these privileges were usually granted verbally by a king, but were then later confirmed in a written charter which could be renewed, amended or cancelled by any subsequent monarch. So in creating Berwick and Roxburgh, Alexander I was basically copying the Norman system in England, while ensuring the loyalty of two important towns (one a vital seaport and the other an important castle), and raising funds for the royal coffers into the bargain.

It is likely that Alexander also had a new castle built at Stirling. This may have been to replace the previous one, for with big open cooking fires and a wet climate, few wooden buildings can have lasted very long without either burning down or rotting away. Possibly he simply wanted to impress his subjects by having a better castle built at his personal command. In 1124 he also founded a new chapel at the castle, and endowed it with teinds or payments in kind from his local lands. In 1122 his wife died and, making no effort to remarry, Alexander himself died in 1124 at Stirling Castle, from where he was carried to Dunfermline for burial beside his mother.

Having no legitimate children, Alexander was followed as king by his brother David. If anything, King David I was even more under Norman English influence than his brother, having spent his childhood in England and married a Northumbrian duchess. He was also brother-in-law to England's Henry I. Not surprisingly Norman ideas, including the feudal system, still more monasteries and abbeys (including Cambuskenneth at Stirling), and the organisation of shires, continued to spread into Scotland. At the same time more burghs were created, and one of the first was Stirling.

Unfortunately nothing remains of twelfth-century Stirling, so to reconstruct this early period is something of a detective story with most of the clues hidden in old documents. For example, it is not even known for certain when David I first established Stirling as a royal burgh; it was probably in 1124 and certainly no later than 1127. During that same period of four years Edinburgh, Perth and Dunfermline were also created, followed soon after by Aberdeen, Renfrew, Rutherglen, Peebles and Hamilton. David I died in 1153, by which time nine more burghs, namely Jedburgh, Lanark, Linlithgow, Inverkeithing, Crail, Montrose, Elgin, Forres and Inverness had also been established, to form the backbone of Scottish urban life for centuries to come. By a twist of fate Alexander I's original two burghs no longer exist today—Berwick is English and Roxburgh has decayed to ruins—so Stirling can now correctly claim to be one of the four oldest royal burghs in Scotland.

Regrettably David I's original charter (if it was ever written) no longer exists. Stirling's oldest surviving charter is dated 1360 from the reign of David II, but fortunately it quotes the full wording of an older charter granted by Alexander II on August 18th 1226, and extended in 1227. Bearing in mind that certain privileges must already have been given by David I when the burgh was first established, and translating from Latin into tolerable English, this is what Alexander II granted: Alexander, by the grace of God, King of Scots: To bishops, abbots, earls, barons, justiciars, sheriffs, prepositi (bailies), officers, and all good men of his whole land, clerics and lay people, greeting.

Be it known to those present and to come that we have granted, and by our charter confirmed, to our burgesses of Strivelyn (Stirling) a market day in our burgh of Strivelyn, that is to say Saturday in every week; and we have rightly given our firm peace to all who may come to that market; and we strictly forbid anyone wrongly to cause injury or molestation or any trouble to those who shall attend our forsaid market, in coming or returning, upon our full forfeiture [ie punishment].

We also strictly forbid any stranger merchant within the sheriffdom of Strivelyn to buy or sell anything outwith our burgh of Strivelyn, on pain of our interdict, but stranger merchants shall bring their merchandise to our burgh of Strivelyn and there sell the same and exchange their pennies.

Also, if any stranger merchant, upon this our prohibition, shall be found buying or selling anything in the sheriffdom of Strivelyn, he shall be apprehended and detained until we have declared our pleasure concerning him.

We also strictly forbid any stranger merchant to cut his cloth to be sold within our burgh of Strivelyn, except from the day of the ascension of our Lord till the feast of St Peter *ad vincula* (Lammas), within which terms we wish that they cut their cloth to be sold in the market of Strivelyn, and there sell and buy cloth and other merchandise in common with our burgesses in the same manner as our proper burgesses, saving our rights.

We command also that all who dwell in our burgh of Strivelyn, and who wish to take part with our burgesses at the market, shall take part with them in contributing to our aids (taxes), whose men soever they be. We forbid also that any tavern shall be kept in any town in the sheriffdom of Strivelyn, unless where a knight is lord of the town and dwells therein, and there shall not be kept more than one single tavern. We grant also to our said burgesses of Strivelyn that they shall have a merchant guild, except the waulkers and weavers.

We strictly forbid, likewise, that anyone dwelling outside our burgh of Strivelyn in the sheriffdom thereof make, or cause to be made, cloth dyed or shorn within the sheriffdom of Strivelyn, other than our burgesses of Strivelyn who are of the merchant guild, and who take part in paying our aids with our burgesses of Strivelyn, except those who have had their charters with this liberty heretofore.

We strictly forbid anyone in the sheriffdom of Strivelyn to presume to make cloth dyed or shorn, upon our full forfeiture. And if any cloth dyed or shorn shall be found made upon [ie in spite of] this our prohibition, we command our sheriff to seize the said cloth and do thereupon as was the custom in the time of King David.

And all these customs and liberties foresaid we grant, and by this our charter confirm, to our foresaid burgesses of Strivelyn.
Witnesses: Thomas of Strivelyn, chancellor;

Henry of Balliol, chamberlain;
Walter Comyn;

Henry of Strivelyn, son of Earl David;
William of Burgh;
Radulph of Champayn;
Hugh of Cambrun;
William of Lyndesey;
John de Vaux
Walter Byset. At Kyncardyn on the eighteenth day of August in the twelfth year of our reign (ie AD 1226).

In a short amendment written the following year, Alexander II granted additional privileges, to do with exemption from tolls and customs on merchant goods throughout the kingdom:

Alexander, by the grace of God, King of Scots: To all good men of his whole land, greeting. Know ye that we have granted to our burgesses of Strivelyn who are dwelling in the said burgh, that they may forever quit of toll and custom of their proper goods throughout our whole kingdom. Wherefore we firmly forbid that anyone, contrary to this our grant, presume unjustly to trouble them in exacting from them toll or custom of their proper goods.

Witnesses: Master Matthew, chancellor;
John, Earl of Huntyngtoun;
Henry of Balliol, chamberlain;
Henry of Strivelyn, son of Earl David;
Peter de Valine;
Walter Comyn;
Alexander of Strivelyn;
Reginald of Crauford, Sheriff of Are (Ayr). At Edinburgh, on the twentieth day of July in the thirteenth year of our reign.

Thanks to these charters, it is clear that by 1226 Stirling was a well-established town with a sheriff, merchants, craftsmen (waulkers and weavers at the very least), and others of lower status, including innkeepers. The town could also produce people of ability and rank, including the king's own chancellor and at least two others fit to witness a royal document. Moreover, reference to 'the custom in the time of King David' makes it clear that trading regulations and punishments existed from the time of the original charter granted to Stirling in the 1120s.

Fortunately, although few scraps of evidence survive from this period, there is at least more than just a couple of old charters. During the period of David I's reign (1124–53) the Court of the Four Burghs was established; the four burghs in question were Berwick, Roxburgh, Edinburgh and Stirling and it is likely that these were Scotland's most important or senior towns at the time. The 'Court' was a body of representatives from these burghs which established a code of laws and practices for burgh administration and the regulation of trade. It is likely that when this code was produced for the first handful of burghs, many day-to-day trading rules already well-rooted in towns were incorporated into it, further indicating that trade and merchants must have existed in Stirling *before* it became a burgh—in other words, before 1124–27. These laws were then enforced in all Scottish burghs as and when more were created; disputes or questions of interpretation were referred back to the Court. In 1369, since Berwick and Roxburgh were in English hands, King David II replaced them with Lanark and Linlithgow, and the Court of the Four Burghs continued until eventually replaced by the wider Convention of Royal Burghs in the 1550s.

The Stirling burgh seal, reverse side showing a castle. The earliest surviving copy of this seal dates from 1296. *Photo:* The Collections of the Smith Art Gallery and Museum, Stirling.

About thirty copies of the Court's code of laws still survive, written both in Latin and old Scots. Over the centuries new laws were added to the list and some were deleted or amended, but the basic code remained as a blueprint for burgh life until the nineteenth century. Today it gives us an idea of how even very early burghs were organised and regulated, and from it a picture of twelfth-century Stirling can be inferred.

More or less from the start, there seems to have been a town council consisting of 'good men of the town'—burgesses or taxpayers, virtually all of whom were merchants and owned or rented property in the burgh. Each year just after Michaelmas (29th September) this council elected a Propositus or provost, and bailies—their original function was to collect the king's taxes, but they eventually became the burgh magistrates and were more concerned with enforcing burgh law. The earliest known bailie is Richard Brice, whose name appears on a document of 1296 together with those of eleven other burgesses, but it is clear that the arrangement of burgesses and councillors existed long before then.

While the king or his sheriff in a burgh might concern himself with important national laws, there were lots of petty regulations which were supervised by the bailies. People haggled about market prices, the quality of meat or weight of bread; folk squabbled about land boundaries and housing plots; they pursued each other for debts, argued about inheritances, accused others of slander, cheating, theft and so on. From the earliest time they must also have been punished in burghs, probably in some central area where parents could watch a whipping or hanging and warn their frightened children.

The Court of the Four Burghs also regulated the first merchant guilds. Based on the original model at Berwick, the code set out who could be a burgess—merchants or craftsmen could qualify, provided they owned or rented property in the town, for which they paid a tax to the king. Then it gave these burgesses privileges by prohibiting all 'outland' or stranger merchants from selling within a burgh; foreign merchants arriving by ship could only sell to merchants from burghs, while certain items such as wool or hides could not be bought except in a burgh. The code also specified market days and the times of fairs and when non-burgess stallholders might sell goods. It detailed which craftsmen could become burgesses, who could take on servants or apprentices, or employ others to work for them (for example, a butcher, dyer or shoemaker could not become a merchant unless he stopped working with his own hands and sold only goods made by servants or others). In other words it created a monopoly trading privilege for merchants and ensured that for centuries to come they were the most important citizens in any burgh.

During the reign of William the Lion (1165–1214) the code was amended specifically to recognise the existence of merchant guilds (which must have existed already, and surely in Stirling since it was one of the Four Burghs on which the code was based). It also added that merchants were free to buy or sell anywhere within the 'liberties' of the burgh—the surrounding area. Wool, skins and hides could similarly only be sold to merchants. Documents from this time also make the first references to market crosses but, of course, this does not mean that there was one at Stirling yet. Stirling's horse market seems to have been especially well-known from very early times. A later document dated 1276 mentions how even the King of England's valet William fitz Glaye sent servants to the fair of Stirling 'to buy horses and other animals for his use'.

What other details of twelfth-century Stirling can be pieced together from surviving documents? During David I's reign he granted to Dunfermline Abbey first a dwelling place at Stirling, then two churches and some land at Stirling, and later a teind or endowment from his lands at Stirling. Then in 1140 King David I also founded Cambuskenneth Abbey (known during its first fifty years as the Abbey of St Mary of Stirling), an Augustinian house built on a loop of fertile carse land immediately across the River Forth from Stirling itself; it was promptly endowed with forty shillings rent from Stirling, a tenth of the royal income from the burgh lands, and part of the produce from one ship per year and one salt-pit in the burgh itself. So not only is it clear that Stirling must have been a place which received ships and had salt-pits, but the royal income from the burgh must also have been large enough to make the king's endowments to these various churches and abbeys worth granting.

The castle was also growing in importance. It is known that David I enjoyed regular visits there and numerous royal documents and charters were signed at 'Striuelin'. A few decades later King William the Lion enclosed the King's Park as a royal hunting ground,

Cambuskenneth Abbey bell tower. The remains of an Augustinian monastery founded in 1140 by King David I.

indicating that he, and presumably a considerable court entourage, also used the castle as a frequent residence. This necessitated a garrison, which must have offered increased business for the burgh's merchants and craftsmen.

By enclosing the King's Park area, the king unwittingly included land which had already been granted to Dunfermline Abbey. A charter survives in which William compensated the monks (who also staffed the chapel at Stirling Castle itself) by granting them land at St Ninians and Cambusbarron—that is, by granting them the rent income from those lands 'to be held in perpetual alms'. This land was then duly marked out by Richard Morville constable of the castle, Robert Avanel the justiciar, Ralph the king's sheriff of Stirling, and Peter of Stirling, a local landowner. (In due course King Alexander III extended the royal hunting lands by creating a New Park, which later formed part of the battlefield of Bannockburn.)

During the reign of William the Lion, the castle fell briefly into English hands—or rather, it was given to them. Put simply, the story is this: when Prince Henry of England rebelled against his father in 1171, he persuaded the Scots to help him by offering Northumberland as a prize. William marched south but was defeated and captured at Alnwick and then imprisoned in the castle of Falaise in Normandy (which was then still part of Norman England). By the humiliating Treaty of Falaise which obtained the king's release, a huge ransom was to be paid and the leading castles in Scotland (namely Berwick, Roxburgh, Jedburgh, Edinburgh and Stirling) were meanwhile to be garrisoned by English troops as collateral for the money. Worse still, the king also had to acknowledge the feudal overlordship of England and marry Ermengarde de Beaumont, a wife nominated by King Henry II of England.

It is possible that English troops never actually occupied the castle. Fifteen years later King Richard I of England restored Scotland's independence, cancelled what remained of the ransom debt and returned the occupied castles, but documents of this arrangement mention only Berwick and Roxburgh (Edinburgh having been returned when William married Ermingarde). Perhaps the English did not bother with Jedburgh or Stirling.

In 1214 after a reign of forty-nine years William's health suddenly broke down during an expedition to the Moray Firth area. He was brought back to Stirling where he died at the castle in December.

William's body was later taken for burial to Arbroath Abbey, which he had founded in 1178.

Nothing is known of the origins of Stirling Bridge, but it must also have appeared during this earliest period of the burgh's history. Wallace's victory over the English at Stirling (see Chapter 3) confirms that a wooden bridge (possibly with stone piers) existed there in 1297. The oldest known copy of the burgh seal is attached to a document dated 28th August 1296 at Berwick; it shows on one side a seven-arched bridge surmounted by a cross, rather like an old burgh boundary marker cross. In Stirling's case this was traditionally the place where the peoples from north and south of the river came to barter or settle accounts. It is not clear from the burgh seal (a medallion of green wax measuring only 3½ inches across) whether this bridge was of stone or wood, but it must surely be the wooden one destroyed by Wallace. In other words, it seems that a bridge existed before 1296, by which time it had already become well enough known to represent the town on its burgh seal.

The Stirling burgh seal, showing what is believed to be the earliest representation of Stirling Bridge, 1296. This was used as the basis of James Proudfoot's drawing of Stirling Bridge on page 30.
Photo: Stirling District Libraries.

The precise location of this early bridge is also open to doubt; various authorities have placed it anywhere from thirty metres upstream from the present 'old' bridge, to the ford at Kildean. The remains of stone piers were said to have been visible in the 1900s about sixty metres upriver from the old bridge, but there is no convincing sign today. What is more important is that, if a ford was enough to draw travellers to Stirling, then a bridge would certainly have been an even greater attraction, from which the burgh must have benefited even more.

Historians are fond of using phrases like 'in the mists of antiquity' or 'in a haze of half-real history' when the details of a period are sketchy. This early part of Stirling's burgh history *is* thin—there is almost no archaeological evidence, and documents tend to mention the castle or religious matters rather than the town itself. But it is certainly clear that a fairly thriving town existed. The buildings may have been only wooden and (like any other burgh) the population barely a few hundred, but there was a burgh council and a merchant guild with enough trading privileges to give the town a chance to prosper. And there were other advantages—crafts and trade and shipping, religious communities, a bridge and a castle. The foundations of the burgh's history were in place.

CHAPTER 3

Wallace and Bruce 1290–1370

During the 1280s Stirling Castle seems to have been rebuilt in stone, perhaps because it had become, more than ever, an important royal stronghold. In 1257, for example, fifteen-year-old King Alexander III was brought to the castle for safety during a struggle for power between rival nobles—Stirling was evidently seen as the safest place for Scotland's king. In 1263 the castle was specially fortified and garrisoned against the Norwegian Vikings whose ships were in the Firth of Clyde. Although they devastated the Kilsyth area, the Vikings never approached Stirling; later they were defeated at the Battle of Largs (as a result of which Scotland later received the Western Isles). This was the only occasion when Stirling Castle was ever prepared for a threat from overseas. During the thirteenth century the Scottish parliament also met periodically at Stirling Castle. As mentioned in Chapter 2, Alexander III also extended his hunting park at Stirling and seems to have improved William the Lion's old park which had become neglected. Stirling was obviously a favourite royal castle.

Alexander III's accidental death on the cliffs at Kinghorn in Fife in 1286 was a blow for Scotland and particularly for Stirling; the town now found itself the centre of warfare for decades to come. It was sometimes said that whoever held Stirling held Scotland, such was its strategic importance—a useful benefit for the town in peacetime but a liability in war.

The king died leaving no children—all three predeceased him, including David who died at Stirling Castle aged only ten. Alexander's granddaughter Margaret was brought from her family in Norway to be queen of a land she did not know, but died on the journey at Orkney aged seven. So ended Scotland's line of Celtic monarchs; from then on they were Normans.

The death of the 'Maid of Norway' sparked a struggle by different families for the Scottish throne. Brought in to arbitrate on who had the best claim, England's King Edward I first demanded that the Scots accept him as their feudal overlord and hand their royal castles over to English governors as a sign of good faith. The selfish nobles, each hoping to rule, accepted and the Scottish parliament agreed, if only to avoid civil war. From 1291–92 an Englishman called Norman Darcy therefore commanded Stirling Castle. It was a disastrous decision by the Scots for it committed them to fight later for the independence they now gave way.

Edward chose John Balliol of the Comyn family to be king of Scotland. He did indeed have a stronger claim than his main rival Bruce, but unfortunately he was also a weak man who could be easily dominated by Edward. Even the Scots came to know him as 'Toom Tabard' or empty coat as, step by step, he submitted to the humiliating demands of an English overlord. Eventually Edward pressed too far by insisting on Scottish troops for his wars in France. The Scots refused and instead formed the famous 'Auld Alliance' with France—a treaty of friendship and mutual support which lasted to the time of Mary Queen of Scots, and beyond. Enraged by this defiance of his power, Edward invaded Scotland in March 1296 and so began the Scottish wars of independence.

The Scots were, of course, no match for King Edward and his powerful English forces—30,000 infantry and 4000 mounted knights. Berwick was captured and its inhabitants slaughtered. The Scottish army was then routed at Dunbar and the country was at Edward's mercy. Edinburgh Castle fell after a siege of only five days. By the time Edward reached Stirling in June the garrison had fled and only the porter remained to hand over the castle keys. In July Balliol surrendered Scotland to the English at Brechin and was then sent prisoner to the Tower of London (from which three years later he was allowed to go into exile in France, where he lived until his death in 1313). To demonstrate his power Edward then marched via Montrose and Aberdeen as far north as Elgin, which he burned. On the return journey he took with him the Stone of Destiny from Scone (which still resides at Westminster Abbey to this day), Queen Margaret's fragment of the True Cross, many of the Scottish records of state, and a list known as the Ragman Roll of 2000 Scottish nobles who now swore loyalty to England—the subjugation of Scotland was complete. The Earl of Surrey was made Governor, with the arrogant Hugh of Cressingham as treasurer, and Edward went off to resume his wars against the French.

At this point William Wallace appeared on the national scene.

Statue of Sir William Wallace at the Wallace Monument. He is looking over the battlefield of Stirling Bridge. *Photo:* Craig Mair.

This is not the place to describe Wallace's background—suffice to say that, when few nobles would risk it, this second son of a Renfrewshire knight took up a guerrilla campaign against the English occupation troops in southern and central Scotland. For a time he raided back and forth with remarkable speed, effectively clearing the English out of the Borders, Lanarkshire, Ayrshire, Perthshire and Fife. In the summer of 1297 he met up with Andrew of Moray who was fighting a similar war in the north, having captured Inverness, Elgin, Banff and other places. Now they joined forces to besiege Dundee. Before long they heard of an English army, heading north under the Earl of Surrey to deal with this upstart Scottish resistance. Wallace and Moray knew that the English would have to cross the River Forth at Stirling, and headed south in early September to intercept them.

It was a situation tailor-made for an ambush by the Scots. The slow loops and bends of the river formed a wide area of marshy pools across the surrounding flat carse land—too spongy for the heavy English battle horses to operate effectively. From Stirling on its higher land a track led down to a wooden bridge across the river. This track then continued by a narrow causeway over boggy moss to higher ground at the Abbey Craig, and from there northwards to Fife and Perth.

From a vantage point on the Abbey Craig, Wallace watched the English army gather on the south side of the river. History has exaggerated the size of this force but it seems to have been around ten thousand foot-soldiers (including Welsh bowmen and the English garrison from Stirling Castle, drafted in to swell the numbers), plus a considerable baggage train of servants and camp followers, and about three hundred mounted knights—the heavy battle tanks of a thirteenth-century army. The size of the Scottish army is unknown, but it was certainly much smaller and consisted mostly of lightly armed spearmen. Wallace knew that cavalry would only be a hindrance on such a marshy battlefield. Few Scottish lords or knights sided with Wallace—being only second or third generation Norman Scots, most were fearful of losing their estates in England and had signed the oath of loyalty to Edward in 1296. In fact James Stewart, Malcolm the Earl of Lennox and several other nobles actually tried to persuade Wallace to give up this foolish idea of a battle.

On the morning of September 11th the English army started to cross the wooden bridge, watched by Scots hidden on the north side waiting for the signal to attack. It took some time, for the bridge was so narrow that the troops could only cross two abreast. The temptation to charge must have been tremendous but Wallace and Moray waited and waited, allowing more and more enemy troops to cross. Then, incredibly, when about five thousand Englishmen were safely established on the other side, they were all recalled because the Earl of Surrey had slept in and had not yet ordered the advance to begin! The English soldiers obediently returned to the south side, and so lost their best chance to defeat Wallace.

Surrey then delayed further by stopping to promote several knights, before finally ordering the troops to cross the river. For a second time the English forces lumbered into action, but just as some reached the other side a party of Scottish nobles approached—again the army was recalled while Stewart and Lennox reported that Wallace had refused to make peace. Surrey then sent two Dominican friars across the bridge to parley with the Scots. Wallace is reported to have sent them packing with the words: 'Tell your commander that we are not here to make peace but to do battle to defend ourselves and liberate our kingdom. Let them come on, and we shall prove this in their very beards'.

By now at least one Scottish knight on the English side was beginning to have serious doubts about the coming battle. Sir Richard Lundie is reported to have said: 'My lords, if we cross that bridge now, we are all dead men. For we can only go over two abreast, and the enemy are already formed up: they can charge down on us whenever they wish. There is a ford not far from here, where sixty men can cross at a time. Give me five hundred cavalrymen, then, and a small body of infantry, and we will outflank the enemy and attack them from behind: while we are doing that, the earl and the rest of the army will be able to cross the bridge in perfect safety'. Had Surrey listened to this suggestion the outcome of the battle would certainly have been different, but he did not, and for a third time the English army began to cross the narrow bridge.

The rest of the story is well known. For most of the morning Wallace watched the English cross and jostle for a dry footing on the causeway track. At the critical moment the Scots were launched into the attack; lightly armed men splashed easily across the marsh-

A drawing by James Proudfoot of the battle of Stirling Bridge, 1297, in which Wallace defeated the English. *Photo:* Stirling District Libraries.

land, seizing the north end of the bridge, dragging floundering, unwieldly knights from their horses and slaughtering most of those who had crossed. The outstanding English knight Sir Marmaduke Tweng was one who did not panic, but hacked his way back across the bridge to safety. But then it collapsed, or was cut down, and the escape route was gone. In those days the River Forth was deeper and faster than today—too difficult for horses or men in heavy armour to cross. Only some Welsh bowmen, who traditionally fought without armour, had much chance of swimming. The English troops on the far side of the river could only watch in horror as their comrades on the north side were butchered. About one hundred knights and perhaps five thousand infantry were either killed or drowned. Among them was the much-hated Cressingham—dragged from his horse and speared to death, before having his skin cut off in souvenir strips by the Scots; Wallace himself had a sword belt made from one portion. On the Scottish side the only important casualty was Andrew of Moray, who was wounded and died a few weeks later.

Meanwhile the Earl of Surrey left the unfortunate Sir Marmaduke Tweng to hold Stirling Castle and with the remains of his frightened army fled in the direction of England (indeed Surrey did not even stop to let his horse feed, and it died at Berwick). At this moment the treacherous Scottish lords Stewart and Lennox appeared like carrion crows to pick off the lumbering English baggage convoy as it was hauled off towards Falkirk—the victory was undoubtedly Wallace's, however.

The Battle of Stirling Bridge is a major landmark in the burgh's local history, but in fact its exact location is vague. As explained in Chapter 2, the precise position of the bridge itself is open to doubt; it was probably just upstream from the present old bridge but the proof is now gone. Even the battlefield is uncertain—somewhere under the Cornton housing estate today, but the fighting may have see-sawed and spread along the causeway track towards Airthrey or Causewayhead. It is quite possible that Wallace High School's rugby and football players regularly compete on a battlefield which is much older than they realise!

Tweng must have watched in dismay as the English escaped—Stirling Castle had no store of provisions for a siege and there was little chance of help coming soon from England. After a short time he surrendered, but Wallace spared him and he survived to fight later at Bannockburn. So the Scots gained Stirling Castle in 1297, and from there soon cleared the English out of all but the strongest castles in Scotland.

When Edward I heard of the defeat of his army he organised a new force of twelve thousand foot-soldiers, including Welsh bowmen, and about two thousand mounted knights. He placed himself in command and set off on a campaign of revenge. The Scottish army of spearmen was destroyed by Welsh longbows at the Battle of Falkirk on 22nd July 1298 and Wallace was forced to flee. He headed for Stirling but it was clear that, for the moment, his cause was lost; the best tactic was to destroy everything in a scorched-earth policy and retire out of English reach. Stirling Castle was dismantled to deny the English its use and the town, together with Perth, was burned as Wallace retreated northwards.

Edward arrived soon after and had the castle rebuilt while he recovered from a kick from his horse. For a year an English garrison of ninety men survived unscathed, but in late 1299 the Scots returned to besiege the castle. The English sent to Edward for help but it was winter and the king could not persuade his nobles to march north again. Instead he authorised the English commander John Sampson to surrender and once again the Scots obtained possession of the castle.

Sir William Oliphant was placed in command but it was a nerve-wracking time for the garrison. The English now controlled virtually all of Scotland; Stirling was but an isolated stronghold in a sea of English power. Oliphant must have wondered how long Edward, by now nicknamed the 'Hammer of the Scots', would tolerate the Scottish flag which flew above Stirling Castle. Twice the English king passed by on campaign with his forces, but did nothing to attack the strongest castle still in Scottish hands. But then in 1304 he returned to besiege the Scots in earnest. Eric Stair-Kerr, in a history of Stirling Castle published in 1913, described the siege:

> The siege began on the 22nd of April and for three months the gallant defenders withstood the attack of the most formidable artillery which the English King could command [there were at least thirteen siege engines—C.M.]. Edward had written to the Prince of Wales urging him to strip the lead from the churches of Perth, Dunblane and other places—leaving only the altars covered—in order to provide weights for the military engines. He commanded also the Sheriff of York to dispatch forty cross-bowmen and forty carpenters to Stirling, while the governor of the Tower of London was required to send north all the ammunition that was under his care in that arsenal. So anxious indeed was the King to secure the assistance of his most experienced soldiers, that he forbade his knights to participate in tournaments without his special permission. While the English battered the walls of the castle with stones and leaden balls, and threw the combustible known as Greek Fire to damage the engines and injure the men, the defenders kept up a constant shower of javelins and other missiles. The King himself was struck by a weapon that lodged in a joint of his armour, and once a large stone fell so near his horse that the animal took fright and fell with his royal master. At last the stronghold was rendered untenable, for the walls were broken down in many places and the food supply was exhausted; but before the starving survivors of the garrison were allowed to issue forth, Edward experimented on the long-

The siege of Stirling Castle in 1304, from a drawing by James Proudfoot. A plaque commemorating Sir William Oliphant's heroic defence against thirteen siege engines can be seen on the King's Building at the Castle. *Photo:* Stirling District Libraries.

suffering fort with his most formidable engine, the War Wolf. The Queen and her ladies viewed this assault from an oriel window constructed for the purpose.

On 24th July 1304 Sir William Oliphant and a handful of defenders finally surrendered. They were brought half-naked and starving to Edward, who would have had them disembowelled except that the Queen begged him to spare their lives. They were sent instead as prisoners to various English castles—Oliphant was eventually released in 1308 on a promise that he would no longer assist the Scottish side. A year later Wallace was captured near Glasgow by Sir John Menteith, another Norman Scot who had sworn loyalty to Edward; he was tried and executed at London. With Wallace gone and every Scottish castle now in English hands, it must have seemed that the war was over.

The peace did not last for long, however. On 10th February 1306 Robert the Bruce killed John Comyn, the exiled Balliol's heir to the throne, and declared himself King of Scots at a secret coronation on 25th March at Scone. At first things did not go well and Bruce lost several battles. With the English and half of Scotland searching for him he was forced into hiding, sometimes in Ireland. His luck turned only when Edward I died in 1307; Edward II was no soldier and it became easier to regain Scotland.

One by one, by daring and trickery, the main castles fell to Bruce until by 1312 only Stirling remained in English hands. In the spring of 1313 the Scots, under the command of Edward Bruce the King's brother, set about a siege. Given the castle's strong position, it was a long and difficult business which went on for months. By November the Scots were still there, not much closer to success but a severe irritation to the English cooped up inside the castle. Then the garrison commander Sir Philip de Mowbray (who was actually a Scot) proposed a bargain, that he would surrender the castle if it had not been relieved by an English army by June 24th 1314, midsummer's day. It is likely that Mowbray confidently expected an English army that summer in any case, and meanwhile it spared him the need to fight on. For the Scots, it released them from a siege which they were not winning, but which was tying down men who could be used elsewhere. Edward Bruce accepted the arrangement.

Robert the Bruce was furious when he heard of the bargain, for it committed the English to come on a rescue mission which the Scots would have to block. The Scots' strength has always been in hit-and-run tactics, not in fighting setpiece battles against the fearsome might of English knights and Welsh bowmen. However, both sides now prepared for the campaign.

Accounts speculate wildly about the size of the English army which marched into Scotland that hot summer. It was probably about 20,000 to 30,000 men, including perhaps 5,000 mounted knights, 8,000 to 10,000 bowmen and a larger mass of spearmen. With them came a huge baggage train of furniture, food supplies, knights' tents, blacksmiths's forges, casks of wine, pay chests and so on. In all, this force straggled for miles along the road, a dusty but powerful, glittering cavalcade, undoubtedly watched with dismay by Bruce's scouts as it marched north in good order. By June 21st the English were at Edinburgh. On the 22nd they were twenty miles closer, at Falkirk. On June 23rd the leading knights were coming down the old Roman road from Torwood to St Ninians and the castle was in sight—but this is where Bruce was waiting.

The size of the Scottish army is not known, but most chroniclers agree that it was about one third to half the size of the English force; it was probably about 10,000 men. Bruce had about 2,000 mounted men but very few heavy battle knights such as the English had. In a full battle the Scottish cavalry would be swept away, but the lighter Scottish horses could be more manoeuvrable on rough or heavy ground. Bruce also had few bowmen—throughout history the Scots have never been good bowmen—and he must have viewed the well-drilled ranks of Welsh longbowmen with much concern. They used fearsome longbows which could penetrate even chain mail, and which had destroyed Wallace's army at Falkirk in 1298. Most of Bruce's army consisted of spearmen armed with the traditional long Scottish pike, and dirks or axes for close fighting. The problem was how best to use this weaker force to stop the English from reaching Stirling Castle.

Where it crossed the Bannock Burn the road to Stirling forked, one branch passing through the wooded New Park, the royal hunting ground, while the other looped onto lower marshy carse-land before joining up again further on. Bruce prepared the better road with hidden pits or 'pottis traps' set with sharpened stakes and scattered spiked iron caltrops. As anticipated, the leading English knights on their heavy chargers took the drier road and soon stumbled into the traps. With the English progress now in confusion, Bruce appeared on a lightweight palfrey horse to steady his troops in case the enemy made a determined attack. As he rode up and down he was recognised and challenged to combat by Sir Henry de Bohun, one of many confident, perhaps arrogant, English knights that day. So occurred the stirring moment when Bruce, on his ridiculous little pony, swerved and ducked to avoid the charging Englishman and with one blow from his battle-axe split de Bohun's skull through its helmet. It was a great moment for the cheering Scots.

At about the same time Lord Randolph was involved in another moment of great valour. Realising that Stirling had yet to be reached before midsummer's day, Sir Robert de Clifford led a party of three hundred fully armoured knights on a gallop towards the castle. Randolph organised a company of five hundred spearmen to block the way, perhaps at the place known today at Randolphfield (where a standing stone marks *something*); with great courage these men held fast against knights who would normally have been expected to overrun such puny opposition. Then they surged forward, forcing the English to retreat with many dead and injured, and Stirling Castle still not reached.

That night the main body of English troops camped on the carse, on safe ground between the Bannock and Pelstream burns, and with the marshlands of the Forth protecting their rear. They were still twice as many as the Scots and with their bowmen still not used must have been full of confidence. But Bruce had drawn first blood and his men were just as ready for battle. They had seen the English baggage train stuck on boggy ground, unable to deliver food to the main camp, and knew that the enemy would be nervous of a night attack.

The next day was June 24th, midsummer's day. King Edward II awoke to find the Scots already in a battle formation which would force the English to fight where they had camped—hemmed in by streams on two sides and with tidal marshy carseland pools behind them. With a better understanding of the meandering Forth, the garrison at Stirling Castle seems to have slipped down to the English camp during the night with planks and even doors to help their comrades cross the wetlands more easily, but it was hardly enough and now the English would have to fight on a battlefield more suited to the Scots than themselves.

The two biggest English threats were their bowmen and heavy knights. Bruce formed the Scots into schiltrons—circular, tightly-packed groups of about 1,000 pikemen, often likened to hedge-hogs since their strength came from a mass of spear-points designed to repel even the most determined knights on battle-chargers. Three schiltrons led by Edward Bruce, Lord Randolph and Lord Douglas formed the front line, with behind them a reserve schiltron under King Robert, a small number of archers and the cavalry under Lord Keith. The particular job of the horsemen was to scatter the formations of English bowmen; at Falkirk the Scottish cavalry had fled without striking a blow, leaving the English archers free to decimate the schiltrons, but Bruce was more certain of the loyalty of his knights than the low-born Wallace had been.

As the English formed up for battle, they watched the abbot of

Inchaffrey bless the schiltrons opposite with a crucifix. As he passed each unit the men knelt down, which made King Edward think they were begging for mercy. 'They do,' Sir Ingelram de Umfraville is reported to have said to his king, 'but not from you. These men will win all or die.'

The Battle of Bannockburn went on till late afternoon. Led by the gallant Earl of Gloucester the knights charged, but made no headway on the soft ground and against the steady schiltrons. Several times they rallied and tried again but the spearmen stood their ground and eventually Gloucester was killed. The longbowmen fired with deadly effect into the schiltron of Edward Bruce but were eventually broken and forced to flee by a Scottish cavalry charge. The main weight of English spearmen pressed forward but was limited to a narrow area by the Bannockburn—most soldiers were well back from the point of battle contact, uselessly shoving forward as they splashed through the pools and marshes of the Forth. Even the Scottish bowmen could not miss as they fired effectively into this heaving mass of bodies.

The see-saw, seething struggle went on for hours, but gradually it became clear that the Scottish schiltrons were driving the English back closer to the Forth. Eventually the enemy troops broke and began to escape as best they could. Then the 'sma' folk' or Scottish camp followers, who had been kept out of danger behind the Coxet and Gillies hills, came surging onto the battlefield, presumably to plunder what they could, and with that the English army disintegrated. For most there was no escape—hundreds were cut down as they splashed through the marshlands. Somewhere in the chaos King Edward, surrounded by a body of knights, galloped off to Stirling Castle but found no refuge; Sir Philip de Mowbray kept his word to surrender the castle and would not give the king admittance. So Edward pressed on to Dunbar where he took a ship for Berwick and escaped.

There are few great victories to record in the long-running story of Scotland's wars against the English, but Bannockburn is probably the greatest of all. No-one knows how many of the English multitude died, but among them were at least twenty-one lords and barons, and perhaps as many as seven hundred knights. Many more were captured including at least twenty-two barons and sixty knights, and these were later ransomed for huge fortunes. The victory did not immediately gain Scottish freedom, but it was the greatest single step along the road to the Treaty of Edinburgh-Northampton which marked England's acceptance of Scottish independence in 1328.

Having won Stirling Castle, Robert the Bruce had it pulled down in case it fell again into English hands. But as the years passed and it became clearer that there was no English threat, the castle seems to have been partially repaired. Bruce himself visited on several occasions, notably in 1326. He also held several parliaments at Cambuskenneth Abbey, particularly in 1314 immediately after his victory at Bannockburn, when all those Scots who had fought on the English side and who still refused to join Bruce had their lands forfeited. At another Cambuskenneth parliament in 1328 Scotland's earls, barons, burgesses and free tenants granted a 'tenth-penny' to the king, an agreement by which Bruce received a loan from his subjects for the government of his realm.

Bruce died in 1329 and was succeeded by his son David, who was aged five. This offered an opportunity to Edward Balliol, son of King John Balliol, who was now living at the court of England's Edward III. Together with an army of disgruntled Scots—mostly those who had supported England against Bruce and had lost their lands as a result—he invaded Scotland and thereby sparked off a new round of battles for power and independence. Balliol had himself crowned at Scone in 1332 but he also declared his feudal subservience to England, which the majority of Scots, now slowly beginning to sense a national identity and patriotism, opposed. In 1333 a Scottish army coming to the relief of Berwick was completely destroyed by Balliol and Edward III at Halidon Hill; Sir Archibald Douglas, regent for the young king, was killed together with the earls of Ross, Lennox, Atholl, Carrick, Sutherland and Strathearn and 'a host of lesser barons, knights and squires' as one account describes it. As a result the boy-king David II was sent to France for safety and Scotland found itself once more occupied by English troops.

Stirling Castle, which seems to have been virtually undefended, was garrisoned by the English under Sir Thomas de Rokeby in 1336. As Eric Stair-Kerr wrote in his history of the castle in 1913: 'The work of renovation was straightway begun. New walls were at once constructed, two wells—one in the castle proper, the other in the nether bailey—were cleared out and deepened; hall, pantry, kitchen, larder, etc., were all repaired, and men were employed in

Gargunnock Wood in hewing down trees for the timber-work of the fortress'. The main defensive walls and turrets, the drawbridge defences and the prison seem to have been made of stone, but most other structures were of wood. A defensive peel or palisade was built inside the castle on the weaker north side, and its wooden walls were covered with mortar to protect it from fire. Living quarters were wooden, with ceilings and inner partitions made of inter-woven sticks known as wattle, daubed with clay. The roofs were of turf.

Across Scotland a campaign was waged to expel Balliol, and in 1337 Stirling Castle was besieged by Sir Andrew Moray. At least two chronicles describe how Sir William Keith tried to climb the walls but lost his footing and died by falling onto his own spear. Just as provisions were running low, Edward III came with troops to relieve the garrison and the Scots were driven off. De Rokeby was able to re-supply his men and the castle remained in English hands.

In late 1341 the siege was renewed by Robert the Steward (later King Robert II) and in April 1342 the garrison was finally starved into surrender; by then it had been reduced to Sir Thomas de Rokeby, Sir Hugh de Montgomery, fifty-seven squires, ten watchmen and sixty-two bowmen. It is believed that during this siege cannon, or 'crakkis of wer', were used for the first time in Scotland. It is likely that they were as dangerous to the Scots gunners as to the English defenders who faced them, for the primitive artillery of those years was notoriously unreliable; King James II was killed in 1460 by a cannon which burst as he watched it being fired in a siege of Roxburgh Castle. Nevertheless, the capture of Stirling in 1342 ended the last occupation of the castle by English troops until the time of Cromwell over three hundred years later. Edward III was now distracted by the Hundred Years' War in France and Scotland was left mostly in peace.

The Wars of Independence must have been a terrible time for the ordinary people of Stirling. They tend to have been overlooked in the more significant story of the castle, but it must truly have been a difficult period for civilians trying simply to survive, marry, make a living and die in peace. On several occasions English troops occupied the castle for years on end and so controlled the town; it can safely be assumed that they treated the locals as occupation forces have done everywhere since time began, with contempt, brutality and loutish arrogance. On top of that Scotland was struck by the terrible Black Death in 1349 and again in 1361; towns, where people were more concentrated, suffered most, but the effect on Scotland's already meagre trade with Europe, where the effects of the plague were even more severe, was also disastrous.

Shipping on the river and general trade was severely disrupted by this plague and the ups and downs of power in Scotland, while the loss of royal custom at the castle must also have been a blow to Stirling's merchants. The bridge, destroyed by Wallace in 1297 in his victory over the English, remained in a dilapidated state (see Chapter 4), which forced people to return to the use of ferries or fords, which in turn must also have had a detrimental effect on trade and travel. Even the town itself, built of wood and thatch, cannot have survived unscathed; it seems to have burned down by accident in 1244, for example. Wallace is said to have burned it down again in 1298 during his retreat from Falkirk, and it would be surprising if the town was not also destroyed on other, unrecorded, occasions during this period. The folk of Stirling, blessed but also cursed by having such an important castle on their doorsteps, must have been very relieved when the wars with England finally ended, at least for the moment.

CHAPTER 4

The Castle 1370–1540

In 1371 David II died without children and was succeeded by Robert II, Bruce's grandson through his daughter Marjorie. King Robert's correct name was Robert the Steward, and so began the Stewart line of kings and queens which was to last into the eighteenth century. King Robert II was in turn followed by his eldest son John (who took the title Robert III on coming to the throne in 1390), and then by a succession of five kings called James. The last of these died in 1542, leaving his daughter Mary to be Queen of Scots. It is this stirring period from Marjorie to Mary which forms the background to the medieval life of Stirling.

During this early span of Stewart kings, Stirling Castle became an increasingly popular royal residence. Three kings were born there, two (and Mary, Queen of Scots) were crowned there, and several princes of the royal family were christened or died there. Thanks to this royal preference for Stirling the castle was almost completely rebuilt during the period from about 1500 to 1600 and came to look recognisably as it does today.

Glimpses of royal activity at Stirling survive from the time of Robert II. For some years the keeper of Stirling Castle was Sir Robert Erskine (whose descendants were to remain keepers, off and on, to the present time), but in 1373 Erskine was replaced by Robert II's second son, Robert, Earl of Menteith and Fife, later known as the Duke of Albany. Surviving records show how the Earl received an annual income of corn and oatmeal from the lands of Bothkennar, plus two hundred merks income from Crown lands around Stirling. He also strengthened the castle's fortifications by constructing outer defences in 1380 and a north gate in 1381—this is almost certainly still recognisable as part of the gateway-building known as the Cunzie House or Mint today, which would make it the oldest surviving part of Stirling Castle.

Robert II died in 1390 but further work continued on the castle. A new tower was built in 1390, a new prison in 1402, a new drawbridge in 1404, and later a wooden mill-house. Alexander I's chapel of St Michael was rebuilt in 1412 (the same year as the creation of the Chapel of Linlithgow Palace), and two new rooms were added to the castle in 1415—signs of considerable royal interest in the castle. It was not long before the prison was required to house some interesting occupants. The king's younger brother Alexander, Earl of Buchan, was better known as the Wolf of Badenoch; as a lawless baron he deserted his wife, plundered the districts of Angus and Moray, was excommunicated from the Church (in revenge for which he burned Elgin cathedral and the town of Forres) but ultimately repented so that he now lies in Dunkeld cathedral. His illegitimate sons, however, continued their father's lawless ways until they were captured and locked up at Stirling Castle under its keeper, their uncle the Duke of Albany.

Another interesting figure who flitted through the scene at this time was Thomas Warde of Trumpington. This half-wit, found in the dungeons of the Lord of the Isles at Islay, happened to resemble Richard II of England whose mysterious death was supposed to have occurred around 1400 (though some said that he had escaped from captivity in Pontefract Castle). It suited the Scots to claim that the fugitive king was now at Stirling, but the poor man died in 1419 without going anywhere near England, labelled forever in history as 'Mammet' or false king. He was buried outside the town at the church of the Black Friars, but no trace remains today.

Robert III died in 1406 and was followed by his son James I, who was aged eleven. (Scotland was bedevilled by kings who succeeded as children—the resulting regencies tended to degenerate into squabbles for power among rival barons; James II came to the throne aged six; James III became king at the age of nine; James IV was comparatively old at fifteen; James V was one; Mary was just one week old; and James VI was two when his mother fled to England and he became king). Unfortunately, just before the death of his father, the boy James was captured off the coast of England while being sent to Europe for an education. He remained a prisoner, first in the Tower of London but later at the English court, for eighteen years without being crowned King of Scots. Meanwhile the Duke of Albany was appointed Governor or Regent of Scotland in his absence. He died in 1420 but was followed by his son Murdoch, the second Duke of Albany.

It seems that the older Duke of Albany had ideas himself of

becoming king. As Governor he certainly acted like a monarch, speaking of 'his' subjects, issuing documents sealed with an image of himself on a throne holding the sword of state, with his coat of arms beside those of Scotland, dated by the year of his governorship and not that of the absent king. His son followed in the same mould. However, in 1423 King James, still a prisoner but now also a well-educated and soldierly knight, fell in love with Joan Beaufort, daughter of the Earl of Somerset; their marriage was soon followed by a treaty with England and James was released for a ransom of £40,000. He was crowned at Scone on May 2nd 1424 and immediately took a strong grip on his kingdom. Top of his list of priorities was to deal with Albany.

That same month a son of the second Duke of Albany was arrested for embezzling funds. Later that year Albany's father-in-law, the Earl of Lennox, was imprisoned. In 1425 Albany himself, with his wife and youngest son, was arrested. At a court in Stirling

The beheading stone, now a prominent landmark on the Gowan Hill and perhaps the site of executions in 1425. *Photo:* Craig Mair.

Castle on 25th May 1425 at which King James appeared in full regalia and robes of state, a jury of twenty-one barons dutifully found all these prisoners guilty. The Duke's eldest son was executed the same day at the Heading Stone on the Gowan Hill beside the castle. Next day he was followed by Albany himself, his youngest son and the Earl of Lennox. Such was the king's revenge on those who had misused his absence, and indeed had done nothing to help obtain his release.

With an iron-willed determination James went on to crush the unruly nobles who had profited so much by his absence. Sir John Kennedy, the king's own nephew, was one who was imprisoned at Stirling Castle. Sir Robert Graham of Kincardine was arrested but escaped. The Earl of Douglas, head of one of Scotland's most powerful families, was also imprisoned for a time, for having signed a 'band' or arrangement with Albany in 1409. Then the Earl of Strathearn was deprived of his title—by now there were several nobles who wanted revenge. The king was finally murdered by Sir Robert Graham and others at Perth in 1437 but Graham was soon captured and brought to Stirling. Here he was nailed to a tree, dragged through the town and tortured for three days with red-hot irons before being executed on the Gowan Hill.

James II was born in Edinburgh in 1430 and was still only six when he was crowned King of Scotland at Holyrood Abbey—the first not to be crowned at Scone. He was nicknamed 'James of the Fiery Face' on account of a large purple birthmark which covered the left half of his face. Once again, Stirling Castle figured largely in this king's life.

As a child he was taken there for safety by his mother—one story says he was smuggled in a clothes chest. However, Sir Alexander Livingstone of Callander, the keeper of Stirling Castle, was one of a rising powerful family with a grip on many royal posts, and he now abused his position to achieve still greater power and influence. When the widowed queen married Sir James Stewart of Lorne in 1439, he had Stewart and his brother imprisoned in the castle dungeons, the queen confined to her rooms at Stirling, and himself declared guardian of the royal child. This thwarted the ambitions of Sir William Crichton, the king's Chancellor and guardian of Edinburgh Castle; in 1440 he collected a band of horsemen and staged a 'rescue' of the nine-year-old king as he rode in the King's Park. The king was taken back to Edinburgh but was later returned to Stirling when Livingstone threatened civil war. He continued to spend most of his childhood there, and the Livingstones, with the king in their custody, continued to grow more powerful.

During this period the castle was improved, perhaps because of Livingstone's royal 'guests'. Exchequer rolls for 1434 refer to the king's and lords' chambers, for example, and most windows in the king's apartments now seem to have been glazed (but not elsewhere in the castle, not even in the great hall or the queen's rooms, where cloth was still used).

Eventually James became old enough to govern for himself. In 1449 he married the Burgundian princess Mary of Gueldres in Edinburgh and later that year held a great tournament at Stirling to mark the occasion. The contestants were two Burgundian knights called Jacques and Simon de Lalain and a squire called Meriadet, against 'three Scottish champions' represented by James the brother of the Earl of Douglas, James the brother of Douglas of Lochleven, and John Ross of Halket. It was to be a fight to the death.

The tournament was held on the Haining, the field presently next to the King's Knot (which did not exist then). Tents and pavilions sprang up around the castle and on the King's Park as knights and nobles came from all over Scotland for the occasion; it must have been a lifelong highlight for Stirling's population, something for them to tell their grandchildren. Before the joust began the six combatants banqueted with the king and were then knighted before taking the field. Eric Stair-Kerr gives a vivid description of the battle which followed:

> After trumpets had been sounded and proclamations made, the warriors eagerly advanced to the contest. The Earl of Douglas's brother and Jacques de Lalain managed to disarm each other and so continued the fight by wrestling; Simon de Lalain's coolness of head enabled him eventually to obtain a slight advantage over the Laird of Halket; the Lochleven Douglas, though twice struck to the ground, persistently returned to the attack, but was hardly able to hold his own with the skilful Meriadet. When at last the King threw down his truncheon as a signal for the conflict to cease, the marshals of the field laid off the struggling champions and compelled them to disengage. Neither side could claim a decisive victory, though the advantage, on the whole, lay with the foreign knights. King James, however, praised the valour of

each individual, and before the Burgundians returned to their own country, he entertained them sumptuously in Stirling Castle and loaded them with gifts.

Having married and taken over the reins of government himself, the eighteen-year-old king moved effectively to strengthen his position. By September 1449 the entire Livingstone family had been thrown out of office and most of them arrested; two (but not the keeper of Stirling) were later executed. Then in 1451 a royal son was born at Stirling Castle and christened James, so providing the king with a clear successor.

Although the Douglases, on the occasion of the tournament, were rewarded by the king as great champions, the fact is that they represented his greatest threat. Their great lands and ambition made the Douglases the most powerful family in Scotland—and with a strong claim to the Crown itself through family lines from Robert II and Robert III. In 1440 there had occurred the infamous 'Black Dinner' at Edinburgh Castle when, in the presence of the ten-year-old king, Sir William Crichton had seized, accused and executed the young Earl of Douglas and his brother. Passions and plots still ran strong among the Douglases. Gradually they rebuilt their power; by 1451 they had made a bond with the Earl of Crawford and the Earl of Ross (who was also Lord of the Isles), with the intention of staging a rebellion against the Crown. It was the most obvious and serious challenge to his power which James II had yet faced.

The king summoned the Earl of Douglas to a dinner at Stirling Castle on 22nd February 1452. Douglas would not attend without a guarantee of safe conduct, which the king granted. After dinner the king took Douglas aside to a small adjoining room where he told him that he knew of the rebellious bond and demanded that Douglas repudiate it. Several times the other refused until, almost certainly in a fit of exasperated passion between two young men, the king's temper boiled over and he stabbed Douglas in the throat. The commotion brought others running, among them the Captain of the Guard who speared the Earl of Douglas several times with his pole-axe to finish the deed. It is said that the body was then thrown out of a window into the Privy Garden, where it was later buried. That area is now called the Douglas Garden and the supposed window still exists; it is now part of a newer sixteenth-century building, but it is likely that the previous building was remodelled rather than replaced; so the window *could* be original.

The new Earl of Douglas promptly swore revenge against the king, and a few weeks later rode at the head of about six hundred men into Stirling brandishing the letter of safe conduct which James had given his brother. He then tied the paper to a horse's tail and dragged it through the muddy streets before declaring that he no longer felt bound by any oath of loyalty to the king. Since there was little prospect of capturing the castle he burned down the town instead. This rebellion was only ended in 1455 when the king's forces destroyed those of Dougas at the battle of Arkinholm in the borders, and captured the Douglas strongholds of Threave and Abercorn (significantly by using artillery—the days when rebellious lords could sit in their castles were over).

James II died at Roxburgh in 1460 when the iron bands on a cannon burst. He was followed by his nine-year-old son who was hastily crowned James III at Kelso Abbey. This boy had spent much of his childhood at Stirling Castle and it continued to be his favourite residence; Lindsay of Pitscottie wrote that 'he took such pleasure to dwell there that he left all other castles and towns in Scotland, because he thought it the most pleasantest dwelling there'.

During James III's reign Edinburgh finally emerged as Scotland's undisputed capital city, but the king nevertheless came often to Stirling. This can be gathered from much smaller-scale activity at the castle; a new gate was built in 1463 and part of the walls were rebuilt in 1467. On March 17th 1473 a son James was born at the castle to Queen Margaret of Denmark (who also died there in 1486). In 1475 James Nory is recorded as having cast cannons at the castle, where they were stored in a special armoury. Clearly James favoured Stirling.

As he grew up it became apparent that this king was rather different from the ideal image of a monarch for that period. He showed little interest in military matters and 'desired never to hear of wars nor the fame thereof'. He had little enthusiasm for the normal knightly accomplishments of hunting, hawking, riding or combat skills, much to the dismay of his entourage, though he did occasionally watch some fencing. Indeed he must have provided quite a contrast to his brothers, the energetic and more dashing dukes of Albany and Mar. The king's main interests lay in fashionable clothes, the arts, and superb jewellery (such as a chain of gold swans set with rubies and diamonds and white enamelled swans set with pearls). The notable poet Robert Henryson lived at this time and wrote some fine work for the royal court. James also patronised painters and musicians and collected classical manuscripts; he particularly enjoyed harp, lute and organ music and choral performances by the choir of the Chapel Royal at Stirling Castle. Perhaps his greatest interest was architecture, however, and during his reign Stirling Castle especially benefited.

Much to the irritation of his nobles, the king surrounded himself with several low-born favourites including Rogers a musician, a tailor called James Hommyl, a bootmaker called Leonard and an astrologer called Andrews—James used to study the stars from the towers of Stirling Castle, perhaps in the hope that he might somehow learn what lay in the future. His most notable favourite, however, was an architect, sometimes referred to scathingly by disapproving chroniclers as a mere 'mason', called Robert Cochrane. He is said to have designed the Great Hall or Parliament Hall at Stirling Castle (although even if he did, work was still in progress on the upper walls and plasterwork as late as 1503, fifteen years into the reign of James IV). In later centuries this building was converted into a three-storeyed army barracks but the magnificent hall can again be enjoyed at Stirling, following many years of careful restoration to its original appearance by the Scottish Development Department.

Cochrane is also reputed to have designed or built a new Chapel Royal for Stirling Castle at this time but nothing now remains except its outline. The building was pulled down and replaced by James VI during the 1590s and only cobblestones mark the original site. During his reign James III founded several other collegiate churches including those at Restalrig, Tain and Trinity College, Edinburgh. He also supervised work on the 'King's Wark' at Leith, the Great Hall at Falkland (burned down in 1654) and at Linlithgow Palace.

One mystery is how James III found the money to finance so much construction work. He is said to have been 'wondrous covetous' and to have amassed a large proportion of Scotland's coinage in a secret 'black box' which he kept at Stirling Castle. This was a period of improving continental trade for Scotland but it actually resulted in serious inflation rather than prosperity, probably because of the king's personal hoard of coins. On the other hand he did spend it again on fine buildings. Nevertheless it was this covetousness and interest in the arts which ultimately caused his downfall.

As with all Stewart reigns, the politics and intrigues are too complex to explain here, but it is clear that James was unpopular with his nobles; he was too different, and easy to criticise. His brothers Albany and Mar were typically greedy for power and in 1482 both were eventually imprisoned for persistant plotting (Albany was in alliance with England, for example). Unfortunately, the Earl of Mar died in prison, and although the king seems to have been innocent of this, he was blamed. Albany escaped by murdering his jailors and fled to England where he was proclaimed 'King Alexander IV' and headed back with an invasion force. The king gathered an army at Edinburgh and went south to face the rebels. Unwisely he appointed Cochrane as Master of the Artillery for this expedition, which seriously insulted his own lords who expected themselves to be the general staff on a campaign like this. At Lauder they suddenly turned on Cochrane and hanged him from a bridge, together with most of the other royal favourites and in full view of the king.

This rebellion died out but trouble flared again several times, particularly in 1484 when Albany tried once more to invade Scotland with help from the Douglases but was defeated—he escaped to France but was killed soon after. It must have been a difficult time for the king; several times his parliament rebuked him for permitting too much lawlessness, for example. Then Queen Margaret died at Stirling in 1486 and thereafter James lived a solitary life at the castle. In 1488 another rebellious alliance of earls led by Home, Angus and Argyll forced the king to gather an army once more. He found support from just as many earls himself, but while he was gone the rebels snatched the king's fifteen-year-old son James from Stirling Castle in a pre-arranged plot with his guardian Shaw of Sauchie. The youth now found himself pushed to the head of a rebellious army against his own father.

There was a skirmish at Blackness but then on June 11th a more serious battle at Sauchieburn (known then as the Battle of the Field of Stirling). The king's army consisted mostly of Highlanders and men from Huntly, Errol and Athol, and was opposed largely by spearmen from the borders—the only occasion when Scottish highlanders and borderers opposed each other in a battle. For a time it was a close contest but the story goes that the king's horse then bolted and dragged him from the battlefield. He fell injured and was carried to Beaton's Mill at Bannockburn where he asked for absolution from a priest. A man claiming to be a priest was brought by the miller's wife but then drew a dagger and 'gave him four or five strikes even to the heart'. One of the suspects was Stirling of Keir, a local man, but nothing was ever proved. The king was buried beside his queen at Cambuskenneth Abbey and the grave, restored for a visit by Queen Victoria in 1842, can still be seen today.

James IV always regretted the manner by which he came to the throne (indeed, he wore an iron chain of penitence for the rest of his life), but the fact is that he was probably the greatest king Scotland had for centuries. At a time of Renaissance in Italy he brought culture and learning to Scotland and particularly to Stirling Castle. Though burdened by guilt over the death of his father and subject to periods of morose sadness (when, according to the contemporary poet William Dunbar he particularly came to Stirling), he was basically a bright and vivacious man who enjoyed music, sport, the arts and good company. He was also devout, brave and admired both by nobles and ladies alike; at least one of his mistresses was housed at Stirling Castle. According to one Spanish ambassador the king was 'of noble stature, neither tall nor short, and as handsome in complexion and shape as a man can be . . . He speaks the following languages: Latin, very well; French, German, Flemish, Italian and Spanish . . . the King speaks, besides, the language of the savages who live in some parts of Scotland and of the Islands . . .'

On the whole James IV enjoyed a fairly peaceful reign. He began well by pardoning all who had fought on either side at Sauchieburn and allowing them to inherit the land of their fathers. He made peace with those lords who had supported his father, and defeated a rebellion by a few who would not accept peace. His admiral Sir Andrew Wood of Largo defeated the English at sea and this was followed eventually by a truce with Henry VII during which James was able to subdue the troublesome Lords of the Isles in the west. War was eventually renewed with England but was patched up again in 1503 when James married Margaret Tudor, daughter of Henry VII and sister to Henry VIII. By comparison to the difficulties which

Beaton's Mill, where King James III was reputedly murdered after the battle of Sauchieburn, 1488. The building was destroyed by fire in 1950. *Photo:* Stirling District Libraries.

his father had struggled against, this was a much easier reign which gave the king opportunities to develop his cultural pursuits instead.

One interest was education. Not only did he provide his two illegitimate sons with an excellent schooling (even in Italy under Erasmus), but in 1496 he also had a statute passed which compelled all barons and landowners to send their oldest sons to grammar school from the age of eight or nine until they had perfected Latin. He was also instrumental in founding Aberdeen University in 1495; King's College was the first to have a faculty of medicine. Then followed the Royal College of Surgeons of Edinburgh (the first in Britain) in 1506, and a new college called St Leonard's at St Andrews in 1512. In 1507 Walter Chapman and Andrew Miller were also encouraged by the king to establish the first printing press in Scotland, at Edinburgh.

By this time work on the new Palace of Holyroodhouse was also well in hand at Edinburgh. Here the king patronised William Dunbar, perhaps the greatest Scottish poet of his day, and who later enjoyed a royal pension of £80 a year—an enormous sum. In one poem Dunbar listed the many other craftsmen and great minds who flocked around the royal court; they included doctors and lawyers, churchmen, philosophers, astrologers, artists, orators, musicians and minstrels, carpenters, masons, shipwrights, glaziers, goldsmiths, jewellers, printers, painters and potters—the list speaks for itself.

Of the buildings which can be seen today at Stirling Castle, the Great Hall was perhaps begun during the time of James III, but the impressive front wall or forework and gateway is undoubtedly the result of James IV's reign. Surviving Treasurer's Accounts show that these were begun in 1500 and were completed around 1508. In 1501 work was in progress on both the central gatehouse and south-west tower (now called the Princes Tower), under two masons called John Yorkstoun and John Lockhart. By 1503 work on the north-east 'kitchen tower' or Elphinstone Tower was also under way and in June 1504 Lockhart supervised the installation of the portcullis to the main gateway. This entrance was completed in 1506 and now Lockhart and Yorkstoun began work on the intervening curtain walls. They were still at this work in 1508 when a gap in the account appears, but by 1511 Lockhart was working on another tower at the Mint and the forework was presumably complete. At that time the towers were much taller—the upper parts were shot away during a siege in 1651 (see Chapter 7), but the general effect is still easy to visualise.

As well as this major construction work, there was an ongoing programme of repairs, enlargements and renovation throughout the castle, in the old church, the chapel, the old hall, the 'King's House', and in the mysteriously named 'cros chalmers'—enough to keep two masons called Walter and John Merlioune in work for years. And of course finishing work on the Great Hall was still underway as late as 1503. That same year the Chapel Royal was provided with enough income from various royal lands and properties to support a larger staff and so it became a collegiate chapel; a year later Pope Julius II appointed the Bishop of Whithorn as Dean of the Chapel Royal at Stirling Castle. The 'coming together' of all this work must have been a great moment for the king.

It is known that there was a garden within the castle walls, but sometime during the 1490s James had another garden built on flat ground below the castle rock, perhaps where the King's Knot is today. It was planted with flowers, vegetables, fruit trees and even vines; surviving records for 1501 show payments made to a French gardener for fetching, transporting and planting 'wine trees' at Stirling. Sadly there are no further records of vines at the castle, no payments to pickers or trampers at the grape harvest, and it

The King's Knot, an ornamental garden overlooked by the Castle. Nineteenth century restoration may have changed its original appearance. *Photo:* Craig Mair.

must be presumed that the vines failed in Scotland's less agreeable climate. On the other hand records for June 1508 show that the gardener at Stirling Castle went twice to Edinburgh with strawberries for the king.

It was at this now-splendid castle with its recently-built Great Hall that James liked to entertain his friends. A colourful assortment of courtiers and ambassadors came to know the place well. Sometimes they went hawking or hunting in the King's Park, or attended tournaments and tilting matches on the Haining; wine apparently flowed so freely that in 1506 one French knight even bathed his horse's feet in Burgundy as an antiseptic. Sometimes the hunt spread beyond Stirling into the highlands, and on these occasions tents were taken for the accommodation of the king and his nobles. Treasury Accounts mention payments to three hundred men after a royal hunting expedition to Glenartney.

One of the more intriguing figures of the period was Perkin Warbeck, a charming and passable impostor who claimed in 1495 to be the son of England's Edward IV; he was so convincing that the king gave him an annual pension of £1200 and persuaded the Earl of Huntly to give his daughter in marriage to this man. Like Thomas Warde of Trumpington who had claimed to be Richard II a century earlier, Warbeck was also housed at Stirling Castle, where he so deceived the king that Scotland even went to war against Henry VII on his behalf in 1496. James eventually realised that peace with England was more sensible and Warbeck was persuaded to leave Scotland in 1497. He later attempted a ridiculous invasion of Cornwall and was executed at the Tower of London in 1499.

Another interesting character at Stirling Castle was a Frenchman (possibly an Italian) called John Damian. Known as the 'French Leech' because of the way he wormed his way into royal favour, he claimed to be a scientist or alchemist and persuaded the king that he could turn lead into gold. James appointed him Abbot of Tongland in Galloway and the revenues from this post financed numerous, but ultimately fruitless, experiments, some of which were conducted at Stirling Castle. Eventually James became so disappointed with the results that Damian feared he was losing his popularity, so in 1507 he announced a new experiment—he would fly from the ramparts of Stirling Castle and be in France before the king's ambassadors.

A large crowd gathered to witness the historic flight. The wings, made of feathers, were fastened to Damian's arms. Then with a great jump and a flapping of arms he leapt from the battlements—and fluttered straight down into the castle midden. He suffered ridicule and a broken thigh bone, but had the dungheap not cushioned his fall it could have been much worse. Legend says that Damian had an explanation for his latest failure; he had used chicken feathers for the wings, forgetting that chickens could not fly! He should, he said, have used eagle feathers. At least he was received again at court by King James, and later immortalised in a mocking poem by Dunbar called the 'Ballad of the Frenzeit Freir of Tungland'.

Tragically, James IV was killed at the Battle of Flodden on 9th September 1513, in another flare-up of war with England but this time to assist France, which was being invaded by Henry VIII. It was a national disaster, for with the king fell the very flower of Scotland's menfolk—thirteen earls, fifteen lords, the Archbishop of St Andrews (one of James's illegitimate sons), two bishops, two abbots and a dean, three highland chiefs, the French ambassador, over one hundred burgh provosts, countless knights and lairds, and an unknown number of ordinary folk from every part of Scotland, including George Campbell the head gardener at Stirling Castle.

As many as ten thousand (half the Scottish army) may have perished. Worse still, the new king was only one year old when his father died. James V was crowned in great splendour in the Chapel Royal at Stirling Castle on 21st September 1513, but the occasion was forever known as the 'Mourning Coronation'; all four royal Jameses had died in tragic circumstances but the death of James IV was surely the saddest of all.

James IV's widow Margaret Tudor became Regent for the young James V, and in view of the dangerous times which every regency seemed to bring, retired to Stirling Castle. Here she gave birth to another son Alexander in April 1514 (he died there less than two years later). Then in August 1514 she unwisely married the Earl of Angus—this provoked such an outcry that she was stripped of the Regency which now passed to the Duke of Albany. Soon after this a deputation of nobles turned up at Stirling Castle gates demanding custody of the royal children but the queen mother had the portcullis lowered and refused to hand them over. This forced Albany himself to come from Edinburgh with an army, whereupon Margaret reluctantly gave him the castle keys. Albany installed a garrison of one hundred and forty men to guard the infant king and Margaret Tudor went back to England. Peace was meanwhile confirmed with both England and France by Lord Arran and the documents were signed at Stirling Castle. Margaret Tudor did return occasionally to see her son, most notably in 1522–23 when she caught smallpox at Stirling and nearly died.

The young king was meanwhile placed under the protection of Lord Erskine at Stirling where, according to one contemporary, he was 'educated with the greatest parsimony'—his Latin and French were barely sufficient. His guiding mentor was the poet Sir David Lindsay, who entertained the king like a favourite uncle with endless stories from history and later became famous for his 'Satire of the Three Estates'. Reflecting the time when young James II was snatched in 1440 from the King's Park, bars were added to the palace windows and a guard of twenty spearmen watched him night and day in shifts of four; if he went out in the King's Park he was accompanied by a bodyguard and six or eight outriders. And so the young monarch grew up, mostly at Stirling.

In 1524 James was declared an independent sovereign but he was only twelve years old and was hardly able to assert any authority at all. Instead he was virtually kidnapped (certainly taken into 'custody') by his step-father the Earl of Angus, a member of the powerful Douglas family, and soon there were Douglases in almost every important royal post, including chancellor, treasurer and master of the household. Twice there were rescue attempts on the king but it was only in 1528 that he finally escaped from Falkland (some accounts say Edinburgh) and came to the safety of Stirling Castle. Here he surrounded himself with a new crowd of nobles and before long the Douglases fell again from power. There is the story of Archibald of Kilspindie, one of his Douglas captors, who came to seek the king's pardon at Stirling in 1534; he waited for James in the King's Park one day and ran beside his horse asking the king's forgiveness all the way to the castle gates, but the king refused to look at him and rode on through the entrance. In due course Kilspindie was exiled to France and was not allowed to spend his last years in Scotland.

It is perhaps unfair to summarise any king in a few lines, but the story of Kilspindie is typical—James did have some unpleasant facets to his character. He showed a vindictive hardness against those who crossed him, especially his border and highland barons. In foreign affairs he schemed and plotted with the English, the French and the Pope, squeezing benefits out of each of them in return for his support; this was the time of the creation of the Church of England by Henry VIII and Martin Luther's protest against Catholicism in Germany, and the Pope was particularly anxious that neither Luther nor Henry's ideas should spread into Scotland. James also found his realm bankrupt when he came to power, largely because of wasteful expenditure during his regency, so he now set out to refill the coffers. He twice married and obtained large dowries, he made frequent levies on the Church, he appointed five infant illegitimate sons as commendators of various abbeys and thus pocketed their incomes, and he regularly fined wealthy nobles on trumped-up charges as a further source of income. When he died he had amassed a fortune but it made him unpopular with many nobles and, in effect, split the nation. As Gordon Donaldson has written, 'Taking into account his vindictiveness, his ruthlessness and his cruelty, as well as his acquisitiveness, he must have been one of the most unpopular monarchs who ever sat on the Scottish throne'.

On the other hand, there *is* the story of the Gudeman of Ballengeich. James seems to have been popular among his poorer subjects, who benefited most from the harsh imposition of law and order and were now less likely to be fleeced by the nobility. The king enjoyed travelling in disguise amongst his people and called himself the Gudeman (or farmer) of Ballengeich, a rocky gully between Stirling Castle and the Gowan Hill. As Caroline Bingham has written, 'many tales of his encounters with tinkers, beggars and outlaws, and his seductions of country girls, passed into the folklore of Scotland'.

Stair-Kerr recounts one such tale which, though it could be reworded, is just as well quoted: 'Once when the Court was in residence at Stirling, Buchanan of Arnprior commanded a carrier, who was journeying from Lennox with commodities for the royal household, to leave him the entire load, for which a just price would be given. On the servant's refusing to obey this order Buchanan boldly took possession of the goods, telling the carrier that James might be king in Scotland but that Arnprior was King in Kippen. A day or two later His Majesty rode with one or two attendants to Buchanan's house in Kippen. James was refused admittance by a tall man bearing a battle axe, who announced that the laird was at dinner and would not be disturbed at his meal. A second time the disguised monarch demanded access to the house and again he was denied entrance, but at length he persuaded the porter to carry a message to the effect that the Gudeman o' Ballengeich was desirous of an interview with the King of Kippen. Arnprior at once guessed the truth, and coming out humbly to the King, begged him to enter and grace his subject's board. So well was James entertained that, before returning home he requested Buchanan to take in future such provision as he should need from any royal carrier passing his door; also he invited the King of Kippen to return the unexpected visit by riding to Stirling Castle to see his neighbour; the King of Scots'.

In 1537, after much diplomatic wheeling and dealing, James travelled to Paris and married Madeleine de Valois, daughter of the French king. She came with a large dowry but was a frail girl and died seven weeks after reaching Scotland. James then quickly married Mary of Lorraine, daughter of the Duke of Guise, whom he had met while in Paris for his first marriage. She came with another large dowry and landed at Crail in Fife (then an important seaport). From there she travelled to Edinburgh by crossing the Forth at Stirling, where she first saw the castle that was to figure

The royal palace at Stirling Castle, built 1540–42 mostly by French workmen for Mary of Guise and King James V. It is one of the finest Renaissance buildings in Scotland.

prominently in her later life. She seems to have liked the place for within two years a tennis court was established and building work had started on two kitchens and also the famous Palace block.

The king's most important construction projects were at Linlithgow and Falkland, but the Palace at Stirling Castle became an important additional residence for Mary of Guise and is now considered perhaps the finest Renaissance building in Scotland. Details of its construction are sketchy but in 1540 when work was nearing completion at Falkland Palace, several master-masons were transferred to Stirling and it is assumed that work must have begun there by that time. The name Thomas French crops up in records but there were at least six French masons also working on royal construction projects; they arrived during 1539, invited by Mary of Guise.

Eventually a rectangular three-storeyed building appeared, with a magnificent facade of tall windows and niches containing a fascinating mixture of both grotesque and beautiful statues. The building itself contained two suites of royal rooms—guard or outer reception halls, inner or presence chambers and bedchambers for both the king and queen, arranged round an open courtyard. This yard was known as the lion's den and is supposed to have housed the king's menagerie of wild animals; a lion is said to have been presented to the king in 1539. The king's presence chamber had a particularly fine ceiling studded with over one hundred carved oak heads, probably created by a wood carver called Robert Robertson. The room, with its high airy windows, great stone fireplace, magnificent hanging tapestries and the crowning glory of that wooden ceiling, must have been a truly impressive place. In 1777 some of the heads were pulled down and destroyed but enough have survived and been restored to give a feel of how they must once have looked.

The Palace block was not completed until at least 1542 and it would seem that James V never saw it finished. Yet another flurry of war developed with England but this time everything went wrong. First the nobles refused to campaign and turned back at Fala, then the king fell ill at Lochmaben and then the Scots were defeated by a much smaller force at Solway Moss. When the king, already sick and depressed, heard the news he travelled to Falkland Palace where on December 14th he died. Almost the last words he heard were that he had an heir; just a week earlier Mary of Guise had given birth in Linlithgow Palace to a daughter. At the age of six days she became Mary, Queen of Scots.

CHAPTER 5

The Medieval Town 1370–1542

During the period of the early Stewarts the castle at Stirling was a constant favourite royal residence, but in spite of this the histories of the castle and town did not often overlap. The effects of the castle on Stirling burgh were nevertheless considerable; in bad times its presence provoked the town's destruction, while in good times the royal household generated much trade and craft work, especially from the later fifteenth century.

Although the Wars of Independence were over by 1370, periodic fighting with England did occur—Stirling seems to have been burned down in 1385 by Richard II, for example, when according to at least one chronicler he made an unsuccessful siege of the castle. War was no longer constant or desperate, however, and Stirling's people did have some respite from the English. Trade began to pick up, and though nationally it never quite returned to the successful golden age of Alexander III before Wallace and Bruce, Stirling remained one of Scotland's important ports and markets. In 1525, for example, a Scottish parliamentary document dealing with trade to Holland listed 'the principal towns of merchandise of this realm, that is to say, Edinburgh, Aberdeen, Striveling, St Andrews, St Johnstone [Perth] and Dundee'.

Stirling around 1370 must have been a very small place. On a document from 1365 the names of thirty-one burgesses 'and many others' appear; even guessing at a total of two or three times as many burgess householders and allowing for families and 'unfreemen', this would suggest a population of only a few hundred—sizeable for Scottish burghs of that time, but tiny by comparison with today. These people lived in the area nowadays known as the 'Top of the Town', comprising little more than Broad Street, Bow Street, St John Street and the top end of St Mary's Wynd. So this chapter deals with a very small part of the modern town.

What impression of fourteenth or fifteenth-century Stirling can be pieced together from surviving evidence? There was a sizeable

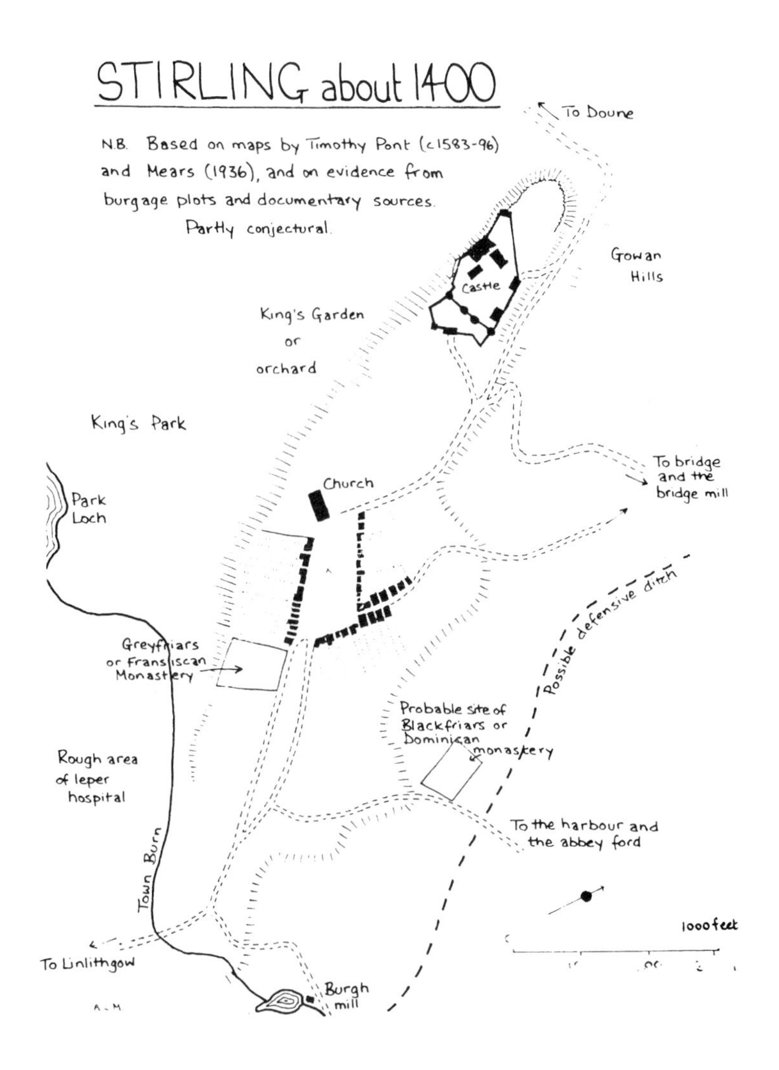

Map of Stirling in 1400.

open area between the castle and the nearest civilian houses, indicated by the esplanade car park today. As at Edinburgh, this was kept clear to provide a field of fire for defenders in the castle and to prevent besiegers from taking cover among houses in the burgh. The first dwellings began at the top of what is now Broad Street, then known as the Hiegait or High Street. It is thought that buildings ran down the north side of Broad Street, across the bottom where Bow Street is today, and up the south side of St John Street. The beginnings of a lane may also have existed at St Mary's Wynd leading to Stirling Bridge, and undoubtedly some sort of track ran down the castle hill towards St Ninians. Another may have branched off down what is now Friars Street towards the monastery of the Black Friars or beyond to Cambuskenneth Abbey. The buildings between Broad Street and St John Street, where Jail Wynd and the tolbooth are today, probably did not exist in the fourteenth century; the entire area was probably an open market space.

In 1982 an excavation was made during the Banks Court housing development in Broad Street. This produced finds from the thirteenth and fourteenth centuries which indicate how ordinary buildings were constructed at that time. The house concerned was timber-built, with an outer covering of thick clay and a clay floor. Since no slates or roof-tiles were discovered, the building, like most others, probably had a straw or thatched roof. A clay oven was found and may have been used by a baker. Several bakers are believed to have lived in this part of medieval Stirling; even the name Broad Street is thought to derive from 'bread', rather than from any reference to the width of the street.

As in other Scottish medieval burghs, houses were built directly onto the street, but each plot also had a long strip of land or 'toft' behind it which ran outwards and down the sides of the castle hill. These tofts were originally farmed; almost all Stirling folk augmented their day-to-day jobs with some additional agriculture. In 1476, for example, William Livingston, a Stirling burgess, sold his feu farm at Kippendavy to Thomas Tailyefeir (Telfer), another Stirling burgess. This included sixteen cows, six oxen, seventy sheep, a horse, five chalders of oats and half a chalder of barley. The toft at Banks Court was certainly ploughed or dug up many times, indicated by the scattered nature of thirteenth- to fifteenth-century pottery fragments; broken pottery was obviously thrown out into the back garden and then gradually mixed up with the soil by later ploughing.

Wooden, close-built, thatch-roofed houses could also burn down easily. Stirling suffered several times, by accident or in war. Unfortunately when one building went on fire others quickly followed and soon the whole town could be destroyed. The house at Banks Court was one example; lots of burnt clay and charcoal were found in the back garden area, suggesting that the building was razed and subsequently pulled down at some time during the thirteenth to fifteenth centuries, and the charred remains then cleared away onto the backyard toft. People owned and cherished so little that it was not such a terrible thing to have to rebuild a house; like the death of a child, it was almost expected to happen.

One focal point in Stirling would have been the church, predecessor to the present Church of the Holy Rude. In the twelfth century the monks of Dunfermline occupied at least two churches in Stirling. One was probably the chapel at the castle but the other, possibly dedicated to St Modan, almost certainly stood on the site of the present Church of the Holy Rude; old foundations were found below the present nave during restoration work in 1912. This previous building seems to have had an eventful history. It appears to have been destroyed in 1406 and perhaps again in 1414 when royal exchequer rolls mention a grant for repair work on 'the burned Church of Stirling'. It is likely that this was at least partially a wooden building and certainly not as large as the present one. It served the town only—the castle had its own chapel. As in most other medieval towns the church had a fairly central location; it may seem to be tucked away in a corner of the top of the town today, but in fourteenth-century Stirling the houses were all nearby. The present church was begun in 1456.

Apart from the parish church, the burgh's most important building was perhaps the tolbooth. Even in the fifteenth century the tolbooth was the centre of burgh life, where the town council met, court cases were heard and prisoners were jailed. The present building dates only from 1703–5 but it is known that an older tolbooth on the same site had become ruinous by 1698, which is why the present one was built. Unfortunately it is not known when this previous tolbooth was first built or what it looked like. Documents show that on 13th November 1473 Malcolm Fleming, son of Lord Fleming, sold land to the Town Council 'forming the site of the tolbooth'. Another early documentary reference mentions a court case heard 'at Strivelin, in the tolbooth thereof' on 26th January 1476. The Burgh Court Book for November 1520 mentions the tolbooth again and infers that it was probably built of stone, but not where it stood. From these references it is tempting to assume that the present site goes back at least to the fifteenth century, but it cannot be proved. If it *were* the case it would indicate that the market area between modern Broad Street and St John Street had already begun to be sub-divided by the 1470s. Even today the buildings there have very short backyard tofts, suggesting that they were squeezed onto the site at a later date than the houses across the street.

By the fourteenth century a mercat cross already existed in some Scottish burghs, but it is not clear in which towns they stood. A national charter granted by David II in 1364 dealing with commercial privileges and merchant guilds states that traders were 'to bring such merchandise to the Mercat and Cross of the Burghs', suggesting that crosses were fairly common in Scotland by then. Since Stirling had already been granted an annual fair and weekly market by royal charter and was one of the most important burghs in Scotland, it would be reasonable to suppose that a mercat cross stood somewhere in the fourteenth-century town. Unfortunately this cannot be confirmed. Moreover, if a cross did exist, it may not necessarily have been where the present one stands. Mercat crosses in other burghs have sometimes been moved about and one study has suggested that if Stirling had a fourteenth-century cross it may have stood more centrally in the then-larger market place, where the houses on the south side of Broad Street were later built.

In most burgh market areas there was also a tron or public weigh-beam, and Stirling was no exception. This was basically a balance-bar for regulating weights and measures, especially the weight of goods brought to market from outside the burgh. The Royal Chamberlain's accounts for 1407 refer to a tron which had been destroyed during a town fire (perhaps the same fire which destroyed the church in 1406), but there is no way of knowing where it stood or how long it had been there. Common sense would suggest the market area of Broad Street (where a later tron *did* stand) but this cannot be proved.

Although Stirling burgh stood on a naturally defensive site, it was probably also protected by some sort of fortification. The present walls were built in 1547 and improved in 1574 (Chapter 6) but it is very likely that something preceded them. The burgh records mention a 'port of the burgh' in 1477, for example; the word 'port' means a gate, which suggests a wall or rampart for the gate to pass through. Records for 1522 also mention the Barrasyet, later known to have been the main entrance into the burgh; this reference also pre-dates the present walls—so what *did* exist? Nothing survives today, but from what is known of other medieval burghs Stirling probably had a wooden palisade or earth rampart, perhaps with a defensive ditch for additional protection. In other burghs this ran along the bottom end of the backyard tofts, with each occupant responsible for the maintenance of his section. It would be surprising if Stirling did not have a similar arrangement.

One of the more important aspects of Stirling's history during this period is the question of Stirling Bridge. Victorian writers used to claim that, following its destruction at the Battle of Stirling Bridge in 1297, there was no bridge at all for the next century and travellers had to use a ferry which operated from Raploch to the remains of the causeway on the north side of the river.

In fact the damaged bridge did survive but it was not reopened until 1305 when, following William Wallace's execution earlier that year, and having seen the bridge for himself during the siege of Stirling Castle in 1304, King Edward I ordered the remaining wooden beams to be repaired; a ferry operated meanwhile. The bridge was mentioned again in documents of 1336, when it seems to have been in full use, but it must later have fallen into decay, for between 1361 and at least 1391 the ferry was back in operation. Income from this ferry went to the king, but some time before his death in 1371 David II gifted this to John de Burgh, a wealthy merchant of Stirling. This man left it in his will to the chaplain of the Altar of St Laurence in the parish church, on condition that he 'caused the foresaid ferry to be sufficiently served with a boat, attendants of the said boat, and other necessaries for the foresaid ferry'. The chaplain also received twenty shillings annually from the Crown for taking the king's horses across when required. In 1407, almost certainly following a letter from Patrick the Abbot of Cambuskenneth, Pope Benedict wrote from France: 'We have learned that in the diocese of St Andrews the bridge over the Forth, where the tide ebbs and flows, and as far as which the river is navigable, is in a very ruinous condition on account of its great age, and cannot be repaired unless by the alms of the faithful'. He offered indulgences to anyone who would contribute work or money to its repair—one of those who responded was the first Duke of Albany, who granted £20 from the Gargunnock estate in 1408. Between 1408 and 1415 the bridge was gradually repaired, probably in wood since a few years later an English spy's report stated that it was capable of being broken. Somewhere around 1500 this wooden structure was replaced by the present old stone bridge and its history is told in Chapter 7.

Once into the fifteenth century, Stirling began to develop more rapidly. A visitor to the town would particularly have noted the various church buildings. The Augustinian abbey of Cambuskenneth, just across the river from the burgh and connected to the town by a ford, was perhaps the most obvious. Founded by King David I in 1140, it was already completed in stone by the early fourteenth century with a church, cloisters and other monastic buildings, and a fine bell tower which must have dominated the surrounding carseland view for miles. Unfortunately it also attracted enemies, as in 1350 when the building was seriously damaged by 'diabolical men', and again in 1378 when the abbot reported that the monastery had 'suffered from constant wars, their chalices, books, and other altar ornaments and other goods having been stolen'.

By the fifteenth century the abbey had been granted extensive lands, including properties at Muirton, Cockspow, Cowie, Dunipace, Touch Mollar and St Ninians, plus income from the rents of Crown land around Stirling and fishing rights on the Forth. By this time the brown-robed monks would have been a common sight, offering alms to the poor and hospitality to travellers (sometimes the king himself) or working the fields around Cambuskenneth. Tradition says that each year the monks held a fair for local people at gooseberry-picking time, supposedly to maintain friendly relations with their neighbours—but it is just a story, for monks, unlike friars, generally preferred the quiet tranquility of a cloister to the hurly-burly of outside life.

Closer to Stirling there were at least two more religious communities. On a site in Spittal Street later occupied by the High School, the Grey Friars or Franciscans had a house. Long after it disappeared the site was still known as Friar Yard. Downhill at the foot of modern Friars Street in the area between the Post Office and railway station, the Black Friars or Dominicans also had a community, supposedly founded by Alexander II in 1233. Remains of medieval walls, foundations and skeletons have been excavated in the area. Tradition says that in 1298, following his victory over Wallace at Falkirk, Edward I lodged there while Stirling Castle was rebuilt (the town itself having been burned by Wallace). It is also said that James IV used to stay there during Lent, where he often ate salmon from the Forth. Even after the erection of the present town walls during the sixteenth century, this building was situated outside the burgh limits.

Medieval burghs also had a hospital or almshouse for the poor. Since lepers were sometimes sent there, Stirling's hospital and its cemetery stood a safe distance from the burgh at Airthrey, where the 'lang calsay' or causeway road across the marshes of the Forth reached dry land. The buildings were probably on this higher ground, where Spittal Farm later stood and attractive gardens now slope down to the A9 road at Causewayhead. Income to support this place came from the burgh council, from (small) royal grants and rent from the hospital's own lands which stretched across the carseland towards Cornton. It was probably staffed originally by monks from Cambuskenneth Abbey and is first mentioned in a Dunfermline Abbey document dated between 1227 and 1243. Black Friars from Stirling may have taken over the staffing during the fourteenth century; when the hospital closed, these Black Friars kept the land until the sixteenth century, so ensuring the local name 'Frierskers of Spittal'. The reason for closure is unknown. One tradition says that the hospital was run by the Knights Templar until they were suppressed in 1316, and then by the Knights of St John, but there is no proof of this unlikely theory. More probably the building was plundered so often in wars, or became such a convenient centre for military operations against Stirling, that it was closed by the burgh council. By then a proper leper house had been established anyway.

Leprosy was a much-feared illness, so the replacement 'lepermanis house' was located well outside the town walls in the Allan Park area, probably on the site of the later manse, where there was spring water (believed by Bruce among others to help cure the illness). Inmates were cared for by the Church, which in turn depended on financial help from others; records mention the leper house receiving supplies of grain from the Crown in 1464 but

This plaque is on a house in Spittal Street which stood opposite Spittal's hospital of 1660. It commemorates the town's great benefactor and can be read easily when a V is taken as a U. *Photo:* Craig Mair.

it certainly existed well before then. It seems that, if declared a leper, you would be given a charitable sum of twenty shillings and sent to the burgh leper house to be treated. If you had not recovered by the time the money ran out you were put out to become a vagrant, sitting at the burgh gates with a begging bowl but not allowed to enter the town. Many lepers wore hoods to spare others the sight of their pockmarked faces, and most finished up in a pauper's grave. It was a sad business.

Several other hospitals also existed at different times. The Hospital (or Hospice) of St James stood near the bridge at Spittalmyre, roughly where the present Orchard Hospital stands now—the original hospital owned orchards in that area and fruit trees still grew there until the railway arrived in the 1850s. This hospice was more of an inn or shelter for travellers than a hospital in the modern sense. It was common for the Church to run such stopping-places for people on the road and for a time Cambuskenneth received the income from St James. Later James II granted this money to the burgesses of Stirling to help them recover from the burning of the town by Douglas in 1452. Mary of Gueldres, wife of king James II, is said to have founded another hospital some time before 1462 but this lapsed after she died in 1463. It may be the building referred to in some writings as the Queen's Hospital. Yet another known as the Hospital of St Peter and St Paul was established some time before 1482 but was in ruins by 1610.

Finally there was the Nether Hospital founded by Robert Spittal, one of Stirling's greatest citizens and benefactors. Born around 1480, he had become tailor to James IV and Queen Margaret by 1509, when his name first appears in Exchequer Rolls. The queen was especially fond of setting new fashions and provided Spittal with plenty of work and a good income, which he seems to have invested in property. During his lifetime he gave to worthy causes and is especially remembered for providing the area with three vital bridges, at Doune, Bannockburn and Tullibody. It is hard to imagine a single act more beneficial to an entire community than the provision of a bridge; Alloa particularly gained from the Devon Bridge at Tullibody. In 1530 Spittal established a charitable hospice for respectable poor people, and by 1540 this had been constructed just outside the town 'in the hills', where Irvine Place is today. About a dozen people, mostly men, were given clothes, food, heating and cooking pots to help them survive poverty. In return they wore distinguishing blue or grey cloaks. This hospital moved to new premises in 1660 (Chapter 7).

The most notable religious development in the town must have been the construction of a new parish church during the 1450s. The burning of Stirling in 1452 by the Douglases seems to have caused some damage to the existing wooden parish church, and in 1455 the Douglases appear to have destroyed it again, because in 1456 the king granted money to the town for the construction of a new church. Perhaps he felt some blame for the town's misfortunes, given that he had killed the Earl of Douglas at the castle.

The new church was built of stone from the Ballengeich quarry and in two distinct phases. From 1456 to around 1470 the present nave or west end of the church was constructed, with a fine processional entrance doorway facing onto what is now the graveyard—this is now blocked up. The bell tower was also erected but not as high as it is today so that the church, half the length it is now and with a stumpy tower, would have looked quite different to the people of fifteenth-century Stirling. Inside, the original medieval oak roof still survives, held together with wooden pins and no nails, but the trappings and chapels of the old Roman Catholic church have mostly gone.

The second phase was built between 1507 and 1555 and was therefore begun during the reign of James IV—what an influence that king had on Stirling! During this period the bell tower was raised to its present height and the choir or east end of the church was constructed with stone from the Raploch quarry under the direction of a master mason called John Coutts; burgh records for 26th August 1529 show that he was to 'work and labour his craft of masonry and geometry . . . at all his utter power and possibility . . . and so to continue diligently at his work all years and days during his lifetime'. Various masons' marks around the church still bear witness to his careful work. Tradition has it that James IV may have worked alongside the masons, but it *is* only a story. The names of a few others involved in the work have certainly been preserved in records including Euin Allason who supplied the timber and Robert Arnot who was 'maister of the kirk wark' for which he was later made a burgess in 1529. There are also several amusing little touches in the church, such as the whiskered crowned head on one wall with, opposite, a face sticking out its tongue!

The church, like its predecessor, was under the control of Dunfermline Abbey which also contributed to the building costs. The amount is not known but most of the money was raised by the people of Stirling. Permission and encouragement was given by the Abbot of Dunfermline for the enlargement of the building in 1507 but the fund-raising was a community effort for its own parish church. Early burgh records suggest, for example, that court fines were paid towards the construction work—in April 1520 hucksters or peddlars of fish or chickens were warned not to sell before noon on pain of an eight-shilling fine 'to the Rud wark', while in July the council decreed that anyone selling ale at more than sixteen pence a gallon would similarly pay a seven shilling fine to the 'Rud wark'. By 1519 the burgh had even provided the church with a 'knok' or clock (and possibly a bell—the evidence is not clear).

The Church of the Holy Rude. The nearer end and lower half of the tower were built 1456–70. The far end dates from 1507–55. The church is considered one of the finest great medieval buildings in Scotland. *Photo:* Stirling District Libraries.

Long before the church was fully completed local burgesses began to add private chapels of their own, made by knocking out one window and extending outwards into the church grounds. The first (and only surviving example) was St Andrew's Aisle built by Matthew Forester some time before 1483. Then came St Mary's Aisle in 1484 paid for by Adam Cosour, Bowye's Aisle soon after, and so on until there were at least twenty private altars or chapels within or projecting out of the church. These were sponsored by the guildry, the town's trades (such as the maltmen and the bakers), wealthy individuals such as Alexander Cunningham of Auchenbowie, and royalty—James IV had a chapel built to honour his marriage to Margaret Tudor, and a carved stone thistle and rose can still be seen where the entrance arch was.

To begin with the church was known as the 'Parish Church of the Provost, Bailies, Council, and community of the Burgh of Stirling', or more simply the 'Parish Church of Stirling'. By 1525 this had changed to the 'Parish Church of the Holy Cross of the Burgh of Stirling' and by the 1590s to the 'Rude Kirk of Stirling', closer to its present name. Whatever some Victorian historians say,

Looking up St John Street, once known as the Back Raw, towards the impressive apse of the Holy Rude church. The manse originally stood in the centre of this view. *Photo:* Craig Mair.

the church was never connected to the Greyfriars community which lived further down St John Street, and it was never called the 'Greyfriars Church'.

At the beginning of the Reformation in the 1560s the church became a Protestant place of worship, but until then was Roman Catholic, and full of bustle, colour and song. In September 1520, for example, the burgh records mention that 'John Bully shall make service in the choir, at mass, matins and evensong, with surplice on him, as he did in James of Menteith's time, and after the form and statutes of Synod'. The colourful vestments and flickering candles must have been a fine sight. At that time the floor was not cluttered with pews, and processions of priests and choir-boys could move freely around the interior. Feast days and especially Easter, when the crucifix was taken down from the high altar and placed at a sepulchre in the choir to celebrate the Entombment of Christ, were especially important occasions. Some burials were also conducted indoors; many wealthier Stirling folk were buried under the slabs of the floor. Around 1545 the church was elevated to a Collegiate Church, which would have involved more priests (at least six) and musicians, and a corresponding increase in its day-to-day splendour. Sadly this did not last long, for during the Reformation all these 'Popish' trappings were swept away.

By the sixteenth-century the burgh's trade was developing. In 1386 Robert II granted the town council the right to the Forth fishings—in other words the right to let out or auction this right and to use the money for the common good. In 1447 James II granted the town an additional fair for eight days at Ascension, and in 1452 he freed the burgh's merchants from paying custom duties on salt and skins. In 1467 a parliament held at Stirling regulated weights and measures, while in 1458, 1467 and 1487 further regulations dealt with merchants trading overseas—it may not look much today, but Stirling's riverbank was once a thriving port. It seems, however, that some skippers saved themselves the trouble of navigating the windings by unloading at the royal burgh of Airth. Nevertheless, Stirling's fifteenth- and sixteenth-century merchants were well established, as the frequent regulation of their trade indicates.

Having wealth, merchants were also expected to have a sense of civic duty. A regulation of 1431 said that every gentleman burgess (that is a merchant able to spend at least £20 yearly or possessing £500 of moveable goods) was to be 'well horsed and armed', while those with over £10 of goods were at least to have 'a good doublet or habergeone [neck armour], an iron hat, bow, sheaf [of arrows], sword, buckler, and knife, and he that was no bowman to have a good axe'. This was because merchants were expected to man the walls in case of attack; occasional musters or weaponschaws were organised to inspect the burgess militia and check that they possessed the correct equipment.

Merchants also formed most of the burgh council—the provost, bailies and various other officials—but here they ran into the growing power of the burgh craftsmen who, by the sixteenth century, were also demanding a say in burgh affairs. D.B. Morris in his 1919 history of the Stirling Guildry neatly sums up the problem which regularly burned between Stirling's merchants and craftsmen:

> A merchant was a man who bought goods and sold them. A craftsman was a man who manufactured goods, but he required to sell them as well as make them, and he also required to purchase the raw material

> of his craft. He was thus necessarily both a buyer and a seller; hence the origin of many a bitter dispute. The merchant was of a more aristocratic caste, his hands were not defiled by work, hence arose a pregnant cause of difference, the pride of the merchant being responded to by the resentment of the craftsman. It was not a question of capital and labour, because the craftsmen were never the employees of the merchants. Nor was it altogether a question of wealth, because some of the craftsmen became manufacturers on a scale that brought them riches greater than many of the merchants.

By the fifteenth century various bodies of craftsmen were well established and had formed themselves into incorporations. These were permitted to exist by 'Seals of Cause' or charters granted by the town council. Morris again explains how they came to challenge the burgh power of the merchants:

> [The crafts] became highly organised bodies, which elected their deacons and other officers, prescribed the conditions of entry to the craft and the terms of apprenticeship, and supervised the work of all members, maintaining at the same time a high standard of workmanship and prices sufficiently remunerative. The leading trade incorporations of Stirling were the Hammermen, Skinners, Bakers, Weavers, Tailors, Fleshers, and Shoemakers. For farther protection they bound themselves together in a body known as the Seven Incorporated Trades (which still exists), ruled by a Convener Court, consisting of the Deacon and old Deacon of each Trade thus numbering fourteen, the chairman being known as the Deacon Convener.

In addition to the crafts mentioned by Morris there were also incorporations for the maltmen and barber-surgeons, but these were not included in the top seven and did not belong to the Deacon Court. However, even by the fifteenth century Stirling's craftsmen were organised enough to challenge the domination of the burgh's merchants.

For years the craftsmen demanded a voice on the burgh council and a say in the making of local laws which favoured merchants and put them at a disadvantage; this was, of course, fiercely resisted by the merchants. The success of the craftsmen's campaign varied during the fifteenth and sixteenth centuries. In 1424, for example, the Scottish Parliament allowed crafts to elect deacons, which gave them an official voice with which to demand rights, but then in 1426 it allowed town councils to fix the price of craft goods and wages, which placed burgh craftsmen under the power of merchant councillors, since they could only sell to merchants. In 1427 deacons were abolished again but in 1457 goldsmiths were allowed to elect 'deans'. In 1466 craftsmen were not allowed to use merchandise in their work, such as the litsters or dyers who were prohibited from buying finished cloth, yet in 1469 they were allowed to have a say in the election of the burgh provost, bailies and other officers. In 1496 the town council was again empowered to set craft prices and yet in 1503 maltmen were allowed to sell their malt in the open market rather than through a merchant. In 1554 the crafts were allowed to have four representatives on Stirling's burgh council, but then a year later a royal decree banned all craft deacons. So it went on in a long feud until 1556 when the Queen Regent, Mary of Guise, in a letter written and sealed at Stirling, finally granted full powers and privileges, including the right to elect deacons, to all incorporated crafts in Scottish burghs. Stirling's craftsmen have always regarded this as the time when they were, at last, fully recognised.

This endless bickering was essentially a human story—indeed the story of Stirling is that of real people, whose names have been handed down to us in the burgh records and other scraps of history. There was Duncan Bow, for example, treasurer to the smiths or hammermen, and who failed to produce accounts one year—it is easy to imagine the merchant councillors rubbing their hands and taking full advantage of the occasion. There was also Willie Fidlar, who used 'violent and impertinent' language against a local priest in 1525, for which he was severely warned that if he did so again he would pay forty shillings towards the 'Rud wark'. In 1520 John Blair was found to have 'ane scabit hors' and no doubt the neighbours were scandalised. John Akman was declared a leper in April 1520 and thereafter his whole life must have changed terribly. Marion Cant was found guilty of being a 'common flytar' or gossip, Jenny Murray was found guilty of 'pykry' or petty thieving, Alexander Forrester was elected burgh provost and must have been a proud man, and so on.

There are also many little cameos of everyday burgh life in the records. In January 1520, for example, the keeping of pigs within the town was prohibited. In October 1522 it was 'statut and ordinit' by the council that clothes were not to be washed in the town burn around the Barrasyet because it fouled the water. Candles were priced at fourpence per pound (weight), for which you got either four large candles or ten smaller ones. In 1521 Duncan Lyntoun (Linton) died; his children inherited six pewter plates, six dishes, three saucers, two trenchers, one quart jug, one choppin mug (1½ modern pints), one chandelier, two pots (worth twenty pence each), one pair of sheets, one bed, one square stool, one pair of bowls, one broadcloth, one towel and one small standard counter or desk. It is a striking indication of how little people possessed.

There are also examples of young love. At 8 o'clock in the morning of November 14th 1475, for example, Duncan Aquhonam and Agnes McAlpin became engaged in the office of the local notary 'according to the laws of the church . . . giving their oaths on the holy Gospels that they had not formerly made any contract with any other persons, but that they might lawfully be joined in marriage'. Intriguingly, the next day at 5 o'clock in the morning, the marriage 'was solemnised in face of the kirk between Duncan Aquhonam and Agnes McAlpin, by Sir Nicholas Franch, curate of the parish church of Strivelin, within the parish church of the Holy Rood of the burgh, the parties giving oath as above; whereupon an honourable man, William Stewart of Baldoran, and Malcolm McClery of Garten, gave their corporal oaths that the said Duncan was of lawful age to contract marriage with the foresaid Agnes McAlpin'. There is no mention of a dowry in this case but when Alexander Bissat became engaged to Janet Crechtoun (Crichton) in July 1520 Janet's father George paid Alexander 160 merks while Alexander's father promised the young couple half of his land plus another area of thirty acres.

No doubt Alexander Bissat and his bride Janet looked forward in 1520 to a happy life ahead. What they did not know was that within a lifetime Stirling would be rocked by two of the most dramatic figures in Scotland's history—Mary, Queen of Scots and her great adversary, John Knox.

CHAPTER 6

Mary Queen of Scots and James VI 1542–1603

Mary Stewart was only six days old when her father died and she became Queen of Scots. Almost immediately a power struggle began between nobles who supported England and the anti-Catholic mood which eventually turned into the Protestant reformation, and those who wanted to maintain Scotland's long connection with France and the Catholic faith. This centred on a rivalry between the Earl of Arran, whose family were traditional governors of Scotland during royal minorities, and Cardinal Beaton, Archbishop of St Andrews, who supported Mary of Guise and was determined to stop the spread of Protestant activity from Henry VIII's England into Scotland.

It was a difficult time. The Scottish army had just been defeated at Solway Moss and many Scottish nobles were prisoners in London. The English could also strike again at any time; fortunately they chose not to. Instead Henry VIII persuaded most of the captive lords to support him in exchange for their freedom, and soon the likes of Douglas, Glencairn, Maxwell and Fleming were returned to Scotland; a few months later Lord Arran was chosen governor of Scotland and Cardinal Beaton was temporarily arrested. Meanwhile Mary of Guise and the infant queen were still at Linlithgow.

Soon it became clear that Henry VIII wanted a marriage between the baby Mary and his infant son Edward, and in July 1543 the Treaty of Greenwich was signed to arrange this. The proposal split the Scottish nobles; some now turned against England, even the Earl of Arran who had hoped that the queen would eventually marry his own son. In such a changing and dangerous situation few seemed to think of the child Mary for her own sake. Nevertheless, in later July 1543 Cardinal Beaton (now apparently free again), together with the Earls of Huntly, Lennox, Argyll and Bothwell and an army of 7000 men, marched to Linlithgow and forcibly escorted

Mary of Guise and her baby to the greater safety of Stirling Castle. The castle was, in any case, part of Mary of Guise's marriage dowry from James V and was the most sensible place for her to stay. Here under the watch of John, Lord Erskine, the keeper of the castle, the young queen and her mother were safe. On 8th September that year the Earl of Arran, assisted by the Earls of Argyll and Bothwell (according to a very disapproving John Knox), even did penance for his temporary Protestantism in the church of the Grey Friars at Stirling.

At the age of nine months Mary was crowned on September 9th 1543 in the chapel royal at Stirling Castle, 'with such solemnity [festivity] as they do use in this country, which is not very costly', as an English envoy wrote. In fact, for a poor, faction-torn and battle-scarred country, it was as much as could be expected. The Earl of Arran carried the crown, Lennox the sceptre and Argyll the sword—the pro-English group of lords including Angus, Glencairn, Maxwell, Cassillis and others pointedly stayed away. It was also the anniversary of the Battle of Flodden—an unfortunate omen, for soon there was trouble again with England.

By the Treaty of Greenwich, which Lord Arran signed with Henry VIII in 1543, Mary was to marry Edward, the Prince of Wales, but the document was never ratified, which gave an excuse for the Scots to reject it later. The English retaliated with 'the rough wooing', an attempt to force Mary into marriage by devastating southern Scotland. Twice the Earl of Hereford invaded, in 1544 and 1545, and destroyed almost every town, village, church and abbey in the Borders—some of their ruins stand to this day as evidence. Only Edinburgh Castle survived untaken. During this period Mary was moved temporarily from Stirling to Dunkeld, which was further out of English reach.

Events now moved quickly but in confusion. Arran was such a weak governor that Mary of Guise (who proved to be very capable) joined him as a co-regent, and added more purpose to the government of Scotland. Her French nationality also raised the possibility of French troops coming to the rescue of Scotland if necessary—indeed a string of French ambassadors now joined the craftsmen, teachers, soldiers and others already at court in Stirling. These foreign emissaries may have stayed at the building sometimes known as 'Queen Mary's Palace' and later occupied by the merchant John Cowane. Stirling's burgh records indicate difficulty between the town's merchants and some foreign ambassadors who did not pay their debts for food and drink—diplomatic immunity seems to have existed then as well as now.

From Stirling the Queen mother did her best to control the turmoil of events, but some, notably the steady spread of Protestantism, were beyond her influence. There is no doubt that the Catholic Church in Scotland had become greedy, corrupt and hypocritical. An official report to the Pope in 1556 stated that the Church received 'almost one half of the revenue of the whole kingdom' (about £300,000 per annum, compared to the Crown's £17,500). Many high posts were filled by royal friends and relatives in an obvious racket to siphon off church income. While local priests lived in dreadful poverty and 'the blind, crooked, bed-ridden, widows, orphans and all other poor' were neglected, many church dignitaries lived in luxury. There were also repeated enactments against the keeping of mistresses and the fathering of illegitimate children by churchmen—Cardinal Beaton's concubine was a woman called Marion Ogilvie, for example. It is not surprising that such obvious excess turned ordinary people against the Church. Unfortunately this also split the Scottish nation.

In March 1546 the Protestant preacher George Wishart was burned as a heretic at St Andrews, watched by Cardinal Beaton. Three months later Beaton was murdered in revenge at St Andrews Castle by a group of reformist Fife lairds, who then, with John Knox, locked themselves into the fortress. Arran laid siege but it was a very feeble effort (perhaps because his own son was a prisoner inside the castle). Over a year later the French in exasperation sent a force which quickly ended the affair in July 1547. Knox and the others were arrested and sent as prisoners to serve in French galleys.

In September 1547 the English, again under Hereford, invaded Scotland. A royal proclamation was made at Stirling's mercat cross urging 'all and sundry our lieges, both to burgh and to land, regality and royalty, spiritual men as well as temporal men, yeomen, commoners, gentlemen and other fencible persons whatsoever, of what state, degree or age they be of . . .' to report quickly for military service. For once the Scottish people buried their differences and over thirty-five thousand volunteered, only to be utterly destroyed on 10th September at the Battle of Pinkie Cleuch near Musselburgh. Thousands of Scotland's best young men, including

Part of the town walls, built in 1547 when English raids threatened the infant Mary Queen of Scots. These are the best walls still surviving in Scotland. *Photo:* Craig Mair.

Stirling's provost, died or were slaughtered in the rout which followed. Coming only five years after the defeat at Solway Moss, it was a national disaster and opened up the fear of a complete collapse of Scotland.

Hereford followed up his victory by marauding through the Lowlands 'like a beast of prey' as one historian has written. Some time during the week after Pinkie the little Queen Mary was taken from Stirling to the greater safety of Inchmahome Priory on an island in the Lake of Menteith. Here, in a property owned by her guardians the Erskine family, the child not yet five years old spent about three weeks hidden from the English.

It was a nervous period for the royal family, but also for the people of Stirling. At any time the English might decide to attack the castle from which Mary of Guise governed Scotland. In October the burgh records show that fishing rights on the 'Watter of Forth' were leased to John Forrester for three years at an annual charge of £18—this money, together with donations from various gentlemen, lords and even Mary of Guise herself, was 'expended upon the strengthening and building of the walls of the town, at this present perilous time of need, for resisting of our old enemies of

England'. So began, under the direction of the same John Coutts who had earlier supervised the construction of the Holy Rude Kirk, the erection of the present town wall.

This wall did not entirely surround Stirling. Beginning at the castle, it ran along the south side of the burgh (where it can still be seen) to the main town gate at the Barras Yett (Port Street). There it turned north to the bastion or angle-tower now restored under the Thistle shopping centre. From there a short section continued north-west before petering out. That seems to have left the north of Stirling unprotected but there was probably a water-filled ditch along that side, as well as a fortified gate on Stirling Bridge and another blocking St Mary's Wynd. Householders with properties facing north were also expected to maintain their garden walls to a good height.

By 1548 the English were still in Scotland. The threat of attack on Stirling was obviously still strong, for in February the burgh council called in a debt of £40 from two bakers called Robert Geichane and Thomas Carnis and used it to equip and pay labourers still working on the town's defences. The council also ordained that 'all manner of in-dwellers within this burgh be ready with their bodies, servants and horse, to work and labour for strengthening of the town in all sorts as shall be devised and commanded, and in like manner that no manner of man depart of this town nor leave the same now in time of need, under the pain of loss of their lands and goods, and themselves or their heirs never to have place, freedom or dwelling within this town afterwards'.

In such dire circumstances many Scots began to accept a royal marriage with France as a necessity. Soon a treaty was signed whereby the infant Queen Mary would sail to France for safety and eventually marry Francis, the son of King Henry. In return French troops would be sent to garrison vital castles and help stiffen Scotland's resistance to the English—indeed fifty French military advisers had already arrived and by June 1548 another six thousand experienced troops were in action. By July the little queen was at Dumbarton waiting for French ships to take her to the continent. On August 7th after a tearful parting from her mother, but escorted by Lord Erskine and several childhood relatives and friends including her 'four Marys', she sailed.

What a sad childhood Mary must have had. She may sometimes

have watched the building of the Holy Rude church but she spoke French as her first language and cannot have chattered easily with the townsfolk. Perhaps she played in the castle gardens and parks, or ran about in the draughty stone corridors of the castle, but she was often surrounded by an atmosphere of tension and danger. Twice she was rushed off to safety when the English threatened, and always there were adults around her worried about national events.

For the next eleven years Scotland's child queen lived in France (where she was much happier) and the nation was under the joint guardianship of the Earl of Arran and Mary of Guise. This is not the place to describe the tumultuous and very complex events which occurred during that period. The highlights are that the Protestant reformation gained ground, that Arran was bribed by the French to resign as governor in 1554, leaving only Mary of Guise in control, and that thereafter she used Scotland mainly to suit French foreign affairs. Numerous Frenchmen were given important positions in the Scottish government, for example, and Scotland was dragged into war with England and Spain.

The period from 1558 to 1561 was particularly unsettled. In 1558 fifteen-year-old Queen Mary finally married young Francis in Paris; when King Henry died in 1559 Francis and Mary became joint monarchs of France. Scotland's government now came under the control of 'Francis and Mary, King and Queen of France and Scotland', which disturbed many a patriot and worried the Protestants. In 1558, however, Elizabeth became Queen of England. She followed an anti-Catholic policy which encouraged Scottish Protestants to rise in rebellion against Mary of Guise's obvious Catholic sympathies.

In 1559 John Knox returned to Scotland; his passionate energies and firebrand sermons at Perth and Edinburgh added fuel to the Protestant reformation. Several churches, cathedrals and priories (including Cambuskenneth in 1559) were attacked and pillaged. Stirling's burgh records are missing from June 1557 to April 1560 but most ordinary people seem to have supported the Reformation; it is known that as early as 1559 Knox preached in the Church of the Holy Rude and urged the townsfolk to cleanse the kirk of idols. The church, not even completed yet, was therefore stripped of its altars and statues (the empty niches can still be seen). Another indication of the reformation in Stirling came in July 1560 when, in an argument, John Bethok accused James Oswald of having 'not as yet recanted his old traditions'. In October 1560 John Donaldson was appointed the first kirk minister of the Holy Rude by the burgh council and given lodgings in the town. In December 1560 the records refer to a plot of land adjacent to the 'old Greyfriars yard'—this Catholic house was closed by then. (In 1567 Queen Mary eventually granted to the Council 'the manor places, orchards, lands, annual rents, emoluments and duties whatever which formerly belonged to the Dominican or teaching friars and Minorities or Fransiscans of our said burgh of Stirling'.)

Nationally, a situation little short of civil war developed. French troops scoured Fife for Protestant insurgents while English ships helped a Protestant siege of Leith. During this period French troops may have occupied Stirling Castle and, probably in 1559, the French or Spur Battery was constructed outside the main castle foreworks to dominate Stirling Bridge; it can still be seen today. In June 1560 the long-suffering Mary of Guise died. By a treaty in July both the French and English withdrew from Scotland. The problem of who would now govern arose, but this was resolved in December when King Francis died in Paris, leaving Mary no more than a nineteen-year-old dowager. By August 1561 she was back in Scotland as Queen. For a time Stirling had been the centre of government, the scene of Frenchmen coming and going and messengers bringing news from all over Scotland, but Mary chose to live mostly at Holyrood Palace; the centre of events now moved from Stirling to Edinburgh.

Soon after her arrival in Scotland, the Queen made a tour round her kingdom. She spent two days at Linlithgow, her birthplace, and then in early September reached Stirling; it was not a successful visit. One night a candle set fire to the Queen's bed-curtains; she was saved only by the quick thinking of a maidservant who dragged her clear, and who thereby undid an old prophecy that a queen would be burned alive at Stirling. (Some believe that this maidservant is the Green Lady ghost, who is said to haunt the castle.) On the same visit there was also a bloody fight in the Chapel Royal when the queen's chaplains and singers were attacked for singing High Mass by Lord James Stewart and the Earl of Argyll (Mary's half-brothers, but who had adopted the Protestant faith). While the Queen cried at a scene of split heads and gashed ears, some others laughed. It can hardly have endeared her to Stirling.

In fact the Queen did come several times to Stirling, where she hunted and enjoyed archery in the palace gardens. She also passed through Stirling in August 1562 on her way to Aberdeen, but a more memorable occasion was her stay in 1565 when she came to nurse her Anglo-Scottish cousin Henry Stewart, Lord Darnley, who was ill with measles. For two months she cared for Darnley and fell passionately in love with him at Stirling. Two months later they were married at Holyrood and within a year Prince James was born.

As usual for royal princes, James was sent with a bodyguard of several hundred musketeers to Stirling Castle and at the age of two months placed in the care of Lord Erskine, who was now also made the Earl of Mar. The royal nursery was prepared to the Queen's own instructions—buckets of gold and silver, blue material for the cradle, with blankets, a fustian mattress and feather pillow, and tapestries on the walls.

In the late afternoon of 17th December 1566 the six-month-old prince was baptised in the Chapel Royal at Stirling Castle, in a splendid ceremony which cost £12,000 Scots—there would be no cause for English visitors to complain of cut-price 'solemnities' this time. The godparents were King Charles IX of France, the Duke of Savoy and Queen Elizabeth of England—none actually attended but they each sent high-born representatives. The French king also presented Mary with gifts of earrings and a necklace while Savoy's ambassador brought Mary a fine jewelled fan and Elizabeth gave a magnificent golden font which reputedly weighed two stones (about 13 Kg). Mary was determined to match these with a lavish occasion; she herself paid for her nobles' clothes, 'some in cloth of silver, some in cloth of gold, some in cloth of tissue, every man rather above than under his degree' as one account said. The Earl of Moray was in green, for example, while Bothwell was in blue and Argyll in red—it must have been a fine sight.

While courtiers and barons lined the way with flaming torches, the christening party moved from the nursery to the chapel. First came the French king's representative carrying the baby, followed by a procession of Catholic lords and officials carrying the crown, salt, basin, towel and rood which would be used in the ceremony. They were received at the door of the chapel by the Archbishop of St Andrews and the Bishops of Dunkeld, Dunblane and Ross. The ceremony was according to Catholic rites, and several Scots and English Protestant nobles waited outside the chapel door while this went on. However, the Countess of Argyll (who was also Protestant but was willing to stand in for Queen Elizabeth) held the child up to the font, where he was christened James Charles in honour of his Scottish and French blood. The only deviation from the full Catholic baptism was when Mary refused to allow the ceremony of the spittle, which would have involved a priest spitting into the mouth of the child. Then the guests adjourned to dinner, followed by music and dancing.

Two days later the Queen held another great banquet at Stirling in honour of her guests. This time there were fireworks and specially commissioned poems, and a masked ball. Some Frenchmen came dressed as satyrs and deliberately wagged their tails at the English guests, which caused such a tumult that Queen Mary had to intervene herself to soothe ruffled feelings. This apart, it was another glittering and very successful occasion—even the normally dour Protestant lords danced and caroused. That evening the Queen also announced that she had created her son Prince of Scotland, Duke of Rothesay, Earl of Carrick, Kyle and Cunningham, and Baron of Renfrew.

There was one dark spot in these celebrations. Lord Darnley, who was the baby's father, was present in the castle but refused to attend either the baptism or the subsequent festivities. In return the French representatives refused to see him. Darnley then seems to have moved out of the castle to lodgings in Broad Street—*not* the building now called Darnley House, which is more recent, but another to the rear called William Bell's Tavern, later known as Moir of Leckie's House. He cannot have been there long, for at the end of December he went to Glasgow. This was the beginning of Darnley's estrangement from Mary which ended only with his murder at Edinburgh two months later.

As the foreign dignitaries and ambassadors went home from the royal baptism, it was undoubtedly voted a great success, but for Mary there were worries. Her marriage was failing and her kingdom was disintegrating into rival religious factions; the French ambassador once found her weeping in her room, 'suffering both mental and bodily pain'. One friend was Sir James Melville who, as Stair-Kerr describes, 'seems to have been a person in whom the Queen could confide. One evening, shortly before the baptism, she took him by the hand and led him down to the Royal Park, where they could discuss the troubles of the state without being

The building known as Darnley's House, which faces up Broad Street. It dates from around 1600 and was for long a public house where town council meetings were sometimes held. *Photo:* Central Region Archives Department.

interrupted by the mockery of Court festivities. After humbly proffering his advice and endeavouring to lighten her burden of sorrow, he escorted her back to the castle through the steep streets of the town'. It would be nice to imagine the two of them walking up through Stirling alone, but more likely the Queen was surrounded by bodyguards who pushed people back and cleared a path up Castle Wynd for the monarch.

In fact the Queen seems to have gone into Stirling burgh more than once. William Drysdale quotes another story: 'When Secretary Maitland of Lethington came to Stirling, on 4th September 1566, at night he did lie at Willie Bell's, and on the morrow Queen Mary came to the Secretary, and there did dine with him, and remained a good part of the afternoon with him, and liked him very well. The Queen then returned to the Castle of Stirling'.

In January 1567 the Queen took her son to Edinburgh, but then came trouble and scandal with the murder of Lord Darnley and Mary's interest in the Earl of Bothwell (whom many suspected of Darnley's death). The child was quickly returned to the greater safety of Stirling. Mary came to visit him on 21st April and stayed two days playing with the ten-month-old boy. She did not know that this would be her last sight of Stirling or her son. On her return to Edinburgh she was intercepted and abducted by her lover Bothwell, and so began the tumultuous collapse of her reign. The Queen married Bothwell in May, was overthrown by Protestant rebels in June, and abdicated in July. She was then imprisoned in Lochleven Castle but escaped in May 1568. Within a fortnight she was defeated at the Battle of Langside and forced to flee to England. Mary expected sympathy and help from her cousin Queen Elizabeth but instead she was imprisoned for nineteen years until her eventual execution at Fotheringhay Castle on 8th February 1587.

Mary having abdicated in July 1567, her baby son now became King James VI. On 29th July he was brought from Stirling Castle to the Church of the Holy Rude to be crowned. This time the Protestant lords would have nothing to do with the Chapel Royal and deliberately chose the burgh church for the ceremony; to emphasise the point, perhaps, John Knox was brought to deliver the sermon (which he took from the Book of Kings, where Joas was crowned very young). Significantly, perhaps, only five earls and eight lords turned up for the coronation in a Protestant church. The ceremony was nevertheless very similar to what would have happened had it been a Catholic one. The church was still learning how to change to new ways; some bishops, for example, were now Protestant while others were not. The crown was placed over the infant king's head by the Protestant Bishop of Orkney, and held there by the Earl of Mar who was the king's guardian. The sword and sceptre were delivered by two Protestant superintendents from Angus and Lothian. The bishop then anointed the royal head (much to Knox's disapproval) and the Earls of Morton and Home swore an oath on behalf of the king that he would uphold the 'true worship of God'. The few nobles who were present then approached and touched the crown, symbolising their acceptance of the new king. Thereafter the Earl of Mar carried the child back to the castle while Atholl carried the crown. For the next twelve years James continued to live at Stirling Castle, guarded by Mar. This was important, for the exiled Mary still had supporters—even Edinburgh Castle still held out for her.

During the King's childhood there were four successive regents—the first was the Earl of Moray but he was assassinated in 1570. Moray was followed by the Earl of Lennox but he also died violently, in an attack on Stirling. On the night of 3rd September 1571 supporters of Queen Mary led by the Earl of Huntly, Lord Claude Hamilton, Scott of Buccleuch and Ker of Fernihirst, together with three or four hundred men, made a surprise raid on Stirling, hoping to capture as many Protestant nobles as possible, gathered there for a meeting of Parliament. Leaving their horses at a distance, they crept up to the walls and entered by a secret passage known to one of the men. Then with cries of 'God and the Queen' they burst into the houses of various nobles and easily captured an assortment of lords including Glencairn, Eglinton and Lennox (since Parliament normally met at Stirling Castle, many nobles had houses or lodgings in the burgh at that time). The only fighting occurred at Morton's house, where two servants were killed before the earl surrendered.

The story might have ended there and changed the course of history, except that Scott and Ker's borderers now rushed off to plunder the town instead of escaping while they could. In due course the Earl of Mar 'sallied forth from the castle with a band of musketeers' as one account says, and from the building site of Mar's Wark, where the house was in the process of construction, began firing down Broad Street at every borderer in sight. The townspeople now grabbed what weapons they could and helped to drive the raiders off. In the confusion of the retreat a trooper named Calder shot the Earl of Lennox; in fact his captor, Spens of Wormiston, threw himself in front of the regent but the shot killed them both. A plaque at Randolphfield marks the supposed spot where it happened. What was to have been a bloodless coup turned into a disastrous failure in Broad Street.

The Earl of Mar was now appointed regent but he died a year later; as Stair-Kerr wrote in 1913, 'the cares of state and the worries of civil war seem to have been responsible for the Regent's premature decease, although the usual report of poisoning was given circulation at the time', while Gordon Donaldson wrote more recently that he 'loved peace and could not have it'. Mar was replaced as regent by the Earl of Morton who, in 1573, also captured Edinburgh Castle and thereby further weakened what was left of Queen Mary's support in Scotland. At about the same time a number of Mary's supporters were brought to Stirling Castle. In 1569 Maitland of Lethington was arrested and held at Stirling Castle for being involved in the murder of Lord Darnley (though he later escaped from Edinburgh). In April 1571 the Archbishop of St Andrews was captured by troops who climbed Dumbarton Castle rock; they brought him to Stirling Castle where he was charged with involvement in the murder of both Darnley and the regent Moray. Two days later the same man who had assisted at Prince James's baptism in the Chapel Royal was hanged at the mercat cross. With the capture of Edinburgh Castle in 1573 the next few years were peaceful. Stirling's walls were nevertheless strengthened during 1574.

Up at the castle, King James was now guarded by Mar's brother the Master of Erskine. With a small circle of friends including the young Earl of Mar and Lord Invertyle, he received an excellent education from two tutors—the famous, brilliant, but very stern Protestant scholar George Buchanan, and the gentler Peter Young. By the age of eight he was able to translate from Latin into French any chapter chosen at random from the Bible, and could also give an exhibition of dancing to the English ambassador. Lord Melville noted in 1574 (when the king was still eight) that 'I heard him discourse, walking up and doun in the auld Lady Mar's hand, of knowledge and ignorance, to my great marvel and astonishment'. He was also 'a tireless and a reckless horseman' as Caroline Bingham has written, but was evidently not fond of martial sports.

Encouraged by his tutors, the King assumed full power himself in 1578 when he was only twelve years old, and the regent Morton was relieved of his post.

Inevitably there was an outbreak of plotting while the King was still so young, and much of this centred on Stirling. Civil war threatened almost immediately; rival armies gathered at Edinburgh and Stirling but fighting was avoided. In 1580 rumours swept Stirling Castle that the King would be kidnapped and spirted off to France; guards were posted inside and outside the royal apart-

The outer courtyard of Stirling Castle in 1600. This view shows, left to right, the entrance gateway, the palace block and the great hall. From a drawing by James Proudfoot. *Photo:* Stirling District Libraries.

ments and the plot failed. Within a year the Earl of Morton was hanged in Edinburgh for his persistent scheming for power. Then in 1582 the King was successfully captured at Ruthven Castle by Protestant nobles worried that James was coming too much under French influence. The sixteen-year-old monarch was brought back to Stirling where he was then allowed to reign again.

Much the same happened in 1584, when Protestant nobles again became concerned at French influence; this time they gathered an army of five hundred horsemen and on 17th April seized Stirling Castle. When the King approached with an army of his own, however, they fled. James then hanged the castle's Constable and three men for their presumed complicity in the matter. In due course the Earl of Gowrie was also hanged just outside the castle walls. In 1585 there was yet another attack on Stirling when rebel lords organised a force of nine hundred men at St Ninians and on 1st November crept into the town at dead of night. With the town easily captured they then surrounded the castle, foiling an attempt by the King to escape, and eventually forcing him to meet their demands. There was no attempt to harm the King himself in these affairs—simply to keep him on the straight and narrow path of Protestant government and away from French influence. Fortunately this jostling for power among the nobles ended in 1587 when James passed his twenty-first birthday and gradually assumed real power for himself. He proved to be an extremely able and clever king and thereafter steered Scotland into a period of stability and greater prosperity—not a moment too soon for the poor citizens of Stirling!

In 1589 James married Anne, second daughter of the king of Denmark. The wedding was at Holyrood but in February 1594 their son Henry was born at Stirling Castle. To celebrate the young prince's baptism, the old Chapel Royal was demolished and the present building was constructed at a cost of £100,000 (including some refurbishment of the Palace). No building accounts survive but it is known that the best workmen were employed and urged with 'large and liberal payment' to have the place ready for the christening on 30th August.

On 24th August three heralds and two trumpeters proclaimed the coming baptism at Stirling's mercat cross, requiring all lords and barons to attend and warning them of feuding or brawling at Court. One by one foreign envoys and ambassadors gathered at the castle from various countries including France, Brunswick, Magdeburg, Denmark, and the Low Countries—Queen Elizabeth of England was represented by the Earl of Sussex. In the days before the event tournaments and banquets were held, building up the atmosphere for the great day while workmen feverishly prepared the new Chapel Royal.

The baptism itself was a memorable event. When guests entered they found the chapel hung with tapestries and velvet, and a new pulpit hung with fabulous cloth-of-gold in the centre of the hall. Sussex carried the baby into the chapel, walking under a canopy supported by four Scottish lairds from Dudhope, Cessford, Buccleuch and Traquair. Behind him came Lord Hume with the prince's crown, Lord Seton with the basin and Lord Livingstone with the towel to be used in the baptism. This was performed, in Latin, by the Protestant Bishop of Aberdeen who named the child Frederick Henry.

That evening there were memorable celebrations in the Great Hall. The King, Queen and foreign ambassadors sat at a top table, with more tables down the sides of the hall to leave the centre area open. Ladies of high rank sat between each Scottish noble and foreign guest. Rennie McOwan has described what happened next: 'After the first course the trumpets played a fanfare, and there was then appreciative murmering from the guests. The second course, a dessert, was carried in on a table placed on a chariot twelve feet long and seven broad. The chariot was moved by men hidden within it and screened from the guests by hanging cloths. It was led by a blackamoor dressed in rich clothes and wearing a harness of pure gold. It was accompanied by six ladies, three in white satin and three in crimson, with features and jewels on their heads. Each lady carried a badge to denote her identity, plus a motto. They represented Ceres, the goddess of agriculture and civilisation, and such themes as Fecundity, Faith, Concord, Liberality and Perseverance. They served the dessert to the guests, and then they and the chariot left the hall, amid applause.'

The next course was an imitation dish of seafood actually made of sugar, and delivered by an extraordinary ship. This vessel was eighteen feet long and eight feet wide, with a forty-foot high mast, red silk rigging and thirty-six brass cannon, the whole thing weighing several tons. It came rolling in mounted on hidden wheels worked by a squad of men somewhere underneath the decks. At least thirty people were crowded on board including a pilot and five sailors, fourteen musicians, various nautical characters such as Neptune and Arion and a bevy of mermaids, all laughing and waving to the guests. All wore colourful and glittering costumes—Neptune, for example, wore cloth of silver and silk, the musicians wore red and gold, and the mermaids were draped with pearls, coral and shells. It must have been a sensational entry.

Having reached the top table, the ship then dropped anchor to a blast of trumpets. Then while the crew played harps and sang songs, the sugary crabs and lobsters and shellfish were unloaded in beautiful glass dishes and presented to the various guests. Having raised anchor, the ship then withdrew, firing all its guns just before it disappeared from sight. And so the party went on long into the night. It was an occasion talked about all over Europe for a long time—except by the English, whose envoys did not mention it in their reports to Queen Elizabeth. Perhaps she would have been jealous.

Henry was the last royal prince to receive an upbringing at Stirling Castle. Taught by Adam Newton, he grew up a confident and kind-hearted young man, with a particular passion for horseriding. According to the French ambassador he also played tennis and golf and enjoyed archery and gymnastics. Sadly the young prince who had been given such a spectacular baptism died aged eighteen and it was his younger brother Charles who inherited the throne.

During the sixteenth century Scotland's monarchs often lived at Stirling, but at the castle. Burgh life did go on, but tends to have been overshadowed by greater national events. Burgh, church and guildry records are, in any case, largely missing for this period and it is difficult to paint a picture of everyday town life in the later sixteenth century. Nevertheless some indicators have survived and help to show how people lived.

Somewhere between 1544 and 1550 a rough population count of Stirling was made and jotted into the back of a council minute book. This list was made to help four town bailies keep the law in their appointed districts of the burgh. The census gives the names of 105 persons including 24 females living in 'The Mary Wynd, Castall Wynd and the north part of the Hie-gait (Broad Street)'. Another 98 names including 14 females are given for the Back Row (St John Street), the south side of the Hie-gait and the bottom end of the Hie-gait. The 'south quarter' below Bow Street (Spittal Street and the south side of modern King Street) contained 99 names including 22 females, while the north quarter (Baker Street and north side of King Street) offered another 103 persons including just 9 females. There were also 35 property-owners who lived outside the town. If these 440 people are regarded as heads of families (which is not certain), it would suggest a population of perhaps 1500 in Stirling.

Among these people crafts evidently flourished. Even in the few pages of burgh records which have survived, mention occurs of the baxters (or bakers), fleshers (butchers), skinners, websters (weavers), coopers, maltmen (brewers), cordiners (shoemakers), bonnetmakers, tailors and others. Merchants also crop up, including reference to wine sellers. The schoolmaster and kirk minister also occur. From time to time the prices of goods are also mentioned; in 1564 the provost and bailies of the burgh council decreed that double-soled lined boots were to cost 24 shillings, single-soled boots 16 or 18 shillings, best quality single-soled men's shoes 3 shillings, lower quality men's shoes from 2 to 3 shillings, double-soled shoes for women 2 shillings and 6 pence, single-soled women's shoes from 16 to 20 pence, good quality children's shoes from 7 to 9 pence, and so on. The leather was also to be 'wele barkit and wele laborit' on pain of confiscation of all goods (bark was used to make pits of tannic acid, which rotted hair from the hides and so, after curing, produced leather). Similarly, in 1598 ale was set at one shilling per Scots pint (three English pints), a 14 ounce wheaten loaf was also to cost a shilling, and a pound of tallow candles was fixed at two shillings.

One interesting note mentions coins from the period around 1560: 'Robert Cowsland appeared in judgement, in presence of the provost and bailies, and there offered payment to Alexander Hog for payment of certain meal bought by him from the said Alexander, and to that effect produced a leather wallet with gold, silver two shilling pieces, plaks, bawbees, hardheads, and other such usual money, and the said Alexander refused to receive any English money . . .'. In a will from the same year an even wider variety of coins is mentioned, including pistol crowns, ducats, angel nobles, testoons and groats. There was a mint at Stirling Castle, perhaps in the building known as the Cunzie House (cunzie means coin). Metal for Scotland's plaks and bawbees is supposed to have come from the Airthrey copper mines; an air vent can still be seen in the Mine Woods behind Bridge of Allan, and tunnels still run under the village.

In 1547 a council deputation went to inspect George Spiers's house and workshop, probably a brewery since it stood beside the town burn, and which had recently been repaired. From this we know that the dwelling was 'well thatched with thatch, well timbered and beamed and raftered above the hall board, the windows well glazed and latticed within and without as usual, with door slots and covers, and the rest of his tenement even to the yard standing sufficiently in large timbers such as the joists, and in beams, wattles and straw, thatch and divot, soberly appeared watertight; and the yard thereof with a stone dyke at the west end of the same, and the said work house with furnishings, leads and vats, well walled and timbered, soberly watertight as said, with the yard thereof dyked with stone and mortar'.

By examining the will of Duncan Kerr, a burgess skinner who

died in 1560, we can also discover what sort of possessions people of craftsmen level had. Apart from his money and a pile of over four hundred skins and hides, Kerr left a coat, a pair of blue hose, bonnet, cloak and doublet, a sword and dagger, and a saddle. Household goods consisted of a large and a small cooking pot and a pan, a plate and pewter dish, two bowls, two bowls with handles, four plates, a ladle, a horn, a silver spoon, a candleholder, a tub, a meat vat, a barrel, a trencher, a saltpot, a pint and a quart tin jug, a set of balance scales with weights, and a chimney with racks, tongs and shovel. Kerr's furniture comprised a standard bed, cot and a feather bed with bolster and three pairs of sheets and blankets, a desk, a cupboard, one long wooden seat, a bench, a chair, a spinning wheel with a pair of carding combs, a chest, a broadcloth, a shelf for dishes, a small cabinet and a brewing vat. These were the sum possessions of a successful craftsman.

We do not know why Duncan Kerr died, but he left a wife and two bairns; perhaps he was still a young man. Disease was widespread in Stirling; the records mention several people who were 'fund lipir', for example. The pest or plague was another dreaded visitor, and crops up in records for 1546, 1548 and 1549. People who suspected plague in their household were supposed to lock themselves in and get rid of anything thought to harbour the sickness, on pain of severe punishment. In 1549, for example, the council found that 'James Hall has failed to put forth clothes and divers stuff out of his house, having a woman servant suspect and sick with the pest, and therefore decerns him to be punished in his person, and all his goods and freedom to be confiscated at the provost's will'.

Crimes and punishments also occur in the records. In 1546 Donald Duncanson waited until his master John Lanorok was asleep and then took 'ane gret hevy stane' and bashed his master's head in, 'and thairefter cuttit his throte'. He then robbed the house and body of clothing, money and goods but was chased by Janet Menteith the master's wife, and Bessie Lanorok his sister. Donaldson was eventually caught, found guilty of murder and hanged.

Most criminals were thrown out of town, however, such as George Moncrieff, James Wilson and others including Maddy Bathelem who were all found guilty of burglary; since Bathelem had been banished before, she was also branded on the cheek with a hot iron and all were threatened with hanging if they ever returned to Stirlingshire. Similarly in 1562, two women were drummed out for being witches. On the other hand, in 1547 when Janet Bell accused Janet Sharp of having David Sibbald's child, she was made to walk through the town one Sunday morning dressed in just a shirt, asking the forgiveness of Janet Sharp and her husband and crying out for all to hear 'tongue you lied on her'.

Over the years the burgh also developed. In 1548 John Forrester and Walter Cousland who were bailies enhanced their status by providing Stirling with a windmill, in return for seven years' exemption from tax and a supply of meal for nineteen years. That same year William Kerslaw was paid forty shillings by the council to keep the town clock in good repair—there was a clock in the tolbooth tower already in 1519 when surviving records begin. In 1557 William Gullein, master at the burgh's Grammar School, received an assistant called David Elles who was to help with the teaching of reading, writing and counting, and with the under-six year olds; there was a school by 1522 and undoubtedly long before then. In the Church of the Holy Rude burials under the floor were ended, but in 1598 John Forrester of Logie, a past stalwart of the burgh council, somehow got himself buried indoors. Perhaps to make his name in the new century, Robert Forrester of Boquhan gave fifty merks to the masters of the hospital in July 1600, to be used to buy land which would, in turn, provide annual rent income for the care of the poor. Since Catholic-run hospitals no longer existed after the Reformation, burghs had to support their own poor, and looked for charity from their wealthier citizens.

In 1603 Queen Elizabeth died and James VI became king of England through his ancestor Margaret Tudor who had married James IV. On 5th April of that year he set out for court at London, promising that he would return at least every three years to Scotland. In fact he came only once, in 1617. Though Stirling did not realise it at the time, its days as a centre of royal life and national intrigue were finished. The burgh did not decline—indeed it grew—but it was never the same again, for the royal ingredient, that hint of spice and interest, was lost.

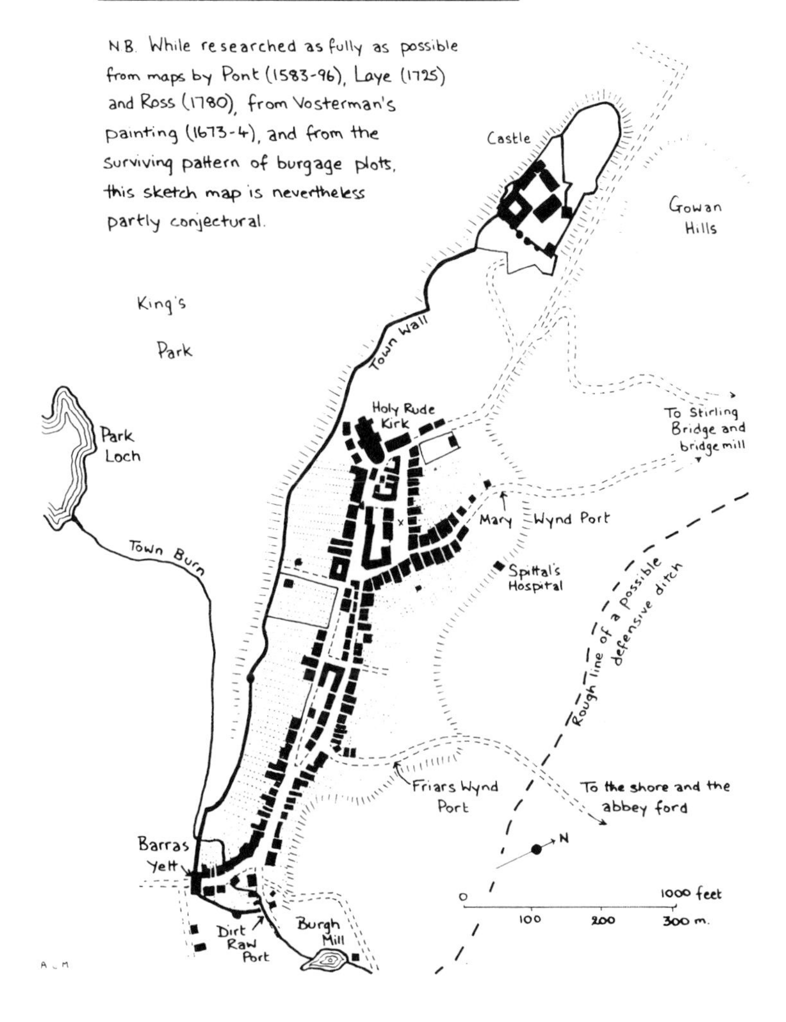

Map of Stirling in 1600.

CHAPTER 7

Everyday Life in the Old Burgh 1603–1707

By 1603 Stirling was a snug, compact burgh enclosed by its defences and entered only by one of its five gates. Housing ran from the Castle downhill to the Barras Yett or Burgh Gate where Port Street is now. The only important side streets were St Mary's Wynd and Blackfriars Wynd (now Friars Street). At one time Spittal Street and Baker Street formed a wider area but, like St John Street and Broad Street before them, they were split apart as housing pressure grew and shops appeared. In the seventeenth century there was no low road to bypass Stirling; since Stirling Bridge was the only crossing point to the Highlands, travellers heading north had to come through the Barras Yett, move up what is now King Street and Baker Street to Bow Street, and then head down St Mary's Wynd to the bridge. With a constant stream of traffic (mostly packhorses or two-wheeled carts) passing through Stirling, the entire thoroughfare was paved with stone. Spittal Street, St John Street and Broad Street, which were away from the main road, were less congested and more pleasant to live in, but seemingly were not paved.

Broadly speaking, folk who lived higher uphill were from a higher social class. Over a dozen nobles had their large and sometimes fancy houses around the Holy Rude church and in Castle Wynd; according to Nimmo they included the Earls of Morton, Glencairn, Cassillis, Eglinton, Lennox, Montrose, Linlithgow, Buchan, Argyll and Mar, plus Lords Semphill, Cathcart, Ochiltree, Glamis, Ruthven and Methven. Mar's Wark and Bruce of Auchenbowie's house in St John Street are the only surviving examples from this period (the Argyll Lodging was not built until 1630).

Those with an important standing in the burgh came next. Broad Street and St John Street tended to be occupied by merchants, with the occasional lawyer or more successful craftsman. Their houses, though with narrow frontages, were tall, built of stone and sometimes quite elegant, and the burgage strips behind were usually long, a reminder that this was the oldest but least crowded part of Stirling. Further downhill were the weavers and bakers, butchers and maltmen; St Mary's Wynd contained at least four bakers, two fleshers, a maltman and a tailor, while Friar's Wynd is known to have included at least two maltmen and a weaver. Spittal Street (being quieter and therefore more desirable) housed at least three merchants, four weavers, two bakers, one cutler and a gunsmith. Here the houses were more crowded, with short burgage strips behind them showing how they were squeezed later into open spaces where possible. Sometimes shops occupied the ground floor and outside stairs or turnpike turrets led to upper levels.

The poorest folk lived at the bottom end of town, where sewage and filth gathered from up the hill. Here in a jumble of wooden huts and thatched sheds and workshops around the Dirt Row Port (the very name says it all) were the potters and brewers, tanners and candlemakers—those with unpleasant or smelly occupations, or no money. One account suggests that the 'lowest of the low' in burghs also included midwives, night-soil carriers and prostitutes. That left just the lepers who were so low that they actually lived outside the gates on the Lepercroft, where the Allan Park area is now.

As the town developed, workshop industries sprang up on many of the burgage strips or backyards, and so little alleys or closes appeared, leading off the street and 'through the back' to a host of merchant warehouses and craft workshops. They could be found everywhere from Broad Street to the Barras Yett, through an arched pend or up a narrow, airless entry to the toft behind. Sometimes the same entry was shared by several people, and even by their cattle as they came home to their byres each day from grazing on the burgh croftlands. Weaving was Stirling's most important craft, and could be done in any backyard shed in any part of town. Tanning and brewing, on the other hand, needed water and were located at the bottom of the burgh where the Town Burn flowed (everyone drank beer because drinking water was polluted). Candlemakers, blacksmiths and others who used furnaces or kilns were also confined to the lower end of town to minimise the risk of fire destroying the entire burgh—particularly the top end where the councillors who made fire regulations lived. Bakers seem to have been an exception to this general rule and were to be found all over the burgh. Coal for these industries came mostly from the Auchenbowie mine near Bannockburn—Alloa's coal mines were more famous, but most of their output went to Holland.

Stirling's markets were found in various parts of the burgh, off the main thoroughfare where there was space for goods to be delivered and stalls could be erected. Ordinary stalls, where everyday things like bread and vegetables were sold, stood around the mercat cross and were open from ten o'clock until midday on Wednesdays and Saturdays (the Saturday market was changed to Fridays in 1648 'for better keeping of the Sabbath day').

In addition, there were several specialist markets. Shoes were sold in Broad Street just above the present Jail Wynd. The grassmarket was at the top end of Spittal Street, confirmed in the records for 1639 when the council ordained 'the grass market to be transported and changed from the Hiegait (Broad Street) to be Back Row in front of James Couper's house on the north side and Thomas Allan's house on the south side'. The meal market was further down Spittal Street; here the town's bakers and maltmen bought grain, and farmers could buy seeds. The horse and timber markets needed more space than the others and were located outside the burgh walls. Horses were sold around what is now the

Broad Street today, the scene of Stirling's old markets. Jail Wynd is on the left and the ruins of Mar's Wark face down the street. *Photo:* Craig Mair.

Lady's Rock in the Holy Rude graveyard, while the timber market was outside St Mary's Wynd port, roughly where the Cowane Centre is today. That left just the fleshmarket; at that time the Holy Rude manse stood as an island at the top end of Back Row (St John Street), and meat was butchered next door, downhill. The disgusting smells and sight of blood or offal trickling down the slope of Back Row were a source of regular complaint to the burgh council. A building was erected by the council to spare people at least the sight of animals being butchered, but as early as 1560 there were complaints that its neglected condition was offending people's sensitivities.

By the seventeenth century shops had begun to appear in Stirling. Merchants originally had booths or stalls or just trestle

The building known as Sir John Dingley's House in Broad Street. The dormer windows, in line with the building next door, almost certainly indicate the original front line of the building, which has later been extended forward over a foreshop. *Photo:* The Collections of the Smith Art Galley and Museum, Stirling.

tables, which they set up on market days and then dismantled. Later they began to erect 'foreshops' or lock-up booths which jutted into the street from existing buildings—these were not always owned by the same people who had the booths. By 1600 many foreshops had become more substantial, being properly built with a serving counter and sometimes an additional room upstairs, so pushing the entire building further out into the street. The council disapproved of these if they narrowed the main through streets and caused traffic congestion, but shops were allowed to develop in Broad Street and down Spittal Street.

In 1603 work began under the direction of James Short, master of works, on an improved quayside and pier on the River Forth, 'considering the great decay of the shore'. Money for the work was raised from anchorage and shore dues, by diverting money raised in fines, and from renting out the Bridgehaugh grazing for three years. The work seems to have taken several years. By 1604 a barge was in use carrying stones and timbers, and the work was under way. There seems to have been a shortage of labour, for in 1606 the council warned people to stop criticising James Short and threatened heavy fines on those who persisted. The council also

The 'shore' or harbour at Stirling lost its importance when ships became too large to manage the river's shallow fords. Shipping nevertheless continued well into the twentieth century. *Photo:* Stirling District Libraries.

ordered that eight male or female servants were to be sent to the shore each day to help carry rubble, and threatened that anyone who avoided this would be fined five shillings, which would be used to hire a substitute worker. The council also ordered one guild brother and one craftsman to attend the work on a rota each day, on pain of a ten-shilling fine on the Dean of Guild or Deacon Convener of Trades if they did not.

Burgh accounts list shore and anchorage dues from 1607 onwards, suggesting that the work was completed by then and river trade was back to normal. Merchants were taxed on anything which they imported or exported by ship, and a list from 1603 survives. This shows that most cargoes going out of Stirling were bales of cloth, cow hides and sheep, lamb or goat skins—not surprisingly skinners, tanners and weavers were among the most important people in the burgh. Cargoes coming into Stirling included tallow, bark, lime, wool (mostly from Norway) and a few tuns or large casks (about 250 gallons) of wine. A lot of timber was also imported including barrel staves from Danzig and 'deals' or sawn planks from Norway (the Norwegians had the advantage of circular saws, unknown at that time in Scotland).

Stirling was not an important seaport—the river windings and shallow fords prevented this. What export trade there was went mostly to the Dutch town of Campvere (now called Veere). Here lived an expatriate community of Scots middlemen through whom Stirling's merchants bought and sold their goods. Scotland was undoubtedly one of the less sophisticated European nations—English merchants did not demean themselves by purchasing small quantities of goods such as the Scots did, and there are frequent references to the impression of poverty conveyed by Scottish merchants in their dress and manners compared to the more cosmopolitan French, Italians and Germans. In 1625 therefore, following the visit of a Campvere factor to Stirling, the burgh council fined Robert Brown and Thomas Anderson for wearing bonnets instead of hats more befitting merchants; Anderson was fined much more than Brown because his bonnet was blue, the colour normally worn by ordinary citizens!

Punishing a man for the style of his hat might seem beyond the power of any council, but not in the seventeenth century. The burgh council was, along with the Guildry Court and the Kirk Session, the body which ran everything in Stirling—indeed all three bodies often included the same people, since only burgesses could vote. Elections were held annually on the Monday preceding the Friday before the feast of Michaelmas. About one-third of the council stood down from re-election each year, but in practice the same body of men elected themselves or their friends annually, and so held all the power in Stirling.

The election of the burgh council in 1610 is an example. On 28th September the 'provost, bailies, council and deacons of craft of the burgh of Stirling, representing the whole community thereof . . .' met in the tolbooth under the chairmanship of the Earl of Mar to choose the new council. They elected twenty-one persons, consisting of Provost James Short (a merchant, and probably the same man who had previously been Master of Works), four Bailies, a Treasurer, Clerk, and Dean of Guild, plus another eleven merchants and two craft representatives. From among these others the lesser officials were chosen, such as Visitors to various markets (who checked on the quality and price of ale, flesh, timber and so on), Officers to enforce law and order, and the Master of Works. The proportion of craftsmen on the council later improved—by 1620 the seven craft deacons were entitled to seats, one of whom was also to be made a bailie, but that still left the merchants with an overwhelming superiority. They used this advantage partly to benefit themselves, by forcing craftsmen to sell their products cheaply to merchants, for example. This apart, however, the council ruled strictly but wisely for the burgh's 'common good' or general benefit.

Burgh income came from a wide variety of sources. Customs or dues were levied on anyone bringing goods in to markets or fairs from outside the burgh, for example. These were paid at each burgh gate, and on Stirling Bridge for those coming from across the river. Burgesses and freemen of Stirling paid much less than outsiders or non-burgesses; typical bridge dues in 1641 included two pence per sack of wool, cloth, skins, lint, hemp or plaidings (non-burgesses paid twenty-four pence), six pence per load of butter, cheese, tallow or iron (non-burgesses paid twelve pence), four pence per ox or cow to be sold (non-burgesses paid eight pence), and so on with sheep, pigs, wine, beer, ale, coal, salt, fruit and vegetables. Market dues were not levied at all on burgesses; outsiders paid eight pence per load of skins, hides, wool, hemp or lint, four pence per horseload of meat, fish or grain twelve pence per score of geese, two pence per stone of butter, cheese, tallow, and so on in a sliding scale which varied from time to time.

Yet another source of money came from 'ladle duty' by which an official took a scoop or ladlefull of grain from every firlot or container brought to market; these scoops of barley or wheat or oats were collected and later sold to swell the burgh's income. In 1613 the council accused the crafts of hoarding grain 'in their barns, lofts and girnals' to force up prices and thus compensate themselves for the loss of ladle dues; with the exception of maltmen keeping malt or bakers storing wheat, they therefore taxed people on what was in store. This led to a tremendous legal row between the burgh's craftsmen and merchants. The Stirling bakers successfully took the merchants to court, and to the Convention of Royal Burghs, in a case which dragged on from 1612 to 1616. At high moments during this turbulent time the bakers' leaders were jailed in the tolbooth (so the ex-deacon of the skinners took the key by force from the jailor and released his friends), the craftsmen marched fully armed through the town, the Earl of Mar was called in to mediate, the Craft leaders were jailed in the Edinburgh tolbooth, and the dispute was eventually settled only by the intervention of the Holy Rude's minister Patrick Simpson—all over the imposition of ladle duty!

The burgh's various grain mills were also taxed. All grain produced within the burgh's boundaries had to be dried in a burgh kiln and ground at a burgh mill, and there was sometimes quite a queue of local farmers waiting to have their oats or barley threshed and ground at Stirling. The Bridge-end mill stood at the Stirling end of the bridge; it was driven by a stream which flowed from Cambusbarron into a small loch below the castle cliffs at Raploch, and from there into the river. The Burgh mill stood below the Craigs and was powered by the Burgh Burn which ran roughly where Dumbarton Road is today; it is presently piped under the Thistle Centre. You paid, of course, to have your crops ground, and the miller was then taxed on this income (brewers were then also charged excise duty). As a result, quite a lot of illicit grinding and brewing went on.

Dues were also charged at the harbour, on fishing rights and fish sales, for the right to graze on burgh lands (mostly acquired from the Church during the Reformation), for the right to collect and sell muck off the streets (which made good manure), on goods weighed at the tron, and so on. Most of these dues were 'rouped' or auctioned to local burgesses who kept a proportion of the income in return for acting as collectors or 'customars'. In addition to these revenues, court fines were often imposed on wrongdoers (which contributed to burgh funds and saved the cost of prison food and warmth).

The money raised from these various sources went on schemes for the common good, such as repairs to public buildings including the kirk, tolbooth, harbour, Stirling Bridge and Spittal's bridge at Bannockburn, or the paving of the High Street. More was used to employ a number of public servants, such as the town bellman, who made public announcements at the mercat cross, and the town drummer; new council regulations were advertised round the town 'by tuck of drum, that none may pretend ignorance thereof'. In 1642, for example, Duncan Ewing was appointed to be 'drummer of this burgh during the town's good will and his ability and good behaviour . . . to tuck his drum nightly at seven hours and every morning at four hours, beginning at the Lady Vennel and from there through the whole town . . .'. For this he was paid £60 yearly, together with a livery of clothes every two years.

There was also a burgh executioner or hangman (who mostly administered other punishments such as whippings and brandings—actual hangings were very rare). One example was David Murray, appointed in 1633 'to the town of Stirling during his lifetime'. Then there was the burgh piper—his job was to provide entertainment on public occasions such as fairs. In 1607 the council ordered the burgh treasurer to 'provide and furnish George Crawford, drummer, and John Forbes, piper, each of them, with breeches and stockings of red stemming (woollen material)'. Forbes did not last long, for in 1614 Harry Livingston was employed as 'minstral and piper of this burgh to serve till Martinmas 1615, and the council allows to him such fees and casualties [tips] as others have had before'. Most councils did not offer long contracts of employment, for pipers were often rogues, drunks and womanisers. They may have been colourful characters always popular with the townsfolk, but to socially-conscious councillors they were an embarrassment, too often found sobering up in a tolbooth cell.

Others on the council payroll included the masters or 'doctors' of the grammar school. In 1625, for example, David Will was appointed for five years 'to instruct and teach the whole youth of this burgh . . . in all the parts of grammar and authors, both Greek and Latin', for which he was paid £100 Scots and a quarterly fee of six shillings and eightpence (half a merk) per child. The council also decided which school books would be used and set school holidays, as in 1663 when 'a supplication, written in Latin, was presented from the scholars of the grammar school craving the vaccance (holiday) for such time as the council should think fit, which being considered by the council they, for the encouragement of the said scholars, and according to the ancient custom of this burgh, have empowered the provost and bailies to go presently to the school and grant the supplicants fourteen days vaccance'. For years all lessons were in Latin. Some young Stirling merchants spent 1679 to 1681 in Holland learning arithmetic and accounting, which were still not taught in Scottish schools.

The council also appointed the kirk minister; in 1620, for example, the 'provost bailies and council of this burgh, representing the whole community thereof, after trial and cognition taken by them of the literature, life and conversation of master Joseph Lowrie, minister at the kirk of Lenzie . . . have conduced and appointed with him for his acceptance of the said ministry . . .', for which they paid him £500 Scots annually and provided him with a manse.

The day-to-day work of Stirling's burgh council can be illustrated in many ways. Most obviously it made laws; in 1608, for example, it decreed against those who sat up 'under cloud of night, drinking and playing in other men's houses' and imposed a fine of £40 on anyone who thereafter sat up 'drinking or playing or walking on the streets after ten hours at night'. The council also threatened all brewers, ostlers and vendors of wine or meat with a similar fine if they sold anything after ten o'clock.

The council also controlled building regulations; in 1614, for example, the council warned inhabitants not to enlarge their houses onto the main through-streets, especially in St Mary's Wynd, on pain of a £100 fine. In 1629 a merchant called Alexander Cunningham was given just forty-eight hours to demolish an extension in Broad Street and 'make all again in as good a state as it was before', on pain of a £40 fine. Later this function was taken over by the Dean of Guild's court (and continued so until 'regionalisation' in 1975).

Once a year, on the first Monday after 'Pasch' or Easter, the entire council accompanied by the burgh piper and drummer 'rode the marches' or inspected the town's boundaries. This included the bridge and the causeway road, the mills and their lades, and a check on boundaries to ensure that neighbouring landowners had not encroached onto burgh lands. During the next century these boundaries were properly marked by march stones, but at this time a regular procession round the town's lands was the only way of reminding everyone where the limits were.

Another important event was the waupenshaw (weapon show) or general muster of the town's fighting men. This was supposed to be done annually, normally in June, but was often neglected and then done hurriedly when danger threatened the town. When a muster did occur, the town's burgesses turned out with all their weapons and armour, the Crafts and Guildry each with their banners, as well as the King's standard. In 1627, for example, the Guildry records state that 'Alex Allan, depute to John Cowane, Dean of Guild, is ordained to carry the merchants' ensign upon the twelfth day of next June, which is the muster day of this burgh'. Occasionally this led to an improvement in the burgh's readiness for danger, as in 1638 when, following a muster, the Guildry ordered all its members (on pain of a £5 fine) to reconvene in fifteen days, each properly armed with a pike, breastplate and sword, or alternatively a musket and sufficient quantity of ammunition. The same happened in 1647 when members were each ordained to produce a halbert within twenty days or be fined £5.

One important function was the supervision of market weights and measures. For centuries the Court of the Four Burghs looked after Scotland's national measures. Edinburgh guarded the standard ell, a measure 37.2 inches long used for measuring cloth and the like. Other burghs sent for a copy from Edinburgh and often (as at Dunkeld or Dumfries but seemingly not in Stirling) this was fastened to a wall in the market area for people to use; an ell wand or stick can still be seen in the Smith Museum in Stirling. Lanark kept the weights, from which all others, from the Lanark stone down to the tiny ounces and drops, were copied; two large weighing stones, probably from the burgh tron, are stored at the Smith Museum. Linlithgow guarded the firlots or grain measures; from time to time, as in 1598 and 1620, Stirling's firlots, pecks, half pecks and quarter pecks were taken to Linlithgow to be re-measured by that town's bailies, after which they were stamped as true measures.

Stirling itself had charge of Scotland's liquid measures. In 1599, for example, a pewterer called Robert Robertson was told by the council that 'all stoups, such as quarts, pints, chopins, to be made by him hereafter, shall be agreeable in measure to the jug and stamped with the town's stamp'. The famous Stirling pint jug (which actually holds three English pints) is on display in the Smith Museum; it is said to date from 1457.

The council also set market prices. Instances go back to the earliest surviving burgh records but in 1614, for example, malt cost £6 per boll, ale was one shilling a pint, wheat was £8 per boll, you got fifteen ounces of bread for one shilling, candles were three shillings per pound, and so on. By 1642 when Duncan Ewing was town drummer at £60 per year, candles were four shillings per pound, ale was one shilling and eightpence a pint and bread was one shilling and eightpence per pound, which was expensive for someone living on just over £1 a week.

As well as the weekly markets, Stirling had the privilege of several annual fairs. In 1600 there were two fairs, held in early September and mid-October, but this was later increased by the addition of another in early May, and then another in July. On the May or 'Riding Fair' the burgesses, many on horseback, would parade from the bridge to the town to the sound of bells and celebratory gunfire. Women and servants were not allowed to participate. In 1705 Stirling petitioned the Scottish government for two more fairs and these were granted to be held in December and January.

Fairs were important but festive occasions with entertainers, sports events and competitions to attract visitors and sellers from far and wide. There were foot races, horse races (for a silver cup or bell) and boat races at various times in Stirling. Unlike weekly markets, cattle and horses were often sold along with the more usual weekly market products. Custom dues were charged on goods being brought in to town for sale, and the lets on stalls for fair days were auctioned to local citizens—two vital sources of revenue for the burgh. In 1621 the town raised £44 by this means, but it rose to £107 by 1643. In 1666, by which time there were four annual fairs, the burgh's income was £270 and by 1691 it was over £340—so it was well worth the burgh making an effort to attract people to its fairs. Interestingly, most income came from bridge tolls rather than from people entering Stirling through the Barras Yett.

By this time the River Forth was crossed by the present 'old

A view of Stirling around 1695 by Captain J. Slezer. Stirling Bridge can be seen on the right, still with one of its arches where a gate forced people to stop and pay tolls.

bridge', and the previous wooden structure was gone. No evidence survives to confirm exactly when the stone bridge was erected, but it seems to have been around AD 1500. At each end of the bridge was a large stone archway, removed during the eighteenth century but marked by pointed pillars today. An iron gate hung from the northernmost arch, which acted as an outer line of defence for the burgh and a point where customs could be levied on people crossing with goods for market. The customar sat in a little roofed booth situated halfway across the bridge, still marked by a recess today.

As well as fairs there were, of course, other days of fun or festivity. Some of these, such as Michaelmas when council elections were held (followed by a dinner) derived from the old Catholic holy days. Hallowe'en with its traditional guizing was popular, but did not then involve any ghosts—rather, it was a time when young people caroused, and told their fortunes by pulling up old kale plants to read the roots, like tea leaves today. Christmas was suppressed in presbyterian lowland Scotland (indeed during the 1690s the Kincardine-on-Forth kirk session *accused* Edward Bruce of attending a Christmas dinner at the Laird of Clackmannan's house).

New Year was widely celebrated, however, and like today was marked by gifts of coal and shortbread. On the first Monday after New Year (known as Hansel Monday) employers traditionally gave a gift or hansel to their workers, while in Stirling some charity-assisted paupers were also given drinking money on Fastern's E'en or Shrove Tuesday. In fact quite a lot of celebrating involved drink, which sometimes concerned the town council.

The Council was also very concerned about public dungheaps. As in every burgh, people threw all their human and household waste into the street, where the mess was occasionally raked up into midden heaps. Eventually these grew so large that they obstructed closes and even the main streets. The burgh records are full of demands that these be instantly removed on pain of heavy fines, but people kept the habit all through the seventeenth and eighteenth centuries. There were at least stone gutters on through-streets, which inhabitants were supposed to keep repaired, supervised by the Master of Works.

Dungheaps were also associated with disease. Although there are examples in the records of people living to a good age, most were lucky to make it past forty without being affected by insanitary water or food. Alternatively they might die of typhus, tuberculosis, syphilis, meningitis or even malaria; leprosy died out after 1600 and no seventeenth-century cases appear in the burgh records. But the greatest fear was plague or pest. Just one outbreak could destroy a burgh—over six hundred people, perhaps a third or more of the population, died in Stirling during 1606 in a plague which seems to have spread from Edinburgh and Dalkeith. During such emergencies the council was expected to take charge. Strangers were put out of town. Men were appointed to guard the town gates and admit no-one from plague-infected areas. Others were appointed to help the bailies patrol their quarters of town to stop people from wandering around unnecessarily. In October 1606 George Norvell and Alexander Paterson were employed to build a pest-house for 'diseased and sick persons' at Bridgehaugh, which was then some distance from the town.

In a crowded burgh like Stirling fire was another constant danger. Several regulations were made to reduce the risk, as in 1618 when a baker called John Anderson was called before the council for having a kiln in his house and was ordered to move it to the bottom of his back yard. In 1669 the council also provided

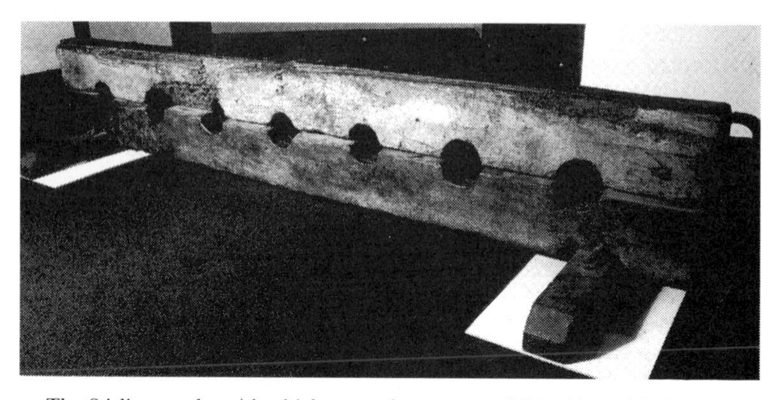

The Stirling stocks, with which wrongdoers were exhibited in public by their ankles in Broad Street. In fact Stirling people were remarkably law-abiding and this instrument was rarely used. *Photo:* The Collections of the Smith Art Gallery and Museum, Stirling.

the town with two dozen leather fire-buckets plus six double and six single ladders. Later it also provided hooks and ropes for dealing with fires.

Punishments were also part of the burgh council's business. On the whole Stirling people were remarkably law-abiding, but there were always some who got into trouble. As John Harrison has shown, the town's butchers (who worked concentrated together at the fleshmarket, and often formed partnerships when buying an animal) sometimes got into trouble for quarrelling or fighting, whereas the weavers (who made few partnerships but worked alone at their looms, scattered all over the town) were rarely in trouble. Another common 'crime' was calling names; women regularly called each other sluts, harlots, whores, adulteresses, brazen-faced and so on, and were regularly warned or made to wear the branks for doing so. (Men took offence when called villains, jackanapes, rascals, knaves, curs, or cuckolds!).

There are virtually no early seventeenth-century references to hangings, stocks, pillories or jougs, but there was the case of Adam Donaldson who, during the great dispute between the Crafts and the Guildry in 1613, assaulted Provost Duncan Paterson with a dagger and a golf club; he was fined £40, put in a tolbooth cell 'during the council's will' and thereafter brought to the mercat cross, where he was to 'openly crave God, the King's Majesty, the said provost and all the magistrates of this burgh, forgiveness for

The gravestone of a merchant in the Holy Rude cemetery. The 'reverse four' symbol was distinctive and is now used as the sign of the Stirling Guildry. *Photo:* Craig Mair.

his offence'. Moreover, he was ordered to pay a £100 pledge against his future conduct and was threatened with banishment from the burgh if he was ever in trouble again. All this was publicly intimated

John Cowane's house in St Mary's Wynd, still inhabited in 1900 but now a ruin. It nevertheless still suggests the wealth and status of a merchant in the burgh. *Photo:* Central Region Archives Department.

at the mercat cross—an effective punishment, and so inexpensive for the merchant-dominated council!

In 1629 several tramps were found guilty of stealing and then selling clothes and plaids. When questioned by the procurator fiscal they lied so much that trial by a full fifteen-man jury was held. They were found guilty of being 'idle and sturdy vagabonds, common thieves, evil liars, and haunters and resorters of evil company', for which James Ramsay was 'scurgit' or whipped through the town to the Barras Yett and there branded on the shoulder, before being banished with the others on pain of death if they ever returned. A gallows stood outside the Barras Yett, roughly where the Black Boy statue is now, and doubtless made its mark on those who came and went from the burgh. This gibbet still stood in 1785, but it is not known when it was finally removed.

Second only to the town council in importance was the Guildry and its Court. This was an association only for merchants—traders who bought and sold things, as opposed to craftsmen who *made* things (even if they first bought the materials and later sold the product). Brewers, bakers, tailors, butchers and so on were therefore craftsmen, whereas wine-sellars, cloth traders, spice importers, sellers of hides and such like were merchants. You could not be a merchant unless you were also a Guild member, or brother, and for this you obtained a Guildry 'ticket'. To have this later confiscated or torn up for wrongdoing was therefore to lose your livelihood.

To join the Guildry you had to be accepted or elected by the Dean of Guild and the other brethren. You normally also had to be resident in Stirling, and to prove that you had enough stock or capital for trading; this varied from £500 Scots to £1000 depending if your family were already Guildry members. There was a sliding scale of entrants, beginning with the oldest sons of existing members (who in 1671, for example, paid just ten merks to join or half a merk if the father was dead), down through a hierarchy of younger sons, sons-in-law, apprentices and 'strangers' (who paid £60 Scots to join in 1637, for example). Some women were also Guildry members—daughters married to apprentices, for example—and it was not uncommon to find women shopkeepers. For a time members were also supposed to possess armour and weapons (usually a halbert or Lochaber axe), to help defend the burgh in times of danger or suppress disorder in the streets; Stirling's merchants had a banner under which they fought at Flodden, Pinkie and several other battles. Finally, there was also an oath to be taken upon joining, in which the entrant swore to be faithful to the Dean of Guild and the brethren, and not to make trading or business partnerships with unfreemen or non-members of the Guildry.

The Guildry regulated almost everything to do with Stirling's trade, either directly through the Dean of Guild's Court or through the town council, on which merchants had a majority of members. It set prices and market times, inspected the quality of goods for sale, and held the weights and measures by which merchandise was weighed. It also regulated the activities of chapmen or pedlars and acted against unauthorised markets and fairs, such as those at Falkirk or Polmaise which sprang up to challenge Stirling's trading privileges.

The Guildry also regulated the question of apprentices. Most apprenticeships were five years long, which consisted of four year's unpaid work and one year as a journeyman for which the young man was paid and fed by his master. Most masters were not allowed to have an apprentice until they had been Guild brothers for five years. An entry fee was also paid to the master; this varied from time to time to regulate the numbers of up-and-coming merchants, or to discourage 'stranger' apprentices when there were enough merchants' sons in apprenticeships. In 1660 the entry fee was 400 merks, but in 1671 'strangers' were made to pay 500 merks. Sometimes the Guildry contributed to the cost of fees paid by the sons of their own members.

A well-documented example is that of Duncan Fotheringham, who, with the consent of his father and two guardians as 'cautioners' or guarantors, became 'bound as an apprentice and servant' to a merchant called John Crawford on 1st May 1649. He promised to 'serve his master loyally and truly both night and day, holiday and workday, in all things Godly and honest' and agreed to accept a punishment of two days' extra work after the end of his apprenticeship for every day of absence, and to repay two pennies for every penny carelessly lost. He also agreed to serve an additional three years' unpaid work if found guilty of fornication or adultery during his apprenticeship. In return, Crawford bound himself to provide the boy with bed, board and clothing, and to teach and instruct him in all the points and practices of trade, including a period overseas for experience after the first two years of training. Finally, Duncan's father James agreed to provide his son up with a new suit of clothes and a bed before handing him over to Crawford.

Following his apprenticeship, the young man (now about eighteen to twenty years old) could enter the world of trade by working for an existing shopkeeper, or starting up for himself or in partnership. He would submit a bill of entry to the Guildry 'setting forth particulars of his apprenticeship and praying to become admitted into the freedom and liberty of a guild brother' as Whitbread describes it. For a time new entrants were also supposed to pay money, wax and wine for a dinner—the money went towards the Guildry mortcloths used at the burials of Guild brothers, but during the seventeenth century this 'bankeit' money was discontinued.

The Guildry was particularly anxious to enforce both respect for the Dean and a good public image. Offenders such as Andrew Thomson, who slandered Dean of Guild James Short in 1601, were invariably punished (Thomson was fined £2 and made to crave the Dean's forgiveness in public). Moreover, when James Forsyth was jailed by the Dean in 1612 but would not accept the Dean's authority to punish, the town council did so instead (Forsyth was imprisoned by the bailies for two days, fined £6 and threatened with expulsion from the Guildry). There were also punishments for not attending church, such as half a merk for wandering through the fields during time of service, or drinking before the service, or opening a booth during time of service. Some of this was prompted by concern for the Guildry's standing in the burgh—what would people *think* if merchants were not regular church attenders? For the same reason, the Guildry loft or balcony in church was usually more lavishly decorated with drapes and fringes than any other except the King's; it was especially better than the Crafts' loft.

Although the Crafts played a lesser role on Stirling's burgh council, their Incorporations were nevertheless important. In particular they vigorously enforced the craft monopolies which each trade had by its Seal of Cause. Each craft group held regular meetings (usually outside the town on the Gowan Hill) and had an elected leader or Deacon, a treasurer (or boxmaster) and a clerk. Arguably most important of all, however, as an identity of the various crafts, was the trade banner—most crafts had one, under which they fought in battles and paraded through the town. A few worn remnants of these flags are kept at the Smith Museum today.

As with the Guildry, craftsmen had to apply for entry to a craft, which usually involved an 'essay test' or practical task to prove the applicant's skill. Prospective bakers were usually asked to make a chicken, veal or pigeon pie, while entrants to the tailors were required to make 'any piece of work which shall be fashionable either for men or women, as the Deacon and Trade shall appoint'. There was also an entry fee, which went in to the 'box' to be used to help the impoverished families of members, or perhaps to send their children to school. In some burghs each Craft had its own box, but Stirling's crafts shared one box between them; this chest, with seven separate locks (one for each boxmaster of the seven incorporated trades) is displayed at the Smith Museum. Rule books for some of the Crafts could be very long and detailed. They regulated their own quality controls for malt, bread, cuts of meat and so on, and (sometimes through the council) inspected premises such as kilns or vats. Like the Guildry, the Crafts also indented apprentices, usually for five years—indeed the oldest known apprenticeship in Stirling was a tailor in 1545. Although each Craft kept its own records and ran its own affairs, they also belonged to the seven Incorporated Trades; this body still survives today but, like the Guildry, its place in burgh life has sharply declined.

Another important part of everyday burgh life was filled by the Kirk, particularly the work of the Kirk Session. This comprised the minister and elders, who included the Provost, at least two bailies, and other respectable citizens, mostly merchants. The Session was concerned with many aspects of everyday life including, for example, the school (such as what was taught, or the spiritual suitability of the teachers, and dealing with truants).

The elders were also troubled by people's moral behaviour, for which they punished offenders. The Holy Rude church records are full of examples, as in November 1663 when 'Marjorie Gardner, fornicatrix with John Steinson'; and 'Christian Park, fornicatrix with John Sumervel', were interviewed by the Session. Although pre-marital sex was not a crime, it was a moral offence, so the two women were required to make a 'public profession of repentance in the ordinary place before the congregation'; this absolved them of their sins and they were then received back into the communion of the church. Sumervel and Steinson were ordered to repent the next day—which they did obediently, for as in a modern fundamentalist Islamic state, the power of the Kirk in Scotland was overwhelming. Of all matters dealt with by the church during the seventeenth century, that of punishing fornicatrixes was the commonest—on 16th October 1695 (just a typical example) five Stirling women were punished in one week. Adulteresses were usually shorn of hair and carted through the streets in shame.

In the same way, everyone was expected to attend church regularly and to participate enthusiastically. David Hairt was fined in 1621 for playing Sunday golf on the King's Park, for example, while

Thomas Morris was ordered to repent for not singing the psalms properly. John Smyth was punished for 'wandering through the fields unnecessarily in time of sermon. Elders were sometimes sent through the burgh when the service started, to round up all those who were not in church. The punishment was usually 'to stand before the pulpit in time of sermon' (some other churches had a 'stool of repentance' at the front for the same purpose). Kirk sermons could sometimes last two hours, and those standing before the pulpit were often cited as examples of sinners for the benefit of others in the congregation. It must be emphasised, however, that such punishments were not imposed simply to humiliate people—spiritual guidance and counselling was sometimes also included, for the Kirk was more concerned about eventual salvation that mere earthly behaviour.

With Town Council and Kirk Session working together, the practice of 'penny bridals' or weddings was also suppressed. Although laws governed where you could marry and the number who could attend the celebrations, some wedding receptions were little more than organised drinking sessions, with musicians and 'promiscuous dancing' and undoubtedly much sex. The burgh records contain numerous enactments against such occasions, and yet by 1680 the council was still complaining of the 'great abuse committed at penny weddings', and in 1716 yet another 'Act for strict execution of law against disorderly marriages' was sent round the town by tuck of drum.

There was little persecution or torturing of witches in Stirling, unlike many other Scottish burghs where hundreds of women were pricked, hanged and burned. Although the Kirk Session, or sometimes local noblemen, did occasionally send accused women to the town council, the bailies did not share the same zeal for witch-hunting and usually just threw the unfortunate women out of town (as in 1677 when a warlock and three witches were 'transported').

Much more importantly, the Kirk Session worked hard to alleviate poverty in the burgh. This occurred for many reasons. People were left destitute by fires or plague; epileptics or those who were 'braincracked' (as the records sometimes called them) could not find work; folk came into the burgh seeking food during times of famine; old soldiers or sailors wounded in battles sat around begging; orphans and the blind needed care . . . and so on. And for the most part the Kirk Session coped admirably and sympathetically, year after year, distributing whatever it received in the weekly church collection.

The work of the burgh council, the kirk and the guildry can perhaps best be summed up in the life of John Cowane, widely acknowledged as Stirling's most eminent benefactor. From around 1520 when the Cowanes first seem to have lived in Stirling, they quickly established themselves as notable burgesses. John Cowane's grandfather, John, was a merchant, and between 1525 and 1528 supplied honey, vinegar, prunes, saffron and such-like delicacies to King James V at Stirling Castle. He seems to have been burgh provost at some time during the 1550s. This John Cowane had several children including three sons, of whom Andrew fathered the future eminent John Cowane. Andrew was another great citizen of Stirling—he died in 1617, having served the burgh for years as a town councillor, Dean of Guild and kirk elder.

Andrew's son John was born around 1570, almost certainly at the house in St Mary's Wynd still called Cowane's House (although it was much smaller then). He was well educated at the burgh grammar school in Castle Wynd and went on to serve an apprenticeship with his father before becoming a wealthy and successful merchant himself. In keeping with the times, he had several strings to his bow, being simultaneously a merchant and trader with Holland (he visited Campvere several times, and ran a foreshop facing up Broad Street), a shipowner and occasional financial backer for Fife pirates, a farmer (he farmed several teinds or sections of land around Stirling), and sometimes a moneylender.

Cowane's father, with whom he was in partnership, died in 1617 when John was 47. Thereafter he rapidly became a notable citizen in his own right. He was first elected a burgh councillor in 1611, when he was immediately also appointed as a bailie. He then opted out of these duties until 1623 when he was again elected and served continuously to his death in 1633. He also served Stirling for years as a representative at the Convention of Royal Burghs, and eventually emerged as one of its most influential members, being several times nominated to deal with delicate or difficult matters of the period; in 1627, for example, he was sent with the Town Clerk of Edinburgh to petition King Charles I in London on a question of burgh trade. He met the King at Whitehall in late May and returned successful in June with a letter granting what the burghs sought.

During those same years John Cowane served as Dean of Guild

The statue of John Cowane which stands above the doorway of the Guildhall. Nicknamed 'Staneybreeks' made in 1649, the figure is said to jump down from its perch and dance every Hogmanay. *Photo:* Craig Mair.

from 1624 to 1630, and from 1631 to his death in 1633. His combined offices of Dean and town councillor fitted him to act as the burgh's Member of Parliament from 1625 to 1632. Cowane served the burgh well; at that time Stirling was ranked fifth in Scotland after Edinburgh, Perth, Dundee and Aberdeen, but with a new king determined to raise money by further taxation in Scotland he managed to negotiate a reduction in Stirling's contribution to half of Glasgow's and less even than that of St Andrews. He was also personally involved in a long struggle between the Scottish parliament and the king over church lands, and later was on a parliamentary committee set up to deal with Scottish fishing rights; this question ran for years, during which Cowane seems to have met the king several times in 1632.

Cowane never married, but he fathered at least one son by another merchant's servant girl called Agnes Cowane (no known relation), for which he was rebuked and fined £6 by the Holy Rude kirk session—she was fined two merks and ordered to make public repentance in church for six weeks. In spite of this error in his ways Cowane was a regular attender at the church of the Holy Rude. He was never made an elder, but he did often help the church in various ways, such as fundraising and auditing the kirk's accounts. In 1618–20 and 1630–32 he participated on kirk committees established to appoint new ministers to the vacant Holy Rude kirk.

John Cowane died suddenly in October 1633, having just been re-elected again as Dean of Guild. He made no will, but on his deathbed explained his wishes to his brother Alexander, a local surgeon. From a considerable personal fortune he left various sums, including five hundred merks to the Church of the Holy Rude and, especially, forty thousand merks for the provision of an almshouse or hospital for twelve 'decayed' Guild brethren of Stirling.

Having thanked God 'who moved the said late John's mind to so good a work', the town council organised the demolition of several derelict properties close to the Church of the Holy Rude (on land also gifted by Cowane), and in May 1637 construction work began. The almshouse was built by James Rynd and a gang of workmen at £4 per week, under the supervision of a merchant called James Robertson, younger, who was appointed treasurer and master of work. As with the erection of a Mar's Wark in the 1570s, some of the stonework was obtained from the defunct Cambuskenneth Abbey, whose lands were acquired by the Erskines (later the Earls of Mar) in 1559 at the beginning of the Reformation. Although the building bears dates of 1638 and 1639, it was not finished until 1649, almost certainly because of plague in the town during 1645, and a mercat cross call to arms during the Civil

The Guildhall, built 1637–49 as an almshouse for merchants with money left by John Cowane. It is now the meeting place of the Stirling Guildry.
Photo: Craig Mair.

War. However, as Harold Whitbread wrote in his 1966 history of the Stirling Guildry:

> The scourge ran its deadly course, and then subsided, the survivors amongst the fighting men returned, and others who had sought safety in flight reopened their doors; work began again on the almshouse walls. But it was not until the year 1649 that the structure was finally completed, with the shining copper weathervane turning in the breeze and the statue of the founder installed in its niche in the wall of the tower.

That statue of John Cowane, resplendant in his merchant's finery, was executed for a fee of £255 Scots by a master-mason called John Mill in 1649 as a portrait. Having been made within easy memory of Cowane's death, it is accepted as a good likeness of Stirling's greatest benefactor.

Even after 1649 the hospital was not long in use, for in 1651 Stirling was occupied by Cromwell's troops and the building was requisitioned for military purposes. During this period some pensioners were cared for in their own homes—indeed out-relief, in the form of money and an allowance of oat or barley meal, continued even after the English soldiers left in 1660, and later became the normal form of assistance. During the 1660s land around the almshouse was paved and planted with grass and trees, beds and bedding were installed, the hospital well was improved and a bell was acquired, but the number of occupants is unknown. No evidence of the almshouse in action survives from before October 1671, when the Masters were ordered to have the place ready to receive inmates by Martinmas (11th November). This included providing them with plates, cups, spoons, sheets, candles, peats and coals for each room (one weekly load in summer, but two in winter). Each inmate was also given 40 shillings Scots weekly to live on—this was paid from income received from lands and town feus rented out by the Trustees (the town council and kirk minister). Several portions of land were acquired over the years for this purpose, at Shiphaugh, Raploch, Bridgehaugh, Cambuskenneth, Ladyneuk, Spittalmyre and elsewhere, and some still provide income today.

The building itself consisted of seven small bedrooms for inmates, plus a hall, dining hall, a business or charter room and accommodation for the Keeper and servants. Bedrooms were plain but sufficient, containing two beds and bedding, two chests, a table, a fireplace and some pots and pans. Today the interior of the building is quite changed, but the main hall used to consist of two floors, with the inmates' bedrooms on the upper level reached by a spiral stone stair.

Inmates did not wear a distinctive uniform, but there were strict rules and persistent offenders could be debarred from receiving any help. Excessive bad language (which, as Whitbread says, 'had to be very foul before attracting official condemnation, for it was prevalent among all classes'), drunkenness, absence from daily prayers in the hospital hall or church on Sunday, damage to such things as bed clothes or furniture, quarrelling and marriage (!) were all punishable, usually by fines, on a sliding scale for subsequent occasions. Drunkenness, for example, was punished by a fine of 6s 8d (half a merk) for the first offence, rising to ten shillings for a second and 13s 4d for a third offence, subtracted from the weekly allowance; subsequent offences were dealt with by a magistrate.

Even by 1700 the 'Over Hospital' (as it was called to distinguish

Norrie's house in Broad Street, as it looked around 1900. This house was built for Stirling's town clerk James Norrie in 1671, and survives today as a fine example of seventeenth-century architecture in the burgh. Since local taxes were charged on the width of a house, Norrie built his tall but narrow. *Photo:* Central Region Archives Department.

it from Spittal's 'Nether Hospital' down the hill) was going out of use. Most pensioners preferred out-relief in their own homes and the building was rarely full. For a time help was given only to those who agreed to enter the almshouse; two needy boothkeepers called William Anderson and William Smith were told they would only qualify 'provided they were content to reside in the said house', while a minute for 1710 records: 'It was proposed by the Masters of the said Hospital that the whole pensioners thereto belonging should conform not only to the practice of this burgh, but also the practice of other burghs, should reside within the Hospital House'.

In spite of this effort to keep to the letter of Cowane's legacy, the almshouse declined and eventually only out-relief was provided for decayed merchants or their families. One room was rented for a time by a music teacher, and in 1712 part of the ground around the building was converted to a bowling green, for which the Masters provided seaside turf for a green, a summer house, 'byass bowls', a pretty Dutch garden, a gardener and a caretaker (whose duties included stopping the town's boys from breaking the church windows or climbing on its roof). By 1724 the building was known in records as the Guildhall, and so it has remained since, though its uses have been varied, including a dancing school, a lawyers' library, a courthouse, a theatre, a church and a cholera hospital. The bowling green (one of the oldest surviving in Scotland) remains a peaceful corner of old Stirling, however, and is still used.

CHAPTER 8

Stuarts, Cromwell and the Union of 1707

During the seventeenth century many important events occurred in Stifling, highlights in the day-to-day lives of the town's people. In 1617, for example, King James VI came to Scotland, having last seen his native land in 1603. Of course he came to Stirling, where he had spent most of his childhood, and naturally the town waited to greet him with mounting excitement. No doubt it reminded some of the good old days when royalty often came and went through the town. By May 1617 preparations for the royal visit were in full swing. The Barras Yett, through which the King would enter, was renovated with two hundred loads of stone cut from a quarry in the Craigs. Scaffolding was erected around the tolbooth to let workmen re-lead the roof, and Stirling Bridge was also repaired. The royal coats of arms on the mercat cross and tolbooth were specially gilded with gold leaf, and by the time King James arrived in July everything was ready. Schoolmaster Robert Murray was appointed to make a speech on the occasion of the King's entry, and he was then probably welcomed by Provost James Short.

In the wake of this visit, a host of royal friends and retainers were made honorary burgesses of the town, at no charge. They included various equerries, gentlemen pensioners and gentlemen of the privy chamber, descending through royal cupbearers, the sergeants of the scullery and the cellars, the clerk of the royal wardrobe, the yeoman of the buttery, the master of the King's carriage, the master of the treasury, the groom of the royal bed-chamber, a groom from the royal slaughterhouse, someone from the royal wine cellar, and so on—indeed anyone even remotely close to the King. The burgh council presumably thought that this would stand the town in royal favour later on, and who could tell when that might not be useful? After spending several days at Stirling the King travelled north to other towns, but on his return south he called again, and on that occasion several more royal hangers-on who had somehow been previously overlooked were also made burgesses.

Up at the castle another interesting event occurred when King James interviewed the Regents of Edinburgh University in the Chapel Royal and listened to them discuss philosophy, mostly in Latin and Greek. The rumour was that the King had intended to close Edinburgh and Aberdeen Universities, but he was so pleased with the discussion that he praised the professors and even allowed them to place the royal coat-of-arms on their college gates.

A similar excitement swept the burgh in 1633 when King Charles I paused briefly in July during a short tour of Scotland. The country had expected a royal visit soon after Charles' coronation in 1625; in 1631 it was again thought that he might come north and the royal apartments at Stirling Castle were prepared. People were even forbidden to hunt hares within eight miles of the castle, in case the King came. When he finally announced a visit in 1633 this prohibition was reintroduced.

In fact the King's journey round Scotland was not a great success. Not only did Charles I have a haughty manner and an expensive retinue of over five hundred courtiers (including the little-liked Bishop Laud), but it transpired that the real reason for the royal visit was to introduce the English form of Prayer Book into Scotland—which, as is well known, provoked a riot in St Giles Cathedral in Edinburgh and thereby led to the signing of the National Covenant and thus the bloody history of the Covenanters.

At Stirling the royal party stayed only two days, during which the town appointed several honorary burgesses (including Laud) and the King again met his old acquaintance John Cowane, who was then Dean of Guild but died three months later. Although he was presented with a special silver and gold cup, Charles I did not pass through Stirling on his return journey south. The whole occasion must have been something of a disappointment to the townsfolk, who no doubt hoped for a brief flurry of the glamour and colour of the old days.

As King Charles travelled uphill to the castle gates, he would have passed a new residence then being built by Viscount Stirling, Lord Alexander of Tullibody. This house in Castle Wynd is now called Argyll's Lodging but around 1632 it was a very much smaller building undergoing extensive and ornate enlargement by its new owner—the Argyll connection came later. William Alexander was a fine poet and a court favourite of Charles I, having made his name with a scheme to colonise Nova Scotia. On the King's visit to the

An engraving of the Argyll Lodging, originally built by the Earl of Stirling whose coat of arms is above the front door. The dates 1632 (shown as a detail) and 1674 (above the door to extreme right), record the building's two main stages of development.

castle in 1633 he was created the Earl of Stirling, Viscount Canada, and the initials WES (William, Earl of Stirling) can still be seen on the building's decorative stonework. Stirling died in 1640 and the building passed to his son Charles. It then passed to the Town Council which considered using it as an almshouse; fortunately it was bought instead by Archibald, 9th Earl of Argyll in 1666 and he further enlarged it into the magnificent town house which still stands there today—the finest of its period in Scotland.

In 1644 Civil War flared between the Covenanters and the Catholic troops of the Marquis of Montrose, but this mostly passed the town by. Stirling Castle was garrisoned by Protestant troops and there were complaints from some burgesses about the unfair numbers of officers billeted on them, but it was little more than an inconvenience. Having conducted a brilliant campaign in the north, Montrose crossed the Forth by the Ford of Frew and avoided Stirling. The nearest fighting was in August 1645 at Kilsyth, where Montrose again won, but then he lost at Philiphaugh and eventually was executed at Edinburgh for having supported King Charles.

Montrose may have skirted Stirling because of the plague; in July 1645 another serious outbreak began. With a council well versed from previous emergencies, the usual precautions were taken. Burgh gates and the bridge were closed and guarded to prevent strangers entering. A pest house for victims was established on the Chirmerland, an area outside the burgh on the east side of the road from Stirling Bridge to Causewayhead. Four gravediggers (including two women) were appointed and pest graves were dug on the chapelcroft, roughly where Viewforth is now (James Davis was given exceptional permission to bury his daughter in his own back yard). Council meetings were held in 'the park' and council records and charters were placed for safety in chests. Bailies were ordered to patrol their quarters of the town to keep people indoors as much as possible, but those with plague in the house were to declare this on pain of death (usually done by nailing a piece of cloth on the front door).

In October the plague declined, and quartermasters were now appointed to distribute help, including coal, to needy people and orphans. Cleansers were also found, including some from Linlithgow and Bo'ness, to fumigate property (even rolls of cloth at six shillings and eightpence per roll), and surviving citizens were taxed to pay for this. The exact death-roll is not known, but in January 1646 Stirling council petitioned Parliament for exemption from monthly taxes 'in respect of the great death of the neighbours and inhabitants thereof of the plague, and in respect of the great losses sustained by the town . . .'. Coming just one generation after the loss of over six hundred people in 1607, it must have been a devastating blow.

The pest may have been of most immediate concern to Stirling folk, but beyond the town national events still raged. Royalist 'Cavaliers' and the 'Roundhead' troops of England's parliament were at war. Most Highland clans supported the king, but lowland Scots had divided loyalties—Charles was a Stuart, but he was also an Episcopalian (if not, indeed, a Catholic). In 1646 and again in 1648 the burgh was required to provide men for the army—twenty-nine were subsequently made burgesses in gratitude for having volunteered to go. In England, however, King Charles I was defeated, then tried and beheaded, and Oliver Cromwell became 'Lord Protector'. The dead king's son, also called Charles, meanwhile escaped to France. Scots now waited to see what life would be like under English rule. In 1650, however, King Charles II returned to Scotland from exile in France and was crowned at Scone. In July he came to Stirling and lodged at the specially prepared and redecorated castle, 'delighting the townsfolk with his courtly manners and reminding the old inhabitants of the splendid days that had gone', as Stair-Kerr puts it. But the visit cannot have pleased everyone. With Stirling in a run-down state, and some houses even in ruins following the plague, there was a shortage of accommodation for the 'diverse persons of quality' who now came to attend court at the castle; the council was therefore ordered to evict as many non-burgesses as necessary to provide lodgings for the King's courtiers.

Strictly speaking, Scotland could have been ruled by Charles II even if England was not; the two countries were separate states,

The main gates at Stirling Castle. The towers were originally much higher but the upper parts were destroyed by General Monck's artillery in the siege of 1651. The lower parts are still peppered with bullet marks from that time, while the upper battlements are obviously of newer stone. *Photo:* Loch Lomond, Stirling and Trossachs Tourist Board.

with separate parliaments. This fact, however, was disregarded by Cromwell who, roused by the king's presence in Scotland, sent an invasion force north. Following a victory at Dunbar, General Monck and an army of over five thousand 'Roundheads' quickly subjugated most of central Scotland and then turned on Stirling Castle itself on 6th August 1651. Faced with such a formidable and disciplined army, the town wisely capitulated next day without a fight, in spite of its defensive walls. At one o'clock in the morning the English marched in. Under covering musket fire from the tower of the Holy Rude church, they then began to construct earthen artillery platforms to besiege the castle. The defenders replied, and the resulting bullet-marks can still be seen peppering the church tower and the castle walls. The siege itself was short—after only three days of serious bombardment from Monck's cannon and mortars the castle, especially the gateway, was badly damaged and Colonel Cunningham's Highland troops mutinied. He surrendered and marched out with three hundred men. (The upper part of the gateway towers remained broken and ruined for years, but were eventually lowered and repaired to the height they stand at now.)

Having placed many valuables in the castle for safety, the townspeople rushed to help the victorious troops carry everything back out—and were surprised to discover that, thanks to iron discipline, little had been looted. Numerous cannon, barrels of claret, the Earl of Mar's coronet and parliamentary robes, two coaches, a collection of royal hangings and tapestries, and Scotland's national records were taken as spoils of war, however. The records were sent to London, but most were then lost at sea in 1661 while being returned to Scotland. With the capture of the castle, English troops occupied the fortress until 1660 and the Earl of Mar was suspended from his duties as Keeper of the Castle. Monck presumably thought an Englishman would be more faithful to Cromwell's cause—the deposed king was, after all, Scottish. Charles, meanwhile, escaped again to France.

In 1652 Stirling's bailies and officers were made to swear an oath of loyalty to Cromwell's government: 'You shall swear that you shall be true and faithful to the Commonwealth of England as it is now established without a King or House of Lords; you shall well and truly execute the office of . . . [e.g. bailie] . . . within the town and burgh of Stirling and the liberties thereof according to the best of your skill, knowledge and power. So help you God'.

In general Stirling's people supported their King, even if they disputed his right to interfere in church matters. The period of English occupation was therefore an uneasy time, for in their hearts Stirling folk wanted the exiled Charles II on the throne; they saw him as the legitimate ruler of Scotland. This dilemma was brought to a head by the minister of the Holy Rude church.

In 1649 the Rev. James Guthrie was persuaded to leave Lauder and come as minister to Stirling. He was a staunch Protestant and had particularly resisted moves by the King during the 1630s and 1640s to introduce Episcopalian bishops into Scotland; on the other hand, he did support the King's right to govern and described Cromwell as a usurper of the crown. His uncompromising sermons worried the council, some of whom were more Episcopalian than he was. On the other hand many townsfolk supported Guthrie's more hardline Protestant views. The town was split to such an extent that in 1656 the Church of the Holy Rude was solemnly divided and bricked up to create two churches, with Guthrie and his followers in the choir and his former assistant Matthew Simpson in the nave. This particularly irked the council; the records for September 1656 mention 'James Guthrie, sometime a minister in this congregation (but now deposed by the church) and a few persons of the incorporation (whereof some pretend themselves to be elders) . . .'. In other words, when the crafts and most other townsfolk supported Guthrie, the merchant-dominated town council was peeved.

Guthrie then acquired a new assistant called Robert Rule. His appointment was challenged by the council but General Monck supported Rule's appointment, which forced the councillors to back down and confirmed the creation of rival congregations. This situation lasted into the 1930s, long after the original passions which had caused it were forgotten. On the other hand, the division of large church buildings also happened elsewhere, including St John's at Perth and St Giles in Edinburgh. Furthermore, both halves of the church were not always in use; on several occasions one or other part was leaking or needed repair and went temporarily out of use.

In 1660, following Cromwell's death, King Charles II returned to a great welcome in England and Scotland. With an Episcopalian on the throne the downfall of some of the more extremist Protestants followed. In 1661 Guthrie was arrested for his uncompromising

The statue of James Guthrie which stands in the Holy Rude cemetery. Guthrie was minister at the Holy Rude church until executed for his Protestant views in 1661. He was the first Scottish Presbyterian minister to be 'martyred'. *Photo:* Craig Mair.

views; following a trial in the Great Hall at Stirling Castle where the minister impressed many with his arguments, he was found guilty of treason and hanged at Edinburgh Cross. His head hung for twenty-seven years from the Netherbow Port—the first Presbyterian minister to be executed in Scotland. His statue stands in the Holy Rude graveyard.

Religious discord troubled Scotland for decades to come, and sometimes Stirling was involved. The castle, always loyal to the King, was often used as a prison. During Charles's reign several notable Protestants were jailed there, as in the 1670s when there was much Covenanter unrest in south-west Scotland. On the other hand, when Protestant monarchs ruled later, a string of Catholics including the Duke of Perth occupied the cells instead.

Charles II never returned to Stirling after the Restoration in 1660, but in February 1681 the castle was visited (in thick snow) by his brother James, Duke of Albany and York. The royal guest spent the night at Argyll's Lodging rather than the castle; by this time Argyll had added to the Earl of Stirling's house; the date 1674 can still be seen above the south-east turret doorway. By then it looked much as it does today—the finest surviving townhouse of its period in Scotland, with extensive gardens and a magnificent view across the Carse of Stirling to the Ochil Hills.

The next day Prince James visited the castle, to the sound of a cannonade in honour of the occasion. He was met at the gates by the Earl of Mar and the garrison lined up for inspection, and from there was conducted on a tour of the ramparts and most important rooms. As he left, the great guns fired again in salute to yet another royal visitor. By one of those ironies of fate, the Earl of Argyll in whose house Prince James lodged in 1681 was the same Argyll who refused to swear loyalty to King James VII when he came to the throne in 1685, and who then organised a rebellion in Scotland which failed and for which he was executed. Similarly the same loyal but Protestant Earl of Mar who, as Keeper, had greeted Prince James at the castle gates was later to have this traditional office stripped from him when James became King.

The century ended on another turbulent note. James VII was overthrown in the 'Glorious Revolution' of 1688 and went into exile in France. William of Orange came from Holland to be King of England and, in spite of Bonnie Dundee's highland rebellion in 1689, was also accepted as King of Scotland. With a Protestant monarch on the throne the people of Stirling were more comfortable but much of the Highlands remained Catholic and there were many besides who felt that the Stuarts were still Scotland's true kings. Indeed in 1689 Lord Kenmure wrote that he would rather his men were not billeted at 'that disaffected town of Stirling' where so many still had Stuart sympathies.

When Queen Anne (who never came to Stirling) ascended the throne in 1702 she recognised this danger and strengthened Stirling Castle. General Monck's siege in 1651 had shown that the castle walls were no match for modern artillery. By 1700 military engineers had solved this problem; walls were now made lower, much thicker, and often with a grassy top to absorb the impact of cannonballs. Between 1708 and 1714 the castle's present outer defences and ditch were constructed. As you enter Stirling Castle now, the road passes first through two gates from Queen Anne's time before approaching the original outer towers of King James IV's defences. Queen Anne's initials AR can still be seen above an outer gate.

In 1691 a hearth tax was levied by the government on all fireplaces, including smiths' forges, ovens, vats and kilns in all parts of Scotland. It was based on the assumption that the rich lived in larger houses, in more rooms with fireplaces, and could afford to pay more; the charge was fourteen shillings Scots per hearth. The returns for Stirling survive and have been analysed by John Harrison to provide an interesting snapshot of the town near the end of the seventeenth century.

In some ways the town had changed little over three generations. On balance the wealthy still lived at the top of the town, while dangerous or messy industries were still concentrated at the bottom end around the Dirt Row Port. Most fleshers were still around the Back Row (St John Street) close to the fleshmarket. The social ladder remained much the same too; country gentry still owned or rented their town houses, merchants still strutted around looking down their noses at the craftsmen (though some craftsmen were just as wealthy), apprentices still hoped to follow their masters into craft or trade, servants still toiled in many Stirling houses, and the poor were still poor. On the other hand, new occupations such as mechanics (builders) and maltmakers had appeared and the town *was* slowly changing. (The mechanics were also associated with the introduction of Freemasonry to Stirling, probably around the 1670s.) It was also easier to become a burgess—you did not need to own a house, for example, and even twenty-one 'workmen' were burgesses, though women were still barred. The first suburbs had also begun to develop, particularly on the Castlehill (where numerous weavers lived), but with a scattering of more isolated cottages at Raploch, Bridge-end, Spittalmyre and Whins.

The tax returns list 275 separate properties in Stirling, but many of these were sub-let or had rooms for rent, for the list also indicates 639 households and names 503 male heads of households. However, it is difficult to estimate the population of Stirling from such figures. Some heads of households were undoubtedly soldiers from the castle garrison, which fluctuated greatly in number from time to time. The state of trade, war or famine also affected Stirling's population greatly. Not surprisingly, the hearth tax returns confirm that richer folk lived in bigger houses. Mar's Wark was already in ruins, but the Argyll Lodging had sixteen hearths and Cowane's House had twelve, whereas most weavers had only one. On average, merchants had three or four hearths in their houses while craftsmen had only one or two. Fleshers, tailors and smiths, being more important craftsmen, had better accommodation than weavers, shoemakers or skinners.

The hearth tax collectors of 1691 would not have known it, but the 1690s were to be a disastrous time for Stirling, and indeed for Scotland as a whole. From 1695 to 1699 terrible famine struck the land, during which many thousands died—in some country districts as much as one third of the people may have died. The politician and writer Fletcher of Saltoun estimated at the time that about 200,000 people (out of a total Scottish population of around one million) were vagrants, wandering anywhere for food. Villages and towns fared little better, for most people were at least part-time farmers. In 1700 Robert Christie was a Stirling miller with a staff of five, for example, but he also rented land at Craigforth and did a bit of salmon-netting to augment his income—his crops failed and, in debt now to his landlord, he was forced to leave his holding. Widow Janet Bachope mortgaged her house in Stirling and bought a smallholding at Raploch—then the famine came and she fell into debt, so she was evicted. She died in 1711 still owing John Dick back rent.

Some of the larger trading burghs with sympathetic overseas connections did better. Merchants organised food imports and starvation was eased, but even Leith and Aberdeen were severely affected. Stirling was not a major trading port, and its merchants did not have the same capital or connections to call upon in such an emergency. On the other hand, the town was well known for its two charitable hospitals—Spittal's and Cowane's benefactions attracted many 'stranger' poor from the surrounding countryside, and also the Highlands.

The town was badly affected by famine. Burgh, Guildry and Craft records all reflect very hard times, with business in the doldrums and many people receiving charity. By 1698–99 things were at crisis point. In view of the 'insupportable number of extraneous and vagrant beggars, who daily frequent this burgh to the prejudice and overburdening of the inhabitants', the town council started to banish almost everyone not from the area. In 1698 only two 'strangers' seem to have been escorted to the gates, but in 1699 a total of eighty were banished, mostly over the bridge to the Highlands, from where they (many of them women) had come begging for food. Meanwhile the various charitable organisations rallied round as best they could.

The 1698 accounts for the incorporation of cordiners or shoemakers, for example, record many donations to women, or for funeral expenses, or 'given to ane poor man' and these go on well after 1700. Similarly, by 1699 the minutes of the tailors reflect how slack work was affecting them; some masters were obviously turning a blind eye to 'moonlighting' work done by their apprentices and journeymen, or were undercutting competitors' prices, or were touting for business where other tailors had previously worked, all of which was strictly against the common good of the craft. New regulations threatened fines against members who did so, but it illustrates the pressures forced on craftsmen during the famine.

In January 1699 the Guildry, driven by widespread starvation in the town and the sight of so many poor begging in the streets, started a general subscription of its members to raise money over and above the donations given to their own needy brethren. On 31st May 1699, as on any other week, the clerk of the East Kirk of the Holy Rude recorded the names of those receiving aid from the church. It ran to over one hundred and fifty people, mostly women and mothers, including two blind women, an orphan and several other children, six strangers, the town's officers and hangman, and seven prisoners in the tolbooth, and it ended with 'distributed at the Church door amongst a number of small ones £2 5s 3d'. So it went on, until the famine subsided.

Just as Stirling was struggling through starvation, a great hope emerged—the Company of Scotland Trading to Africa and the Indies, a Scottish answer to England's famous East India Company, was formed. The idea was to establish colonies in Africa and thus stimulate Scottish trade and manufacturing; there was also the attraction of gold and spices and ivory coming back to Scotland, to the benefit of every investor. Coming at such a critical time, it caught the nation's imagination and everyone rallied to the venture. One calculation has estimated that as much as one half of all the capital in Scotland went into this scheme. Every rank in society invested what it could; the Duchess of Hamilton gave £3000 while the Countess of Rothes gave £1000, but the minimum stake was just £100. As one director wrote, 'they came from all corners of the kingdom, rich, poor, blind and lame, to lodge their subscriptions in the Company's house'. Most burgh councils contributed what they could—Edinburgh, Glasgow, Inverness, Aberdeen, St Andrews, Paisley and so on. Lanark's £100 came from £50 out of burgh funds, £25 from the Guildry and £25 from the Trades. Even little Selkirk found £100. Several craft incorporations also contributed, including Edinburgh's cordiners and Glasgow's coopers. All saw in 'the Africa Company' the change to revive dwindling trade and perhaps bring the bad years to an end.

Stirling was engulfed in the same wild enthusiasm. £500 was invested by the town council on behalf of Cowane's Hospital, 'considering that it may be advantageous to the said hospital to give in some money to the Indian and African Company'. Another £500 was given on behalf of Spittal's Hospital, and yet another £200 by the town council itself. The Guildry also gave £200, and the town made a further contribution to the £3000 invested by the Convention of Scottish Burghs. In addition, several Stirling people volunteered to help establish the company's proposed first colony at Darien, in modern Panama. In June 1699 the Guildry ordered the masters of Cowane's Hospital to give £3, plus a fifty-merk advance for clothing, to William Swinton, a merchant, 'whereby the hospital may be disburdened of them'. Swinton, his wife and children, duly sailed off, probably on the *Rising Sun*, to Darien. Others went too, including a merchant called James Keir who was given £60 by the Guildry, and Robert Russell (and six others) who were given ten and a half ells of broad scarlet ribbon to trade with when they got there.

The rest of the story is quickly told. The venture failed in the face of tropical disease, poor leadership, ships lost at sea (including the *Rising Sun* on a homeward voyage), attacks from the Spanish who ruled Darien and regarded the Scots as invaders, and calculated indifference to the plight of the colony's dwindling band of survivors on the part of the English in Jamaica. The scheme collapsed and Stirling, like every other investor, lost its money. Worse, like every other Scottish burgh, it lost hope. Coming together with years of famine, the failure of the Darien Scheme must have been a body-blow.

By the end of the century Stirling was in the doldrums. It had slipped from 7th to 13th place in the list of burghs liable to taxation, its trade was waning and the population had been terribly affected by plague and famine. In December 1699, in one of the last town council acts of the century, bailie John Don was appointed to 'make two hundred lead badges for the poor of this burgh, bearing ane raised S for Stirling, and the year of God, to the effect the same may be distributed amongst the said poor by the elders, to whom the council recommends the same'. Only those who wore a badge had council permission to beg in the streets. Even the tolbooth steeple was crumbling and beyond use—visible signs for all to see of the burgh's sad condition. Would the 1700s bring new hope, or a fresh start?

Early in 1702 King William died and in the Holy Rude kirk the pulpit and various prominent lofts or balconies were draped in black. In April the town drummer and officers proclaimed Queen Anne and on 16th May the provost, bailies and council swore an oath of allegiance to the new monarch; thereafter they reconvened at John Martin's house with Lord Tillicoultry, Lord Aberuchill and various other gentlemen, to toast the new Queen by drinking wine, ale and brandy, and smoking pipes (for which they later claimed over £42 expenses from the council—times don't change!)

Perhaps this *was* a new beginning for the town. In 1702, for example, Alexander Hamilton of Airth was appointed as new minister at the Holy Rude kirk. In 1703 a new tolbooth was begun to a plan by the renowned architect Sir William Bruce of Kinross. The builders were Harry Livingstone, a stonemason, and John Christie, a carpenter, both local men, and their work still stands on the site of the old tolbooth on Broad Street today. Later that year there were more signs of renewed activity; Spittal's almshouse (by now in Friar's Yard on the site of the old Grey Friars' monastery) was repaired; two new fairs were advertised by tuck of drum round the town for December and January; new Acts were made in favour of the hammermen and bakers, and so on.

When the proposed union of Scotland with England (strongly favoured by the Earl of Mar) was announced in 1706, the town was especially stirred. In November the council sent a petition of protest against the union to the Scottish parliament, and simultaneously ordered everyone in the town aged from sixteen to sixty to 'be in readiness with their swords and guns'. However, when some of the inhabitants then actually burned a copy of the Articles of Union at the mercat cross, the magistrates hastily disowned such disloyal behaviour. Such 'manifest contempt thrown upon the Government' had been perpetrated only by 'some drunken people and boys without the knowledge of the magistrates and council, and who were likewise ignorant of the late act of parliament against tumultuary and irregular meetings and convocations . . .'. In other words, as most Scottish burghs have done throughout history (even with the introduction of a Poll Tax in 1989), Stirling protested but in the end obeyed the law.

Stirling Castle was the traditional home of Scotland's monarchs, and Stirling's people may instinctively have felt more than a twinge of regret at union with England. The battlefields of Stirling Bridge and Bannockburn, where Scottish independence was fought for, were also powerfully emotional places so close by. But just as the town council had drunk the health of both the catholic King James VII and, just three years later, the protestant King William, or had rushed to make honorary burgesses of Cromwell's soldiers and Charles's courtiers alike, so now it hastily smothered its feelings about union and supported the majority view. In Glasgow there *were* riots against the union, and trouble flared elsewhere too, but most burghs undoubtedly felt that protest was not worth the damage, imprisonment or killing which might follow—the English army was, after all, at Berwick ready to suppress disorder if necessary.

In 1707 the Act of Union was signed and on May 1st Scotland joined with England. The benefits of such union lay hopefully in better trade, but there was a price to pay. Many features of the old Scots way of life disappeared, including Scots money and measures like the ell and the Scots pint. In their place came English or Imperial measures. In November 1707 the town belatedly sent its famous pint jug off to Edinburgh, 'vindicating the town's right to the keeping of liquid measures', but in January 1708 the council requested 'Colonel Erskine, late provost, and Bandalloch, or any of them, to receive the standard of the liquid measures now come from England in stead of the former jug . . .'. And so Stirling moved into a new era, and a new beginning.

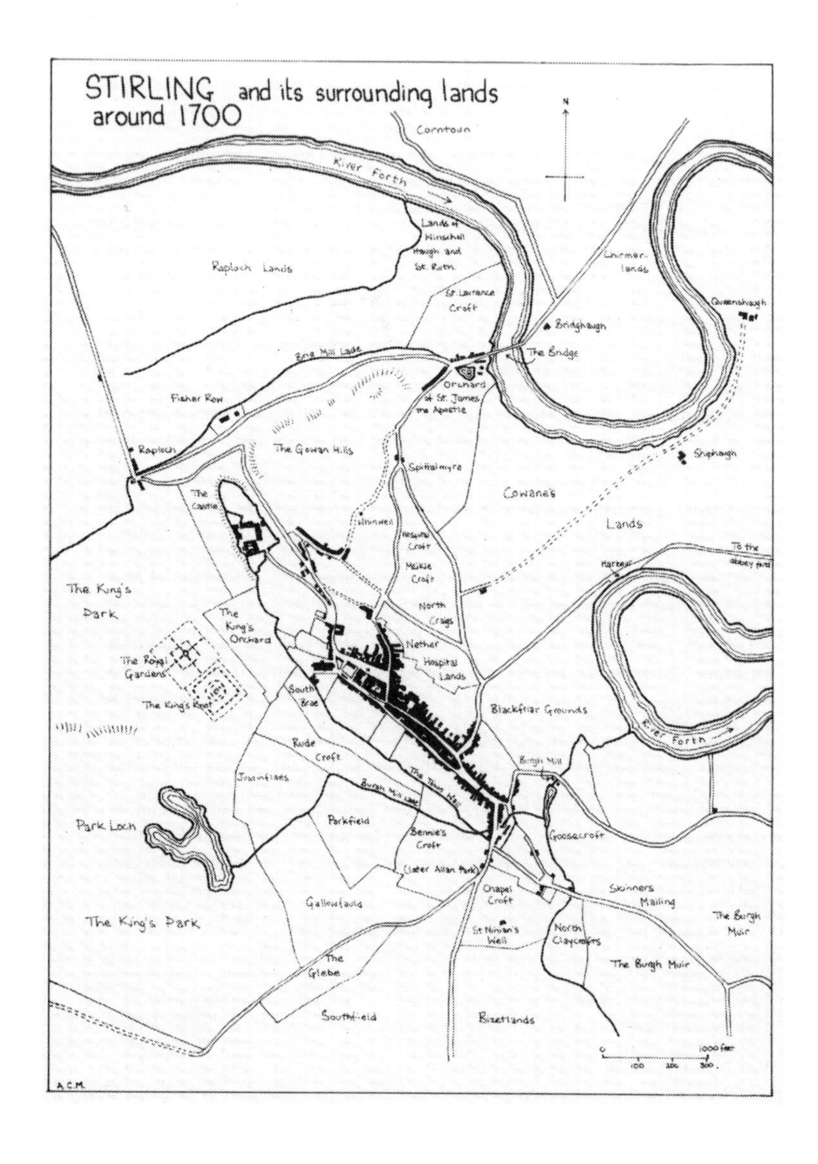

Map of Stirling and district in 1700.

CHAPTER 9

The Time of the Jacobites 1700–1750

The end of the seventeenth century saw great upheavals in Scotland, mirrored in the history of Stirling. On top of plague, famine and disasters like the Darien Scheme came the 'Glorious Revolution' of 1688 and a new line of Protestant rulers. James VII was deposed and exiled, and replaced by his daughter Mary and son-in-law William of Orange. Not everyone in Scotland welcomed the new king. From the north came John Graham of Claverhouse ('Bonnie Dundee' to admirers, 'Bloody Clavers' to his enemies), at the head of a rebellious army of highland Jacobites (supporters of *Jacobus* or James VII), determined to send King William home to Holland. These Highlanders routed General Mackay's government force at the battle of Killiecrankie in July 1689, but Claverhouse was killed and the rebellion fizzled out. William and Mary were confirmed as Scotland's monarchs and burgh councils all over Scotland dutifully promised loyalty to their new Protestant rulers. Within three years even the Highlands were subdued and the clans were forced to swear oaths of loyalty to the Crown—the MacDonalds of Glencoe were late in doing so, and were subsequently massacred by Campbells (but with royal consent) for this display of defiance.

Stirling, as usual, sat uncomfortably in the middle of all this. In a burgh which had long benefited from the Stuart royal family, some folk were still Jacobite sympathisers—in March 1689 Claverhouse quit a convention of Scottish lords met at Edinburgh to offer William the throne and tried to organise a rival Jacobite convention at Stirling, so it must have been a potentially sympathetic place. The convention plan came to nothing, perhaps fortunately, for the castle was a government stronghold and the town had no wish to invite punishment for views expressed too loudly. The burgh council had to tread a very careful path; it was difficult even to protest about local citizens press-ganged into regiments, or the illegitimate children left behind by soldiers, or officers' unpaid quartering bills, without seeming hostile to the Government's troops. In June 1689, for example, (just before Killiecrankie) the magistrates complained of 'abuses committed by the (raw, recently-recruited) soldiers of my Lord Kenmure's regiment to the inhabitants of this burgh through want of their pay to satisfy their diet'. In the end the town lent the regiment's officers enough money to feed their men until the soldiers' pay was received. In the same way, the town councillors were expected to offer suitable accommodation and hospitality to high-ranking officers; burgh accounts refer to wine drunk in May 1689 with Lord Colchester (who commanded a horse regiment) and the Earl of Mar (who died before going on campaign), and with Lords Eglinton and Kenmure in June before they set off for Killiecrankie.

After Killiecrankie military activity died down as regiments marched away, but Stirling was still left with much unfinished business to sort out. Horses commandeered by dragoons, or for the baggage trains of regiments, had to be retrieved. Bailies were sent after some officers to get unpaid bills settled. Some burgesses now sought compensation from the town council for various losses—John Mitchell, however, had to wait eighteen years to be recompensed £20 for a horse killed at Killiecrankie! In October 1689 a soldier was hanged at Stirling cross; records survive for the hangman's fee (£4) and the various costs of rope, nails and having a gibbet built. At the same time the town was careful to make honorary burgesses of important officers in the government army, especially Major-General Mackay himself.

The Jacobites were finally defeated (for the moment) at the battle of Cromdale in 1690 and fears of a Highland rebellion subsided. Any future rebels would probably come across the Forth at Stirling Bridge, however, so here at least there was constant military activity. Once again, Stirling's records do not reflect whole-hearted enthusiasm for the government's cause. In 1696 a Stirlingshire Militia was formed and included twenty-five officers and men from Stirling itself. Although this was a 'fencible' unit intended only for defence of the local district, it required the bailies and town's officers to go through the four quarters of the burgh with 'ane exact list of the whole inhabitants' to produce enough volunteers. That same year there was a petition from the council to have some of the soldiers quartered in the town removed as 'the place cannot accommodate them'. In 1702 the council complained

Stirling Castle and the historic 'top of the town' from the air

Loch Lomond, Stirling and Trossachs Tourist Board

The Guildhall, completed in 1649 as an almshouse

Below
Mar's Wark, built by the Earl of Mar (the Regent of Scotland) in 1570

The Argyll Lodging, considered the finest town house in Scotland

Stirling University, opened in 1967 on the most beautiful campus in Britain

Sunrise at the statue of Robert the Bruce at Bannockburn. *Loch Lomond, Stirling and Trossachs Tourist Board*

that 'several of her Majesty's (Queen Anne) loyal subjects frequenting the market have at several times hitherto been troubled and molested by soldiers, who have offered to press them to military service contrary to a late (i.e. recent) act of Parliament, to the great prejudice of this burgh and discouraging the lieges (i.e. citizens) from coming to the markets'. There is no record to show if these press-gangings were relaxed but military activity, including drilling and equipping the militia, certainly continued.

During this period England was at war with France's Louis XIV in the War of the Spanish Succession (during which the Duke of Argyll fought with distinction, and John Churchill, the Duke of Marlborough, made his name as a general with a string of great victories in Europe). In 1688 King Louis had supported James VII, exiled in France, as the legitimate King of Scotland and England; when James died in 1701 Louis continued to support the exiled King's son 'James VIII' or the 'Old Pretender' as the true monarch. This may only have been to stir up difficulties for France's enemy England, but as long as this support continued, and there were Jacobite followers in Scotland, Stirling remained a garrison town bustling with military activity.

In 1708 Louis sent a battle fleet loaded with an army of 6000 troops and the Old Pretender himself on an invasion attempt to the Firth of Forth. Bad weather and the English navy prevented this force from landing, but the general alarm in Scotland was great. Stirling's town council had no wish to see the burgh damaged by warfare and hastily wrote to Lord Grange, Lord Justice Clerk of Scotland, that 'this burgh is generally well affected to the present government and are willing to stand to the defence thereof but only they want guns and ammunition'. Meanwhile a guard of twenty men was posted on 24-hour watch under the command (in shifts) of the bailies, Dean of Guild and Deacon Convener.

Eventually this emergency passed but the town remained full of troops. The burgh records reflect this in various ways. In 1711, for example, the town council lent 'to Lieutenant Chalmers in Colonel Grant's regiment, £15 Sterling money for the use of the six companies of the said regiment lying here, upon his bill for repayment'. That same year the town council passed an Act 'for the better suppressing of the sin of uncleanliness in this place, that whatever women shall hereafter be found guilty of that sin with any of the soldiers that shall happen to be quartered here . . . shall be subject to the punishment of the cuckstool and thereafter banished forth of this burgh.'

In 1714 Queen Anne (the last of the Stuarts) died leaving no children. Many Jacobites including the Earl of Mar, a member of her last government, hoped that James VIII would now arrive from France to rule; in fact Queen Anne was succeeded by her nearest Protestant heir, George the Elector of Hanover, who now also became George I of Britain. In Scotland his acceptance was pushed through by a small group of lords including the Duke of Argyll (who was later highly favoured for this display of loyal support). Generally, however, although Stirling and other burghs duly proclaimed the new King at the mercat cross, the 'wee German lairdie' was not popular. He spoke no English, he did not visit Scotland, and by now the Treaty of Union (with its malt and salt taxes from a London-centred government) was also unpopular. There were also many Jacobites in Scotland, and not all in the Highlands. The Earl of Mar, suspected by King George of being a Stuart supporter, was deliberately snubbed when the new king arrived at London; soon he was also replaced as Governor of Stirling Castle—a wise precaution by the king perhaps, but a dishonour to the family who had been hereditary Keepers for generations. By August 1715 Mar was in the Highlands gathering the Jacobite clan chiefs together for a rebellion. There were also Jacobites in the Lowlands and in England—the plan was for them to link up in a nationwide rising.

Once again Stirling found itself in the forefront of preparations for war. Under the Duke of Argyll a guard was placed on the bridge and a government army began to assemble on the King's Park—Argyll expected Mar's highland rebels to attempt to cross the Forth at Stirling and was determined to stop them when they arrived. By September the rebels were in Perth with an army of around seven thousand men and still growing. At Stirling the government's army totalled only around 1500 men—had Mar attacked now, he would surely have won. By October the total was up to about 4000, but Mar's army had meanwhile swollen to an estimated 12,000. Fortunately for the Duke of Argyll, the Jacobites delayed instead of pressing on to Stirling, and this gave the government's army time to prepare. An artillery battery covering Stirling Bridge was positioned on the Gowan Hill, for example.

In the town all fencible men between sixteen and sixty years old were called up for the local militia. Semi-retired officers on half-pay were hastily rounded up to prepare this makeshift crowd of conscripts for battle, but it was a difficult task—as with the Home Guard in 1940, there were not enough weapons, for example. In the event a local hammerman called John Stevenson was paid £40 Scots to provide twenty Lochaber axes, and one hundred muskets were borrowed from Major Holburn at Stirling Castle. Meanwhile all burgesses in the town were also made to sign an oath of loyalty to King George.

By now Stirling was crowded with the officers of regiments camped on the King's Park. Of course there were difficulties; in particular, the harvest had been bad and by October hunger was in the town. Down on the carse Argyll had an edict nailed to the door of Logie kirk warning local farmers not to sell any crops to the rebels; soon after, Mar did the same and threatened them with treason if they sold to the garrison at Stirling—such was the lot of ordinary folk in time of civil war.

The greatest strain fell upon John Lowrie, once the burgh's Deacon Convener and now its quartermaster. In September he was granted a payment of £10 'for the extraordinary occasions of quartering that have been within this burgh since Michaelmas last, and great pains and trouble (he) has been put to thereby . . .'. At the same time Adam McArthur was rewarded for keeping the town's guns oiled and repaired. As tension mounted, the stress of disruption to normal life began to show. In early November the burgh council ordered a grain-dryer called John Millar who lived at the bridge to assist the guard in verifying who was coming or going across the river; to compensate him he was paid half-a-crown each week. Upriver, John McFeat was rewarded for keeping a check on everyone using the Drip coble (or ferry). Meanwhile the militia brought every boat on the river as far as Alloa to the south shore, to deny Mar's men an easy crossing.

At this point the Jacobite troops began, at last, to move south to Stirling. About 9000 set out, leaving a force of 3000 to guard Perth. Mar's plan was to march as far as Dunblane, where 3000 men would advance to Stirling and distract Argyll while the rest crossed the Forth near Aberfoyle and pressed on into England. On November 10th the Jacobites bivouacked at Auchterarder and next day they advanced to Ardoch Roman camp at Braco. Argyll's spies kept him informed of Mar's movements and on November 12th he marched out over Stirling Bridge to block the Jacobites at Dunblane. The militia, bolstered by a contingent of five hundred volunteers from Glasgow, was left to guard the town under the command of Lord Buchan, the Lord Lieutenant of Stirlingshire. That night Argyll's men slept in battle order on the rising ground of Kippendavie above Dunblane, while Mar's troops camped three miles away at Kinbuck. Next day, Sunday 13th November, the two armies met in the Battle of Sheriffmuir (originally known as the Battle of Dunblane).

Having hastily recalled food-foraging troops from all over central Scotland, the Duke of Argyll's army numbered about 3500 men, mostly experienced infantrymen and accompanied by five regiments of cavalry. Mar's army, though reduced by desertions to about 8000, was still much larger: 'There were country gentlemen from Angus and Aberdeenshire, riding on stout horses, with sword and pistol, each dressed in his best laced attire, and each attended by serving-men, also armed, and also on horseback. Then there were Highland gentlemen in the more picturesque garb of their country, with obeisant retinues of clansmen on foot. The mass of the army was composed of Lowland peasants, with arms slung over their plain gray clothes, and of mountaineers, nearly naked, or at least wearing little more than one shirt-like garment. Two squadrons of cavalry, which Huntly had brought with him . . . (were) composed of stout bulky Highlandmen, mounted on little horses, each with his petit blue bonnet on his head, a long rusty musket slung athwart his back, and not one possessed of boots or pistols. It sounds like a raggle-taggle army, but Lowland troops could be hard and dour and a Highland charge could certainly be terrifying.

Of the two commanders Argyll was the more experienced, a proven general from Marlborough's campaigns against the French. On the other hand, Mar was 'an inexperienced amateur, whose ablest implement was his tongue' as one account puts it. Before the battle he made a widely-admired speech to his men, but when it came to the fighting he had not the same skill or decisive leadership.

The exact site of the battle is uncertain, but it most probably occurred north of Dunblane beyond the Queen Victoria School, on the undulating fringe slopes of the Sheriffmuir. Almost certainly it did *not* happen where Ordnance Survey maps indicate by the Wharry Burn, nor around the Clan MacRae memorial cairn near the Sheriffmuir Inn.

Both armies were arranged in two lines. The Jacobites had ten battalions of MacDonalds, Macleans, Gordons and other clans in the centre of the front line, with cavalry on the flanks (including a 'Stirling squadron' which carried the royal standard, but of which little is known). Their second line and reserves included men from Huntly, Inverness, Atholl, Perth, Fife, Angus and elsewhere. The Earl of Mar positioned himself in the centre-right of the front line. Opposite the Jacobites, the government army was similarly organised, with a front line of six seasoned infantry battalions guarded by troops of dragoons (including the Scots Greys) on the flanks, and a second line behind. Argyll commanded the battle from among his cavalry on the right wing.

The fighting began about noon, on a frosty, chilly day. Argyll's right flank was uphill from the rest of his force, stretched out down the slope towards the outskirts of Dunblane. From his higher vantage point the Duke could see the Jacobites advancing, but because of undulations he could not see the lower, left-hand end of his own army. Suddenly the clans on Mar's left, opposite Argyll, launched a ferocious charge; two thousand Highlanders fired their muskets, then threw them away to attack with dirks and broadswords into the crumbling ranks of Argyll's infantry. The government troops were saved only by a charge across frozen marshland by Colonel Cathcart's cavalry troop which broke the Jacobite onslaught and forced the rebels to retreat northwards to the River Allan, where the escape was blocked. Six times the Highlanders faced about to repel cavalry charges, but although they fought on for three hours, many were now killed. On Sheriffmuir, the MacRae memorial says that their clan fell almost to a man. Argyll himself was heard to cry 'Oh, spare the poor blue-bonnets!' for which momentary display of feeling for fellow Scots he was later censured. As far as Argyll could see, however, his small army had now won the day.

Argyll was wrong. While his cavalry was cutting down the Jacobite left wing, the Earl of Mar's right wing was outflanking and destroying Argyll's left. Later some shepherds described how, from a distance, they watched 'a diamond-shaped patch of scarlet, gradually diminishing in a darker setting'—one of many bands of redcoats surrounded and wiped out by Highlanders. In just seven minutes the MacDonalds of Clanranald and Glengarry broke and scattered the enemy, sending cavalry and infantry alike fleeing past

Dunblane and across the Bridge of Allan towards Stirling. With the Jacobite cavalry, including Mar, in hot pursuit, the chase went on for half an hour as far as Cornton and Stirling Bridge itself. The sight of this slaughter certainly worried those who watched from Stirling Castle. Lieutenant-Colonel John Blackadder, deputy governor of the castle, wrote in his diary: 'Being under arms all night, I slept two hours on Sabbath morning, and then went to church. At the dismission we were alarmed (i.e. the alarm sounded), and, upon going out, I saw one of the most melancholy sights I ever beheld in my life—our army flying before their enemies. . . . I went down to the bridge with a heavy heart, the runners-away coming fast in, and everyone giving a worse account than another—that all was lost and gone. Indeed seeing is believing; all the fields were covered with our flying troops, horse and foot—all had the appearance of a routed army'.

Like the Duke of Argyll, the jubilant Earl of Mar believed that he had won. In fact the battlefield was virtually deserted for a time, with Argyll's right wing chasing Jacobites off towards Greenloaning and Mar's right wing pursuing Hanoverians to Stirling Bridge. Eventually Argyll re-formed what he could of his force and returned to Sheriffmuir, where he found part of Mar's force ready for them on a hillock. For a time the two sides watched each other warily, well within pistol-shot range, but made no attack. Then Mar returned with his victorious men from Stirling—had he now attacked Argyll the Jacobites might still have won a victory, but Mar hesitated and the thirst for more battle drained away from both sides. This went on till dusk when, protected now by the arrival of three fresh regiments, the government troops marched off to Dunblane. When Argyll returned next day, intending to continue the fight, he found that Mar and his army had slipped away in the dark to Perth.

Considering that most of the fighting was over quickly, there was great loss of life at Sheriffmuir; most estimates agree that each side lost at least six hundred men. When the men of Bridge of Allan went next day to the battlefield they found, as Catherine Steuart later wrote: 'many and many a new-made grave. Savage and unkempt creatures wrapped in tartan plaids were wading and searching in the icy stream (the River Allan). Every now and then one of these, with a wild and dolorous cry, hailed his comrades, and a stiff and ghastly form was lifted from the water. When they arrived at the farm-town of Linns the little party spoke with a poor trembling old woman, who shuddered as she told how she had seen eleven soldiers killed on her own midden before the door, after which the Highlanders had burst into the house with their bloody swords. They saw hundreds of dead bodies lying still unburied upon the frozen heather, whilst the poor people of the neighbourhood, sorry enough, but desperately hungry, were spreading on the ground the plaids of the dead Highlanders, into which they were emptying the stone of oatmeal, carried by each man in his wallet . . .'

Finally, there remains the question of Rob Roy Macgregor and his part in the battle. He *may* still have been arriving over the hills when the fighting started, having been delayed waiting for the Macphersons to join him at Balquhidder. Cameron of Locheil, a Jacobite survivor from Sheriffmuir, later wrote that, as he tried to rally men in the fighting by the River Allan, he saw Rob Roy still on his way to the battle: 'At the same time I perceived Rob Roy Macgregor on his march below me coming from Doune, he not being at the engagement, with about 250 betwixt Macgregors and Macphersons. I marched towards him with the few I had got together. Perceiving Argyll opposite us, I entreated, he being come fresh with these men, that we would join and cross the river to attack Argyll, which he absolutely refused . . .'

The more usual story, however, is that popularised by Sir Walter Scott: 'During this medley of flight and pursuit, Rob Roy retained his station on a hill in the centre of the Highland position; and though it is said his attack might have decided the day, he could not be prevailed upon to charge. Mar's positive orders reached Rob Roy that he should presently attack, to which he coolly replied, "No, no, if they cannot do it without me, they cannot do it with me". . . . Rob did not, however, neglect his own private interest on the occasion. In the confusion of an undecided field of battle, he enriched his followers by plundering the baggage and dead on both sides'.

Scott seems to have obtained his facts from a history of the rebellion written in 1717 by the Rev. R. Patten, a Northumbrian Jacobite who turned King's evidence to save his own life—and then wrote his account of the battle (which he did not even attend). In neither version does Rob Roy come out with honour, however, though he may well have shown good sense to keep out of such an indecisive battle. As one observer noted, Rob Roy fought neither for King George nor King James, but for King Spoils.

Technically the result was a draw, but while Argyll's small army marched back to Stirling with fourteen captured banners, four waggons, six enemy cannon and a string of over two hundred prisoners including Lord Strathallan, Drummond of Logie-Almond and Lord Panmure (who later escaped), Mar's men lamented the loss of the Earl of Strathmore and the young MacDonald chief of Clanranald. Mar *should* have won but the result was much better for Argyll. Soon more regiments arrived from England and Holland and the Jacobite cause was effectively lost. In December James the 'Old Pretender' arrived in Scotland, but he soon realised the position and sailed off again to France in February to await another opportunity. The Earl of Mar sailed with him, and with that the clans went home and the rebellion ended. As the well-known rhyme says:

There's some say that we wan,
And some say that they wan,
And some say that nane wan at a', man;
But ae thing I'm sure,
That at Sherra-muir,
A battle there was, that I saw, man;
And we ran, and they ran,
And they ran, and we ran,
But Florence (Huntly's horse) ran fastest of a', man.

For some local people the aftermath of Sheriffmuir went on for quite a time. Following a government commission, Jacobite landowners such as the Earl of Linlithgow, Viscount Kilsyth and the Duke of Perth forfeited their estates and titles. Others who lost land included John Hay of Cromlix, William Douglas of Glenbervie and Sir Hugh Paterson of Bannockburn. Stirling of Keir forfeited his estate, and with it an annual income of over £900 sterling. The Earl of Mar lost his lands in Aberdeenshire and at Alloa and Stirling, and with them an income of over £1650 sterling—the portioners of Cornton, for example, now found a Crown-appointed factor collecting the rent, until their lands were eventually bought by Mar's brother James Erskine, Lord Grange, for £36,000.

Burgh life was also affected by the brief rebellion. With trade disrupted and folk afraid to come near Stirling, William Cowan the burgh's customs collector was given £500 Scots for his loss of earnings. Robert Stirling, whose home at Bridge-end was commandeered as a guard house, was similarly paid £36 Scots in compensation. £215 8s 10d was paid to the Stirling men who had guarded Doune Castle during the emergency, while quartermaster John Lowrie was given another 300 merks for 'the great and extraordinary trouble, pains and fatigue' which he had suffered while coping with the host of soldiers in town, which had taken up all his time and prevented him from following his own hammerman's craft. Several bailies also received compensation for having had to accommodate various officers in their houses; one such was bailie Harry Christie, who received £72 Scots 'for his furnishing Major Stuart . . . with two rooms, bed, coal and candle, for the space of twenty weeks, before and during winter last'.

Something also had to be done with the host of Jacobite prisoners brought into Stirling by Argyll. By New Year the tolbooth was overcrowded with wretched Highlanders, including an additional thirty-four captured at Tullibardine as they headed home from a lost cause. In February 1716 the town council was ordered by Argyll to pay £3 8s a day for the maintenance of some of these people. On 25th February the council also paid 'Archibald Moir, jailor of this burgh, thirty shillings sterling for his extraordinary pains and charge in attending the prisoners that were incarcerated in the tolbooth by the government since beginning of September last, cleaning the prisons, serving the prisoners, and furnishing a servant to his assistance . . . the jailor having received no jailor fee from these prisoners'.

Of course the council intended to reclaim these expenses from the government, and by the end of February an account was drawn up. Before sending this off, the council took the precaution of congratulating the King on the 'happy success of his Majesty's forces against the rebels'. A suitable letter conveying these congratulations was duly submitted by Provost Colonel Erskine to Henry Cunninghame, the local MP, 'to be presented by him to his Majesty by the introduction of such peer as the said Henry Cunninghame shall think fit'.

In April 1716 there was still a 'multitude of prisoners' in the tolbooth and Archibald Moir was again granted two shillings sterling a week for his troubles. During the summer, however, most of these people were taken off to Carlisle for trial. Stirling was made to provide twenty horses to help convey them as far as Kilsyth—help readily given, for it eased congestion in the tolbooth and helped the town return to normal life. Meanwhile General Wade and later General Clayton set to building a network of military roads and barrack forts throughout the Highlands (including Major Caulfeild's road from Stirling to Crieff, constructed 1741–2 on the line of an older gravelled track). A Disarming Act also required Highlanders to hand in their weapons. Apart from these measures, however, the government was lenient—none of the prisoners tried at Carlisle were executed, for example, for the spirit of rebellion was genuinely thought to have been extinguished.

As it happened, the government was wrong. In 1719 another Jacobite rising occurred with assistance from Spanish troops who landed on the west coast. Barely one thousand Highlanders joined them, and the attempt was quickly ended by a government victory at Glenshiel, but even this episode affected Stirling, as the records for 21 April show: 'The magistrates and town council of the said burgh considering the danger wherewith his Majesty's kingdoms are at present threatened by an invasion from Spain, and that it is credibly informed that a part of the descend (i.e. enemy) are landed in the north of Scotland, they, for the better providing the inhabitants of this place with ammunition for defence of the government, appoint the town treasurer to borrow one hundred pound weight of powder from the deputy governor of the castle of Stirling . . .' Once more the bridge was guarded, the town filled with troops, and quartermaster John Lawrie was busy again. The alarm passed, and for a generation there was peace—but then came 1745. The Highlanders were stirring and the town faced another Jacobite rebellion.

In France the Old Pretender's son Charles took up his father's Jacobite cause and prepared to sail for Scotland. In August 1745 he landed with just seven supporters in the Hebrides and from there made his way to Glenfinnan, where he raised his standard and summoned the clans. Some, such as the MacKenzies and the MacLeods of Skye, thought the chances of success very small without substantial help from French troops, and did not join. On the other hand, King George II was unpopular, northern England was said to be full of Jacobite supporters, and a new generation of chiefs was leading the clans. When Cameron of Locheil declared his support, the MacDonalds, Stewarts and more followed to Glenfinnan. On August 21st, with an army of about two thousand men, Bonnie Prince Charlie set off southwards to win the crown of Britain for his father. As he advanced, Lord George Murray and the men of Atholl joined the cause, which encouraged the Macgregors, Robertsons, Mackintoshes and others to enlist.

News of this spread quickly to Stirling, and soon the town was in a bustle as it filled with troops. In command was General Sir John Cope, 'a parade-ground soldier, with an expert knowledge of pipe-clay and button polish, but completely devoid of intelligence and resource' as one account puts it. On August 20th Cope marched out across Stirling Bridge with twenty-five companies of infantry and several cannon. 'Skilfully avoiding the rebels, he reached the shelter of Inverness on the 29th, leaving the road to the south freely open to Charles's Highlanders', as the account goes on. On September 13th, with Cope's men somewhere in the north, the Jacobites suddenly appeared outside Stirling, having avoided the bridge and crossed the River Forth six miles upstream by the Ford of Frew. Fortunately the rebels were pressing on to Edinburgh and skirted round the town, making no attempt to capture it; some of the castle's guns were fired but there was no fighting and the buzz of alarm subsided as the Highlanders marched on to Linlithgow.

On September 17th the Jacobites captured Edinburgh (but not the castle), and at the mercat cross King James VIII was proclaimed. Now the Ogilvies, Gordons, and others joined and swelled the Jacobite army to about five thousand. Some were intercepted by troops from Stirling Castle as they crossed the River Forth at Alloa on October 30th. The *Scots Magazine* noted that the government troops 'wounded some, took several prisoners, some cows, horses, baggage, arms, money and letters; all which they carried into Stirling Castle that night'. Sir John Cope's men meanwhile came by sea from Aberdeen to Dunbar, hoping to intercept the Jacobites' southward march. Instead they were destroyed on September 20th at the Battle of Prestonpans—reputed to have lasted only four minutes, and perhaps the shortest in Scottish history. Apart from a handful of government-held castles, such as Edinburgh and Stirling the whole of Scotland was now open to Prince Charles.

The rest of the story is well known and quickly told. The Jacobites advanced into England through Cumbria and Lancashire. Many people cheered and waved, but except for some men at Preston and Manchester, few Jacobite supporters actually joined the Prince's army and Highland spirits fell. It was now November and many clansmen were restless to get home. Finally at Derby, on December 6th ('Black Friday' as it became known), with London just one hundred miles away and poorly defended, the rebels decided to turn back home. Prince Charles protested in vain that the prize was so near and there for the taking—the Highlanders, laden with booty and worried about the harvest, paid no heed. With government troops now more organised and snapping at their heels, they retreated back into Scotland, straggling back through Dumfries and entering Glasgow (which was staunchly anti-Jacobite) on Christmas Day 1745.

Stirling's town council followed these events as best it could. In November they judged it 'expedient at this time to address his Majesty' and a letter was prepared in the Town Clerk's best handwriting. It was sent by the Dean of Guild to the Duke of Argyll 'desiring his grace to do the town the honour to present the address to his Majesty'. This display of loyalty to King George (when the Jacobites were marching south to London) may have been prompted by the large number of government troops stationed at Stirling (now including the town's own militia of 400 men, placed under the command of Major-General Blakeney at the castle), but it was quite typical for Stirling's council to do whatever it thought would best save the town from harm or retribution.

Meanwhile about three thousand Jacobite reinforcements, mostly Frasers, Mackenzies and Mackintoshes together with some troops from France and Ireland, had gathered under Lord Strathallan at Perth, and about eight hundred of these were now stationed around Stirling at Doune, Dunblane and Bridge of Allan. Opposite them, the militia from Glasgow, Paisley and Stirling guarded the various fords across the Forth. As soon as the Jacobites reached Glasgow, however, the militia were sent to Edinburgh and Stirling's castle garrison and militia were left to face the rebels alone. In late December General Blakeney decided to cut one of the arches of Stirling Bridge to hinder Jacobite communications with the reinforcements at Perth (in fact the Highlanders crossed at Frew by making a floating bridge). Although this decision was a serious blow to the town, records show that by December 28th the southernmost arch was already being dismantled. In its place the council organised a ferry crossing and announced a scale of charges—each single person 6d Scots, each person with a horse 1s 6d, each pack horse one shilling.

Although the castle, with its recent Queen Anne outer defences, was strong enough for a siege, the burgh was certainly not. The Barras Yett was stone-built and robust, but other smaller gateways and alleys had to be blocked with rubble. The walls were also checked, but with the northern part of the town protected only by garden dykes this was the weakest point; several deep trenches were therefore dug on this side. It is not known how well provisioned the town was, but this was midwinter; the town council later claimed to have had only eight days' supply of meal, which is plausible.

On Friday 3rd January 1746 the first Jacobites appeared outside Stirling, but beyond musket range. Next day more arrived and completely surrounded the town. Then several nobles appeared with their contingents from Perth and the town council realised that, when all the stragglers finally arrived, something like eight or nine thousand Jacobites would be available to lay siege to the burgh. From the walls they watched artillery barricades being built, and trees being cut down to help span the bridge's broken arch. Worse, they saw several large cannon arrive; these were of varying size but included at least one which weighed 1¾ tons and required twenty horses to pull. Several of these cannon were floated across the Forth at Alloa—Stirling, on the other hand, had no artillery at all. By now surrounding communities such as Denny, Bannockburn, Cambusbarron, St Ninians and Bridge of Allan were already full of rebels demanding food and accommodation from the helpless locals. It was a frightening, panicky time for people in Stirling.

On Saturday 5th January the rebels dug trenches close to the town and set up their artillery. That night at about eight o'clock a Jacobite drummer approached the Barras Yett with a message, but the inexperienced, nervous town guards fired at him before he could shout anything and he ran off into the dark, leaving his drum behind. This was duly hauled up over the walls like a trophy. On Sunday 6th Prince Charles occupied Bannockburn House, the residence of Sir Hugh Paterson, a local Jacobite sympathiser who had actually had his estates confiscated after 1715 but somehow managed to continue living in his house. The Prince's arrival soon saw another drummer approach the town gates with a demand for the town's immediate surrender. This time it was daylight and the sentinels did not fire. The message read as follows:

Stirling Bridge. In December 1745 the southernmost arch (partly obscured by trees) was broken by General Blakeney to prevent Jacobite reinforcements from reaching the main highland army at Glasgow. *Photo*: Craig Mair.

'CHARLES, Prince of Wales, &c., Regent of Scotland, England, France and Ireland, and the Dominions thereto belonging: To the Provost, Magistrates, and Council of the Town of Stirling.

Intending to take possession of our town of Stirling, we hereby require and command you to give our forces peaceable entry into and possession of the said town, and to receive us as the representative of our Royal Father, James the Eighth, by the grace of God, King of Scotland, England, France, and Ireland, and the Dominions thereunto belonging; and as we have a list of all the persons now in arms in the said town, you are expressly required to deliver up to us all their arms, and likewise all cannon, arms, and military stores presently in the said town; assuring you hereby that if you refuse or delay to receive us, or to deliver up the arms or military stores aforesaid, and thereby oblige us to use that force which Providence has put into our hands, after our discharging one cannon against the said town no articles or capitulation of protection shall be given to any of the inhabitants for their persons, goods, and effects; and as the town is now blockaded on all sides, if any person therein now in arms shall be apprehended without the walls of the town they shall be carried to immediate execution. An answer to this is to be returned to our quarters here by two aclock afternoon this day. Given at Bannockburn, this sixth day of January 1746. (Signed) CHARLES, P.R.'

Castle Wynd with, left to right, the Argyll Lodging, Holy Rude church and Mar's Wark. *Photo:* Stirling District Libraries.

What now happened became a topic of great controversy. The town council held a public meeting—some wanted to make a fight of it, but instead the council sent Provost William Christie and bailie James Jaffray as envoys to ask the Jacobites for another day to consider such a difficult decision, and this was granted. Again there was a frenzied public meeting where argument swayed for and against defending the town. General Blakeney is said to have come down from the castle with the words 'Gentlemen, be true to your religion, King, and country, and defend your posts to the last extremity; and if you are overpowered by the rebels, make a handsome retreat, and I'll keep ane open door for you'. Some said General Hawley was on his way to help them (in fact he was another thirteen days in coming, and then was heavily defeated at Falkirk so that he never actually made it to Stirling). Others feared that if the militia had to retreat into the castle, the Highlanders would plunder and rape freely in the town. Meanwhile the Jacobites fired twenty-seven cannon shots into the burgh, knocking off chimneys to hasten the town's decision.

Wisely, perhaps, the town council decided to submit. There were many, especially among the militia, who strongly disagreed but when they begged General Blakeney to support them he is reported to have said, 'Gentlemen, as your Provost and Bailies think the town not worth their notice to take care of it, neither can I. I will take care of the castle'. Whereupon most of the militia, with as many guns as could be saved, went with him into the castle and at eleven o'clock on 8th January the town gates were thrown open. The first Jacobites entered Stirling at four o'clock.

Looking back now, the town council were surely right to surrender. At the time they were called traitors and cowards by those who disagreed with the decision—some of the wealthier, more episcopalian, council members may indeed have been Jacobite supporters quite willing to submit quickly, but the burgh could not have resisted a siege for long and would surely have been damaged in the process. The militia had been on alert for three days and nights and were exhausted, food supplies were low, the town had no artillery with which to silence the Jacobite guns, and even the most optimistic count of nine hundred men under arms would have been no match for the rebel thousands. As the council later recorded in their defence, even if they had fought and then retreated to the castle, whole families would have been left to the fury of the rebels. There would also have been a great difference 'between the rebels entering on terms and their entering by assault, the consequence of which must have been that our streets would be strewed with the corpses of the inhabitants and others, and the whole effects in the town become their plunder'. Instead, Stirling was not seriously looted, it remained relatively undamaged, and the population suffered no recorded casualties.

Once the Jacobites had possession of the town their attention turned to the castle. From Hexboy's pub in the Bow, Prince Charles first demanded its immediate capitulation, to which General Blakeney replied that His Royal Highness must have a bad opinion of him to think him capable of surrendering the castle in such a cowardly manner. So the Jacobites prepared for a siege. In the town the gates were shut and rebel guards were posted to prevent any citizens from leaving. Military law was imposed by tuck of drum through the town—anyone found near the castle, or harbouring garrison wives or children, would be shot. From among the houses platoons of Jacobite troops kept up an intermittent musket fire against the castle—some bullet marks on the castle walls may well date from this period.

On 12th January three Jacobite cannon were set up between the Holy Rude church and Mar's Wark—the only suitable site, according to Charles' chief artillery officer Colonel Grant, from which the castle could be bombarded level with the fortress. Blakeney's guns soon destroyed this position, but such was the damage to the nearby manse and grammar school, the town council's vehement protests persuaded Charles to move his guns. Colonel Grant must have complained at this, for he was replaced by the incompetent French officer Mirabel de Gordon, who decided that two gun batteries could be set up on the Gowan Hill, just forty yards from the castle, and another on the Lady Rock. On such rocky sites trenches and emplacements could not be dug and the guns had to be protected from enemy fire by woolpacks. Even then, most of the work was done by French troops, since the Highlanders found it beneath their dignity and the Lowland troops were plain lazy.

On 17th January the Jacobites defeated a relieving force under General Hawley at Falkirk, much as Bruce had earlier destroyed at Bannockburn an English army coming to the assistance of the castle. Rebel spirits soared, but twice Blakeney rejected further demands to surrender, saying that he would rather die as a man of honour. Instead, preparations for the siege went on. Some Highlanders actually tried to scale the cliffs below the castle walls, but were driven back with heavy losses by musket fire. Prince Charles himself stood within musket range and had to be persuaded to take more care.

On 29th January, with three of the cannon ready on the Gowan Hill, Monsieur Mirabel (whom the Highlanders called Mr Admirable) declared that the castle would be taken within eighteen hours of the first shots. What *actually* happened was later described by Prince Charles' aide-de-camp the Chevalier Johnstone: 'M. Mirabel, with a childish impatience to witness the effects of his battery unmasked it . . . and immediately began a very brisk fire . . . but it was of short duration and produced very little effect on the batteries of the Castle, which being more elevated than ours, the enemy could see even the buckles of the shoes of our artillerymen. As their fire commanded ours, our guns were immediately dismounted (i.e. destroyed), and in less than half an hour we were obliged to abandon our battery altogether . . .'.

By now another government army was on its way from Edinburgh, this time under the more competent Duke of Cumberland. By 31st January this force was at Linlithgow and next day the Jacobites decided to pull out of Stirling. The plan was to rendezvous at St Ninians, where a rearguard would be chosen to protect the main bulk of the army as it crossed the Forth and headed north. In fact, even before daybreak Highland troops began to disappear upstream to the Fords of Frew. As the Jacobite general Lord George Murray later wrote: 'Never was their (*sic*) a retreat resembled so much a flight, for their was no where 1000 men together, and the whole army pass'd the river in Small bodies and in great Confusion, leaving Carts & Cannon upon the road behind them'.

That morning (1st February 1746), as Lord George Murray rode to St Ninians to appoint a rearguard for his troops, there was a loud explosion. The village church, used by the Jacobites as a powder store, blew up as it was being emptied for the march north. It seems to have been accidental, but the blast demolished the church and left only the tower standing. It still stands today—a silent memory of the last, and probably most futile, attack on Stirling Castle. As Murray rode off and the Jacobites reached Doune and Dunblane, so the Duke of Cumberland and his troops marched into Stirling, to an artillery salute from the castle.

There was little time to make Cumberland welcome. In less than three days government troops quickly repaired Stirling's broken bridge with timber abandoned by the rebels, and by 6 a.m. on 4th February the first troops were able to march out in pursuit of the Jacobites (who were by now at Crieff). The end of the Jacobite story is well known. Cumberland's men destroyed and then butchered the Jacobites at the infamous Battle of Culloden on April 16th, following which they combed the Highlands, burning or emptying villages and capturing or killing most males whom they found. Prince Charles meanwhile hid for five months among the glens and islands of the north-west; despite an enormous reward of £30,000 on his head, he was not betrayed. He finally escaped to France, a disillusioned but legendary figure—the 'Prince across the water'.

In April the Duke of Cumberland was made an honorary burgess of Stirling. His burgess ticket was presented in 'a silver box, richly made and gilded' for £5 sterling by a local jeweller called Ker. According to burgh records, the box was engraved with the town's arms, the wolf on the crag, 'done and executed in the handsomest manner'. In July, when it was clear that Culloden had been a decisive battle, the council 'judged it expedient that they should address the King' and a suitable letter congratulating George II on his victory over the rebellious Highlanders was duly sent off via Mr Erskine of Grange, the burgh's MP. This must have been well received, for the town does not seem to have suffered thereafter for its unseemly surrender to the rebels.

Stirling recovered slowly from the Jacobite period. For months the town was full of troops, including a Hessian regiment from Germany. Many townspeople now claimed compensation for losses to the rebels—Thomas Campbell was paid £30, for example, while John Hall, the local coalman, was granted £9. Several carters from Clackmannan who happened to be in Stirling with loads of coal when the Jacobites entered, and who then had their waggons commandeered, were given £30 Scots towards their losses. 'The woman who keeps the two children belonging to the military left in this place' was granted £12 per quarter. Then in 1748 repair work finally began on the broken arch of the bridge, and with that the Jacobite episode in Stirling's history may be said to have ended.

CHAPTER 10

The Town begins to change 1750–1830

By 1750 the Jacobite threat was clearly over and Stirling's role as an army base was reduced. With a network of military roads now spreading through the Highlands, Stirling Castle was never again seen as a defensive bastion against the north. Over the next century it gradually changed to become a regimental barracks and store. In the King's Presence Chamber the wonderful ceiling with its beautifully-carved oak heads became neglected; when some of the carvings fell off in 1777 orders were given to have the entire apartment stripped and converted to a barrack room. A few years later the Great Hall was similarly altered into barracks. What was once a magnificent hall, the scene of many royal occasions and meetings of Scotland's parliament, became a hulk ruthlessly subdivided into four floors. Then in 1807 the ground in front of the castle was converted to a parade ground—the transition from royal castle to barrack block seemed to be complete.

This change was both good and bad for Stirling. From the time of the Stewart royal family's departure for London in 1603 the town's fortunes had declined. With no court to attract them, every lord and earl had by now deserted the burgh, causing a drop in the import of foreign cargoes such as wine or fine cloth. The Forth's notorious windings and shallow fords were, in any case, awkward for increasingly larger trading ships to negotiate; nothing over about 70 tons could reach Stirling, and the town's sea-trade fell gradually during the seventeenth and eighteenth centuries. The demise of the castle as a Highland guard-post added to this slump, and reinforced the feeling that Stirling was no longer a nerve-centre at the hub of Scottish life.

As a result the town in 1750 still looked recognisably as it did in 1650 and not *very* different from 1550. A population of about 4000 still squeezed into a few streets on the castle hill. Blood and offal from the fleshmarket still trickled downhill from St John Street (still called the Back Row at that time) towards the more squalid workshop district around the Craigs and the Dirt Row Port. Most folk still entered town by the Barras Yett and most streets were still unpaved.

At the top of Broad Street stood Mar's Wark, never completely finished and already in ruins; the Earl of Mar now lived at Alloa closer to the coal mines which made his money. John Cowane's hospital was also neglected, with no inmates and only some rooms rented by lawyers or teachers. Around the town other buildings stood in ruins, neglected since their owners died, perhaps of plague or famine, decades earlier; mostly the town council left them alone, until they fell down. Markets still flourished, including a butter and poultry market in Jail Wynd, but even here some old Scots measures were still used, including the Stirling jug for liquids; even the burgh's own accounts were still kept in old Scots money until the end of financial year 1751–2, while land measures such as acres, roods and falls were still used into the nineteenth century. It was hardly the atmosphere of a town at the forefront of change or innovation.

On the other hand Culloden, the last battle on British soil, marked the end of Jacobite rebelliousness and ushered in a long period of stability and extraordinary development over much of Scotland. Industries sprang up, architecture blossomed, country estates were improved, farm land was made vastly more productive, turnpike roads and canals were built, and with this a feeling of regenerated wealth developed.

Signs of this appeared all around Stirling. The Alloa glass works was founded by Lady Frances Erskine of Mar in 1750 and continues to this day. The Carron iron works, with its modern bellow-driven blast furnaces, opened in 1759 and became a household name for two centuries. An estate map of Bannockburn coal pits in 1783 shows no fewer than seventeen grouped around Bannockburn House, while at Alloa the largest coal mine employed 475 people in 1780; by 1791 this had risen to 520 workers, including 104 children under seven years of age. The route for a Forth and Clyde canal was first surveyed by Smeaton in 1763; digging was under way by 1768 and the first ships sailed in 1775.

There was a similar picture in agriculture. Lord Kames inherited the mossy Blair Drummond estate in 1766 and organised an amazing clearance of 1500 acres of bogland by cutting channels to the River Forth and flushing tons of peat away with a sluice; Kames died in 1782 but his improvements saw previously useless peat bogs (such as can still be seen at Flanders Moss) transformed to the fine carse farmland of today. Similarly there was an outbreak of limekiln building. In 1794 the minister of St Ninians parish described how from April to November each year lime was burned at Craigend and Murray's-hall for spreading on the fields. This employed thirty-three people and Craigend alone produced 2000 chalders of powdered lime a year.

Further afield even more striking developments were happening. Edinburgh's New Town came into being and it entered its period of being the 'Athens of the North'. At Glasgow the tobacco trade with North America produced not just spectacular wealth for the 'tobacco lords' but growth in the city. Ships sailed from the Clyde with locally-manufactured goods such as stockings, ribbons, linen tape, shoes, glass, pottery and iron tools, and returned with half of all Britain's tobacco imports, most of which was re-exported to Europe for enormous profit. When the tobacco trade fell after the American War of Independence these wealthy people invested their money in other enterprises—cotton, coal, bleaching, sugar refining, shipbuilding, iron works and much more. As a result the whole town benefited and thrived. The number of Glasgow-centred ships rose from fifteen in 1692 to 476 a century later—Stirling's shipping meanwhile stagnated. Glasgow's population of 17,000 in 1740 rose to over 40,000 in 1780 and over 80,000 in 1801—Stirling's meanwhile grew from 3951 in 1755 to only 5271 in the first official census of 1801.

Stirling was never really caught up in the wave of development which swept across Scotland—indeed it was more of a neglected backwater. This may have been on account of the Town Council, which was not above corruption and self-interest before the burgh's wider good. Once before, in 1681, the Court of Session heard how Provost Robert Russell and his relations had, during the 1660s and 1670s, 'enhanced the trade of the burgh in their own, and their relatives' hands' and had 'embezzled the common good and invested pious donations . . . [and] by contrivance and combination continued themselves in the magistracy of the burgh . . . these many years gone by'. This was corrected in 1695 when an oath was introduced for town council members by which they bound themselves 'to take no lease of any part of the public property, under their management, nor to purchase any part of it; neither to receive gratification out of the public funds, under pretence of a reward for their trouble, in going about the affairs of the borough (*sic*), or of the hospitals founded in it'.

In 1775 a similar, but worse, scandal was exposed in a leaked secret document known as the Black Bond. By this paper, evidently written in 1771, three Town Councillors called Henry Jaffray, James Alexander and especially John Burd had agreed to 'secure to ourselves the total management of the Burgh during our lives and that will be much for the benefit of Us and our friends . . .'. They agreed to nominate each other's friends as councillors and thus to 'weaken the interest of Nicol Bryce and by degrees to exclude him and his friends from the council altogether . . .' Having secured control of the burgh, they intended to appoint various officials in return for payment—the Town Clerk would pay £25, for example, to be divided among the three of them. Since only town councillors were eligible to vote in parliamentary elections, they would also sell their favours to prospective candidates, and again share the spoils.

The eighteenth century was noted for its corrupt local government and parliamentary elections, but when news of this conspiracy broke even the government could not ignore it. In 1773 the Court of Session declared that year's council election void, 'having been brought about by undue influence and corrupt practices', and suspended the burgh council. In 1776, following a fruitless appeal by Burd and his friends to the House of Lords, the Court of Session appointed David Gourlay esquire of Kipdarroch, Dr John Gillespie, physician in Stirling, and Mr John Glass senior, merchant in Stirling, as managers of the town's hospitals and public affairs. This was to last for three years. In addition the town was disqualified from participating in parliamentary elections, from attending meetings of the Convention of Royal Burghs, and from choosing Deacons of Craft or a Dean of Guild. Bailies or magistrates were to be appointed personally by the new managers.

In 1779, and at a cost of £100 sterling, the managers appealed to the Court of Session to have the burgh's privileges reinstated, but it was not until 1781 that King George III finally restored full burgh rights to Stirling. A preliminary election was ordered to be held in June that year, followed by a return to normality in a proper poll at Michaelmas (i.e. September 29th, the traditional date for burgh elections in Scotland).

The council originally consisted of seven craft deacons, of whom four were replaced each year by new members, and fourteen merchants, of whom seven similarly stood down. Annual elections were therefore held to choose four craft and seven merchant council members. The Provost, bailies, treasurer and Dean of Guild were all merchants. Before any election each craft had to send a short leet of four possible deacons, from which the town council (dominated by merchants) deleted two—craftsmen did not even have a free say in the election of their own deacons. Similarly, while the council included fourteen merchants, ordinary merchants had no say in deciding which seven stood down, or who was appointed to replace them—this was done by the councillors alone. They also had no say in the appointment of the Provost, bailies or even their own Dean of Guild. In other words the outgoing council voted in the new. No-one could serve as an ordinary councillor for more than two years, but by packing the council with friends it was possible for a merchant to serve two years as a councillor, then to be chosen as Provost, Dean or whatever, and then to begin another two years as an ordinary councillor . . . and so on. This is what Burd and his friends had planned to do.

By the new elections called for 1781 each craft was simply to choose its own deacon and between them to elect a Deacon Convener. The merchants were to elect all fourteen merchant councillors and decide from among them who was to be Dean of Guild. The entire elected council would then appoint its own Provost, bailies and treasurer. All craftsmen and merchants who were already burgesses in 1777 were entitled to vote, and during the six days before the appointed election were to bring proof of their eligibility so that their names could be included on a voters' roll. As everywhere else at that time, voting would be done by public declaration, but in an effort to keep the process as free from corruption as possible the Sheriff Deputes from neighbouring Perthshire and Lanarkshire were to attend and oversee this election, and enforce an oath against bribery and corruption on every voter. At the same time the constitution of the burgh was also altered by order of the Privy Council so that after 1781 only four merchants would stand down from the council each year but one would then be appointed Dean of Guild. Four deacons of craft would also stand down, but would be replaced by the crafts alone without having to submit leets first. It may not have been the perfect solution by modern standards, but as a result of these much-needed changes the elections of 1781 were perhaps Stirling's most democratic polls that century.

Although the town's temporary managers were undoubtedly wary of doing anything too innovative or expensive, some hints of a developing civic pride, or a desire to improve, did begin during the 1770s. As a result of council encouragement and public subscription from various individuals and incorporations, clean water was brought to Stirling from the Touch Hills in two-inch pipes; this was stored in a reservoir tank in St John Street and by gravity fed the town's street wells. From the outset the supply—about two gallons per head per day (assuming no drought)—was not really enough, and it was many years before houses had running water. But the supply was pure and for the moment the queues for good water grew longer every day. Lord Cockburn who, as a circuit judge, sometimes came to Stirling, described the queues for water in the town. 'The two or three public wells are also so constructed, having only one spout each, that the poor people are obliged to stand idle and shivering for hours before they can get their vessels filled, to their great discomfort and not at all to the improvement of their manners or morals. I counted about 200 tubs, pails, pitchers, etc., arranged on the street, with the owners waiting their turns from the solitary spouts. I told the Provost that if I was in his place, these evils should be remedied in a month, simply multiplying the spouts at the existing drawing places.'

Other useful improvements were made. In 1773 the town council demolished the arch which had stood for years at the north end of Stirling Bridge. The southern arch was already gone, but for years the northern one had survived because the Bridge gate hung there. The reason given was that the weight of stone was weakening the bridge itself, but their passing was marked by the pyramid-topped pillars which still stand at each end today.

In 1791 the Back walk was extended. This pleasant urban path, often rated still the finest in Scotland, was first provided with money given by William Edmonstone in 1723, but it ran only from what is now Academy Street past the Guildhall to the Valley (or the Lady Rock). In 1791 one end was extended from Academy Street to Port Street, while in 1798 the other end was continued round the Castle Rock to Ballengeich (and eventually in 1832 to the Gowan Hill).

In 1794 the town council moved the weekly Friday cattle market to a new site 'within the town of Stirling, at the ordinary market place between John Graham's house and the Factory near the Bridge . . .'. This was directly under the Gowan Hill, just where Back o' Hill Road begins today, on a site now occupied by a large tenement block of flats.

In 1806–7 a new prison was constructed in St John Street to supplement the tolbooth cells. It was built over two years at a cost of £1978 by a joiner called Thomas Traquair, and Alexander Bowie, a mason normally associated with work on Allan Park houses. The architect was Richard Crichton from Edinburgh.

In 1814 the old Meal Market at the top of King Street was demolished. It was duly replaced by a Corn Exchange which stood opposite the present District Library. Meanwhile an elegant new building known as the Athenaeum was erected on the site of the Meal Market in 1816. With shops at ground level, an assembly room, library and reading-room above, and crowned by an impressive spire, the new building had an immediate impact on Stirling's 'townscape'. A statue of Sir William Wallace was later added, and he still faces down King Street today in one of the best-known views of the town.

During the later 1770s the Barras Yett was demolished (although a customs house was kept and dues were still charged on goods coming into the town). The removal of the narrow gateway invited burgh expansion outside the town walls. Quite soon a number of properties appeared where Port Street is now, and this gradually spread further—street names like Pitt and Melville ring of this period. The most significant development of this time was the creation of the 'terraces' which still exist near the Allan Park cinema and Black Boy statue. These appeared around 1785 when, first, four feus were created to the south of the Stirling-Linlithgow road beside the old St Ninian's Well. These plots, each of four acres, became the grounds of Viewforth, Springbank, Viewfield and Annfield mansions (Langgarth and the present Viewforth are later buildings). As it still is today, the Stirling-Linlithgow road was situated in a gully, so a separate, more level, track was provided for these residences: their location was described in council minutes as being bounded '. . . on the west by the higher footpath or road and the highway leading from Stirling to St Ninians'. Of these four properties, Viewforth was closest to Stirling, and soon the intervening space was feued by the council in smaller lots for further development. So appeared the terraces, largely unchanged today

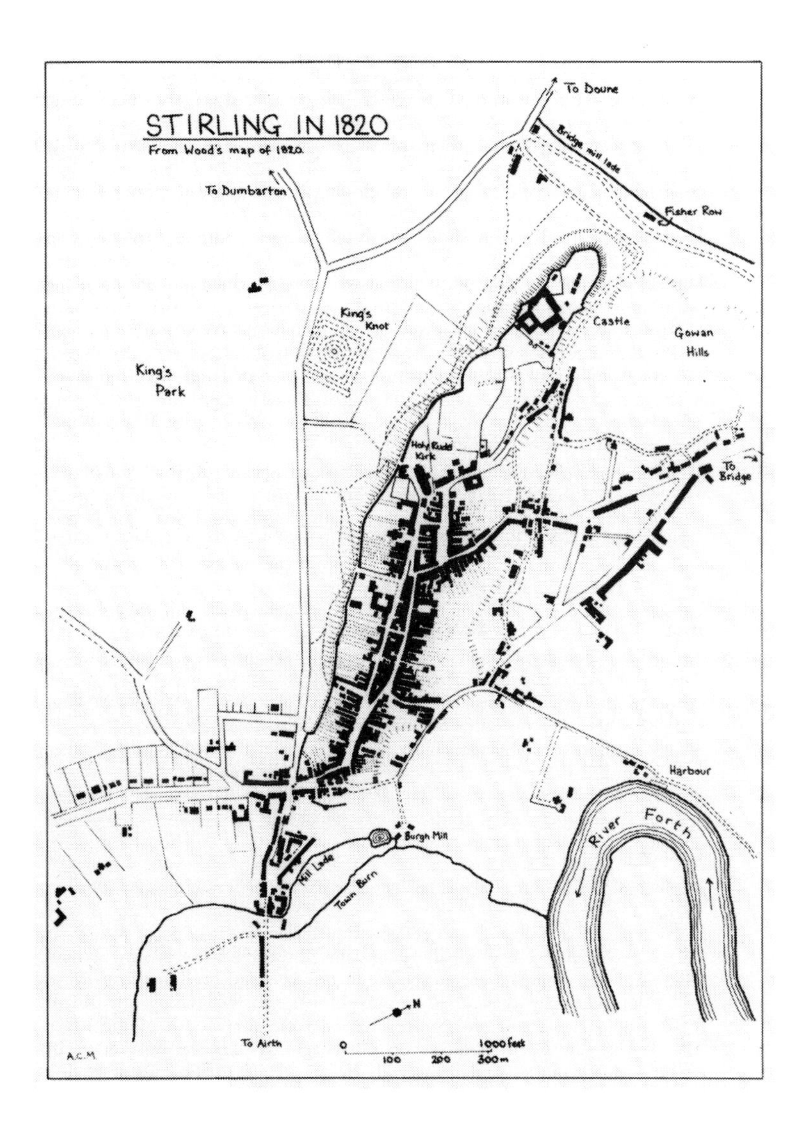

Map of Stirling in 1820.

except that some of the present trees are replacements for originals. By the end of the eighteenth century the approach to Stirling by Port Street must have been very elegant and impressive.

Around 1790 the beginnings of Dumbarton Road were also developing and various feus in the Allan Park area were being acquired by Stirling's wealthier citizens. (On the other hand, when the Town Burn, which ran along Dumbarton Road, was finally culverted by the town council in 1816, gaps were left to allow Allan Park residents to water their cattle!) By 1801 lots one to eight of Southfield, part of the terraces area, had been feued out by the masters of Spittal's Hospital to various merchants and tradesmen. A gradual drift away from the older top of the town area was thus beginning, and would go on throughout the nineteenth century.

New streets and housing then appeared to the north of the town. By the time of Wood's detailed map of 1820 the north side of Cowane Street had been built, and Irvine Place was developing downhill from Upper Bridge Street towards the present Barnton Street (at that time no more than an *intended* street, and with no houses yet built along it). Although named and marked off by 1802 (shown in a beautiful plan by a land surveyor called Mathie, in which he drew each proposed house and marked out even the paths and flowerbeds in each garden), Queen Street barely existed even in 1820. Just one year later, however, sixteen plots were sold off at £8 an acre and thus another new street was born. Murray Place did not yet exist, except as a rough mill-track, so there was no carriage road through or round lower Stirling; traffic entering from Port Street still had to climb the old way up King Street (then called Quality Street) and Bakers Wynd to St Mary's Wynd and so down to Stirling Bridge.

Quite separately, the community of Raploch began to grow. This land, originally sold in the 1670s by the Earl of Mar to the patrons of Cowane's Hospital, was mostly agricultural. During the 1690s the town council had built six houses, known as Fisher Row, immediately beneath the castle's nether bailey ramparts roughly halfway round the Back o' Hill road today. As John Harrison has written, however, the attempt to found a colony of salmon fishers failed with a decline in fish stocks, the disastrous effects of the Darien Scheme, and the terrible famines of the 1690s. By 1735 some of the houses had been demolished and the remaining tenants were farmers.

In 1799 the patrons of Cowane's Hospital (who were, of course, synonymous with the town council) decided to feu out ten plots of land roughly where the present Fire Station is, and so began modern Raploch. This was a more viable community than before; each plot allowed a house, garden and workshed where necessary, at an affordable rent of just over £1 per year, with a 999-year lease. The first tenants included a smith, a builder, a tailor, two shoemakers, four weavers (including one from Glasgow and another from Blairdrummond), and the customar for Stirling Bridge. In 1813 the patrons also granted a salary of £3 3s yearly for a schoolmaster at Raploch—Samuel Forrester is recorded as having been the teacher there in 1818.

The spread of housing also reflects the development of local roads. As elsewhere, roads were originally maintained by the statute labour system, whereby local tenants were supposed to do six days' roadmending work, filling potholes or wheel-barrowing gravel for the surface (Craigforth Road, for example, was made with gravel carried from the mouth of the River Allan across the Forth in sacks on horseback). This never worked well; everyone who could, avoided this duty by simply not turning up or paying someone else to do it for him. As a result roads were generally rough and travel was slow and difficult; in 1742, when Lord Lovat made a journey of one hundred and sixty miles by coach from Inverness to

The Raploch as it looked around 1900. The first community appeared at Fisher Row (not in view) during the 1690s, but this area was first feued for housing in 1799. *Photo:* Stirling District Libraries.

Edinburgh, the journey took eleven days during which there were three broken axles. Similarly, as Drysdale relates, 'In January 1777 the riding post from Edinburgh, in fording a stream near Falkirk, was swept down—boy, bags, and beast; but, mercifully, all were fished out'.

The first turnpike roads appeared around Edinburgh in 1714. These were well-built roads, properly maintained by a trust or committee, for which travellers paid a sliding scale of charges according to their method of transport. Each road required a separate act of Parliament, however, and there was a long gap from the first in 1714 to the next in 1751 when a real mushrooming of turnpike roads began. John Patrick has neatly summed up the result: '. . . by 1844 three hundred and fifty acts had been passed setting up trusts all over the country. Slowly communications improved. In 1749 a coach service was begun between Glasgow and Edinburgh. The forty-six mile journey took twelve hours. By 1799 the time had been reduced to six hours. The service between Edinburgh and London ran twice a day instead of once a month, and took sixty hours instead of a fortnight'.

Not surprisingly Stirling, with its vital bridge across the Forth, soon became part of the turnpike network. Local Turnpike Trust records for the period are missing, but work on the first turnpike began during 1752 when there first appeared 'an Act for repairing the Post Road from the City of Edinburgh through the Counties of Linlithgow and Sterling, from the boathouse ford on Almond Water, and from thence to the Town of Linlithgow, and from the said Town to Falkirk and from thence to Sterling; and also from Falkirk to Kilsyth, and to Inch Bellie Bridge, on the Post Road to the City of Glasgow'. This route passed via Bannockburn, where it still used Robert Spittal's old bridge until 1819 when the present Telford bridge was constructed.

It should have opened up exciting possibilities for a backwater like Stirling, but in fact this first turnpike got off to a bad start when the trustees demanded statute labour from Stirling to help them maintain stretches of the route well beyond the burgh. Town Council and Guildry minutes indicate a readiness to support the road proposal, but also contain a vehement rejection of the idea that the town should contribute workmen for its upkeep; Stirling had its own streets to maintain and besides, surely the tolls charged were supposed to pay for repairs? In 1753 this went to the Convention of Royal Burghs which discovered that other towns like Perth and Linlithgow were experiencing the same demands. As a result the Convention sought (and won) high legal ruling to support Stirling's case (though even in 1754 the council had to form a sub-committee to 'resist demands from Trustees for statute labour on the Turnpikes'). In 1755 work on the road seems to have reached the burgh, however, and the route must have opened for business soon after.

Thereafter progress continued, mostly still evident in the present A-class road network. In 1794 the military road to Dumbarton was upgraded to a turnpike, entering the town by what is still called Dumbarton Road. Mostly this route followed the present A811 to Buchlyvie and beyond, except that it originally passed through Gargunnock and Kippen and was only later realigned to avoid these places. A turnpike link to Glasgow also appeared, branching from St Ninians to Dennyloanhead and Kilsyth. In 1802 a turnpike was built from Causewayhead to Alloa and beyond, augmented in 1810 by another along the hillfoots from Causewayhead to Dollar and Dunfermline via Rumbling Bridge; the Causewayhead part of this road may not have been completed until nearer 1820, however. Remains of the previous statute labour road can still be followed parallel to this newer route along much of the hillfoots through Menstrie, Alva and Tillicoultry. In 1812 yet another turnpike (now the Drip Road) was built through Raploch towards Doune. Mention of its development appears in the Guildry minutes: 'Which day the . . . Patrons of Cowane's hospital being conveened (*sic*) they accept of the offer made by the Trustees of one hundred and fifty pounds sterling per acre for the ground to be taken up by the new turnpike road thro' the lands of Raploch, exclusive of the expense of the new fences, which the Trustees are also to pay . . .'. The Drip Bridge is older and dates from 1769 (but *not* from around 1745 as is often said).

Surprisingly, the causeway which connected Stirling Bridge to Causewayhead was possibly the last to be turnpiked. It was certainly still a statute labour road in 1785, and does not seem to have been improved until the nineteenth century. The road from Causewayhead to Bridge of Allan and beyond (allowing for some later alterations of route) was originally a medieval track, improved in 1742 by the army to link with Wade's road at Crieff. At some point after the Jacobite period it was handed back to civilian care;

an agricultural survey of southern Perthshire published in 1794 reported that this route 'has been greatly repaired in late years', but according to James Bryce of Blawlowan's *Recollections* of 1888, it was not turnpiked until 1814.

Turnpikes led naturally to a development of coaching services. In 1792 the *Courant* newspaper carried this advert:

> The Stirling Light Coach sets off from Robert Lawson's Swan Inn, Grassmarket, Edinburgh, to George Towers's, Stirling, on Mondays, Wednesdays, and Fridays, at 8 o'clock in the morning; and from George Towers's to Robert Lawson's likewise every Monday, Wednesday, and Friday, at 8 in the morning. The proprietors of the Stirling Coach mean to run her at the rate of six miles per hour for speedy conveyance of passengers. Each seat, 8s 6d.

By 1814 there were two coaches daily to Edinburgh, and two more to Glasgow (one passing through Stirling from Perth). By 1835 steamships had captured the trade to Edinburgh, except in winter when two coaches still ran, but there were nine daily coaches to Glasgow, four to Perth, two to Alloa, and one to Callander (except in winter when there were only three a week). Also, as Drysdale reports, 'An omnibus ran four times a day to Bridge of Allan for the accommodation of persons attending the Mineral Wells at Airthrey'.

Several hotels acted as 'coaching inns' (an expression not used then) for these various services. They included Wingate's Inn (later Gibb's Red Lion Hotel) in King Street, now the Golden Lion Hotel, the Saracen's Head Inn and Star Hotel in Baker Street (both gone now), and Sawer's Golden Grapes Hotel in Port Street, which still stands—at the time of writing one of the coachyard stables is a fruit and vegetable shop.

Wingate's had not been open long when Robert Burns paid a visit. This was during his first Highland tour, when he was accompanied by Willie Nicol, a schoolmaster from the High School at Edinburgh. They arrived on the afternoon of Sunday 26th August 1787 by chaise from Falkirk, having just visited Bannockburn. Burns's room on the second floor of the Golden Lion Hotel is still there, but the view of the Ochils which he would have enjoyed is now obscured.

That evening Burns and Nicol strolled up through Broad Street to the Castle from where, as he wrote in a letter that night, 'I have seen by the setting sun the glorious prospect of the windings of the Forth through the rich carse of Stirling'. At the same time the two men were appalled to find the former home of Scottish kings dilapidated and neglected—the great hall was even roofless. Burns's Jacobite or patriotic sympathies must have been aroused, for that night he scratched some lines on a hotel window:

> Here Stewarts once in glory reign'd,
> And laws for Scotland's weal ordain'd;
> But now unroofed their palace stands,
> Their sceptre falled to other hands;
> Fallen indeed, and to the earth,
> Whence grovelling reptiles take their birth;
> The injured Stewart line is gone.
> A race outlandish fills their throne;
> An idiot race, to honour lost—
> Who knows them best, despise them most.

These became known as the 'Stirling Lines', and were to hinder Burns's life for years to come, such was the offence caused to the Hanoverian royal family. As Burns wrote later, when applying to become an exciseman 'I have almost given up the Excise idea . . . I have been questioned like a child . . . and blamed and schooled for my inscription on Stirling window.'

Next day, Monday 27th, Burns made a celebrated trip along the Ochils hillfoots to Harviestoun Castle, from where he explored the River Devon as far as Rumbling Bridge. That evening he returned to Stirling, where he found his companion Nicol much worried by the obvious insults which Burns had scratched on the window. Nicol must have reproached his friend, for Burns is said to have added more, in a sort of mocking penitence:

> Rash mortal, and slanderous poet, thy name
> Shall no longer appear in the records of fame!
> Dost not know that old Mansfield, who writes likes the Bible,
> Says, the more 'tis the truth, Sir, the more 'tis a libel?

By taunting Lord Mansfield, a noted judge of the time, Burns simply made matters worse.

That evening Burns and Nicol dined with three Stirling locals—perhaps at the inn, but it might have been at the castle or in a house near the castle. These three were Dr David Doig the Rector of Stirling Grammar School, Mr Christopher Bell a singing teacher and Master of the English School in Baker Street, and Lieutenant (though Burns called him Captain) Forrester from the castle garrison. Dinner was then whiled away with drink and song—for years thereafter August 27th was observed as a night of Burns Suppers in Stirling.

Next morning Burns had breakfast with Lieutenant Forrester, probably up at the castle. As he later returned to Wingate's, news of the poet's presence in town must have spread, for a crowd gathered to see him. Various gentlemen including John Ramsay of Ochtertyre, Dr Doig from the Grammar School and local poet Hector Macneil chatted with him; outside the tolbooth local schoolmaster Sandy McLaurin offered him snuff, and little Johnny Dick (later Provost of Stirling) noted how tall, but stooped and swarthy, the great Burns was. That morning Burns and Nicol left Stirling for Dunblane and beyond.

This statue of Robert Burns, which stands near the Albert Hall, recalls the poet's two visits to Stirling in 1787, when he lodged at Wingate's Hotel (now the Golden Lion) and wrote the notorious 'Stirling Lines'. *Photo:* John McPake for Central Region Council.

In October that year Burns returned on a more leisurely visit to Stirlingshire, and fell in love with Peggy Chalmers at Harviestoun Castle. He visited John Ramsay at Ochtertyre and the older man advised the 28-year-old Burns to avoid writing satire and study rather the spirit and dialogue of *The Gentle Shepherd.* It is known that Burns lodged again at Wingate's Inn where, having learned to his cost the rashness of his 'Stirling Lines', he belatedly smashed the offending window with the butt of his riding crop. Unfortunately Burns kept no diary of this visit, and little is known of his second visit to Stirling. So much for Burns, and the turnpike road which brought him from Edinburgh.

Turnpikes might also have encouraged the cattle trade, but in fact they were actually avoided by the Highland drovers who brought their beasts to the autumn trysts at Falkirk. The tolls were high—sometimes 2d per cow for just a few miles—and hard road surfaces hurt the hooves. Instead the cattle followed drove roads—ancient tracks across the hills, wide enough to let animals graze as they plodded twelve to fifteen miles a day southwards from the glens. Like streams gradually joining together to form great rivers, these tracks led on to the Stenhouse Muir at Falkirk. Some headed for the ferry crossing over the Forth at Kincardine but most funnelled towards the bridge at Stirling; from Skye, Mull and the Western Isles, the far north and Inverness, Moray, Banff and Buchan, Grampian and Atholl, they came to cross at Stirling.

Crieff was once the main cattle-dealing centre, but by the 1770s it had been replaced by the trysts at Falkirk, held on the second Tuesdays of August, September and October. Here some 50,000 to 60,000 black cattle were sold each year—and most of them passed first through Stirling. When dry summers made it possible, the cattle crossed upstream at the Fords of Frew, but otherwise they came by the bridge. This annual autumn sight must have been tremendous; as early as 1735 the bridge customar was complaining of the jostling cattle and the low parapet, and how two young bulls had fallen off and broken all their bones. The herds then followed the same route as everyone else through the town, up St Mary's Wynd, down Bakers Wynd and King Street, and out by Port Street—the disruption must have been considerable. Drysdale writes, however, that 'about 1824 drovers were informed that they might take their cattle by the Mill Road (now Murray Place), thus avoiding the inconvenience of passing the Corn Market, at the head of King Street'.

By 1800 the first industries had also appeared at Stirling—indeed, by the 1790s as much as one quarter of the population may have been employed in manufacturing. As early as December 1744 the burgh records mention a linen manufactory recently erected near the bridge by a merchant called John Galloway—regrettably there is no further mention of this business. For centuries the town's income had come particularly from wool, however—according to the *Old Statistical Account* of 1792 there were 68 weavers in Stirling compared to only thirty merchants, eighteen lawyers, eighteen shoemakers, fourteen tailors, thirteen hammermen and twelve bakers. Weavers also worked in surrounding communities like Cambusbarron, Torbrex and Bannockburn. *Shalloon,* the coarse woollen cloth typically produced at Stirling, was even exported at times.

The main industrial developments were therefore in textiles, but there was no spectacular growth such as at Glasgow and elsewhere—unlike nearby Alva or Tillicoultry the lack of suitable water power (barely sufficient even for the burgh's grain mills) was a hindrance until steam engines suited to mills became available around the 1780s. Nevertheless the Rev. James Sommerville reported in 1792 that 'there are above 100 employed by one master in this work, in tearing, scourging, and combing the wool, and in making it ready for the wheel'. Robert Belsches in his 1796 *General View of the Agriculture of Stirling* adds: 'A few years ago the manufacturers of Stirling introduced a coarse and thin species of woollen cloth, very much wore (*sic*) by gentlemen in the summer season; and which, from the place where invented, was called *Stirlingette.* The wear was found to be unprofitable, and the caprice of fashion soon drove it out of vogue'. Belsches mentions that local serge sold from tenpence to one shilling and sixpence a yard.

One of the most important eighteenth-century local woollen communities was Bannockburn, where the Wilson firm had a mill (later the Skeoch mill, parts of which still survive) as early as the 1770s, taking power originally from the Bannock Burn. Surviving records also describe the housing erected by Wilsons for their workers during the 1780s; each family had one room, with a box-bed, closet and fireplace. The Wilsons became especially famous for the manufacture of tartan, which had once flourished at Stirling but had subsequently declined. By the 1790s Bannockburn had virtually cornered the entire market, as Belsches described:

'[The village] has, for many years, been famous for the weaving of *Tartan*, the celebrated garb of the Scottish Highlanders. It is believed that the whole tartan employed for plaids, hose etc. of the many battallions of Highlanders in the British army, is manufactured in this village. The wool . . . is brought principally from the counties of Peebles and Roxburgh; it is spun and dyed chiefly in the town of Stirling, and the immediate vicinity, where the dyers have been long famous for their dexterity'.

In 1819 the Prince of Wales (later King George IV), while on a visit to Scotland, had material for a Highland outfit made for him by Messrs John Callander and Company at Stirling. It was later much admired and highly praised in a letter of commendation from the royal clothiers.

Another branch of the woollen business was a local carpet manufactory. In 1792 there were between thirty and forty carpet looms in the town, while in 1796 the price of Stirling's 'Scotch carpet' was from two shillings to four shillings a yard. It proved a profitable industry and a century later the Forthbank carpet works still existed.

By the 1790s cotton was also being made; three Glasgow companies gave out spun yarn to local weavers and the *Old Statistical Account* reports that there may have been 'in all 260 looms employed in weaving coarse muslin'. One company installed spinning jennies in 1791; within a year it had fifty looms in operation and was employing nearly one hundred people. About forty little girls were also employed in cotton embroidery.

Some other industries had also appeared by 1800. The development of a substantial coal industry was well under way at Plean and Bannockburn, and by 1794 was producing 600 tons of coal a week. There were four nail-making manufacturers at Whins of Milton, near St Ninians—the *Old Statistical Account* mentions that 113 hands (who would have been mostly little boys) were employed, producing between 1000 and 1200 nails each, per day (further described in Chapter 11). In addition there were several breweries, distilleries (six in St Ninians, according to the *Old Statistical Account*), brickworks and tanneries. By the 1790s paper making was also established at Bridge of Allan, though at this point the product was not for writing on but was used as a sandwich layer in the making of felt.

Industries led in turn to other developments. Capital was needed

The Royal George mill, a remnant of Bannockburn's great days as a weaving town, when it made most of Britain's tartan cloth. This building probably dates from around 1825. King George IV visited Scotland in 1819 (as Prince of Wales) and 1822. *Photo:* Craig Mair.

and several banks appeared in Stirling. Early examples included the Stirling Banking Company (1777–1826), the Merchant Banking Company of Stirling (1784–1814) and Belsh and Company, which was founded in 1804 but collapsed in 1806. A branch of the Bank of Scotland was also established before 1800, and eventually branches of the National Bank and the Commercial Bank followed.

Harbour improvements did not occur until the 1850s (when it was too late), but during the 1820s the Stevensons (who include Robert Louis Stevenson among them, but were otherwise eminent civil engineers) worked on cutting a channel through the numerous rocky fords which bedevil the River Forth from Alloa to Stirling. Low summer tides still sometimes reveal these great slabs of rock, and the passage blasted through them by Robert Stevenson. This increased the size of vessels able to reach Stirling to around three hundred tons, but did little to arrest the decline of Stirling's harbour. Some ships preferred to unload downstream at South Alloa, and by the 1850s the railways had come.

Improvements were not easily afforded by a town as small as Stirling. At that time there were no domestic rates or community charges to provide a town with income. Except when benefactors donated money for specific projects, everything spent on public works came out of the burgh's common good fund. This accumulated from such things as shore dues, the roup of local salmon fishings, customs from the bridge and Barras Yett entry points, fees from horse sales, and rents from burgh lands. As Finlay McKichan wrote in 1978, the town had 'frittered away' most of its lands by 1800, and though customs over the bridge continued to grow for several decades yet, income from fishings fell. There was little scope for much development, or for meeting emergencies.

This can be shown by looking at Stirling's attempts to cope with periodic famine. During the early 1780s dreadful weather saw crop failures all over Scotland. Stirling Presbytery minutes for 1782–3 (when there was, quite simply, *no* summer) refer to the 'backwardness of last season and the lateness of the harvest'. In the Highlands especially, some women reapers with their sickles stood in deep snow, still trying to harvest crops in January 1783. The Church seems to have felt that this was the hand of God, punishing folk for their impiety and immorality. Meanwhile ministers were urged to 'let aside a day for solemn fasting and humiliation, that they may implore of God the forgiveness of their sins . . .'

There was little else that could be done, and little money in the burgh coffers with which to help. As in previous centuries, many country and Highland folk came as starving destitutes to Stirling, hoping for something from the Cowane and Spittal charities. The town's accounts show that charity payments in the three years prior to 1782–3 averaged around £19 a year; payments in 1782–3 were £34 10s 4d, and a year later rose to £47 19s 1½d before subsiding as improved harvests returned.

In 1799, during the Napoleonic Wars when grain trade with Europe was impossible, a much worse famine struck Scotland and paled all previous relief efforts into insignificance. Charity payments noted in the burgh's accounts climbed to £152 16s 6d for 1799–1800, and then to £238 16s 5d a year later, before falling to around £83 for the next two years. But that was only what came out of the burgh's common good fund. This famine was so great that every possible source of revenue was tapped to help the town council meet the crisis.

In December 1799 the council, in 'consideration of the present state of the poor from the high price of provisions, and to devise the most effectual means of their relief', decided to subsidise the price of grain at the town's meal market. To do this, £500 was borrowed from the Stirling Banking Company, to which the council added £20 of its own, plus £20 from Cowane's accounts and £5 each from the Spittal and Allan funds. The Guildry and Trades were also urged to 'contribute such sums from their respective funds as they can afford for the above laudable purpose'. That effort helped only for the first year.

By February 1800 a soup kitchen was established for the 'relief of the poor during the present season of scarcity'. In May, as winter turned to starvation in spring, the 'Fishing Company' was persuaded to sell all fish caught to the town, and not for export (which might have made more money). A price was fixed at 3d per pound salmon and 2½d per pound of grilse. By June lists of needy people were being drawn up, while Kirk Session minutes show people being given handouts until September, when it was expected that the harvest would be in. During October £6 more was borrowed from town funds, then from Cowane funds, and later another £4 from Spittal funds. Then the crops failed again, and in November the town was forced to buy grain from America. £300 was now raised from the burgh's funds, plus £300 from Spittal's hospital and £500 from the Cowane bequest. And even this was not enough.

In February 1801 the Kirk Session, 'considering the present clamant situation of the poor, and that the funds that had been deposited for their support in the hands of the treasurer are completely exhausted, unanimously agree to authorise Mr Murdoch their treasurer to borrow £30 sterling to answer the present exigencies'. By June this money was gone and Mr Murdoch was empowered to borrow another £30. In October all the orphans supported by the church were called before the Session and told that their pensions would be continued until the next meeting—there was no way of anticipating beyond that. Then someone made an anonymous donation of £50 to the church to help the poor, and in November another £10 10s came from the will of Alexander Jaffray of Glassingall, 'to be applied to the purpose of relieving the wants of the poor of this parish'. In June 1802 the Session treasurer was again allowed to borrow money from the Stirling Banking Company, and still the famine went on. In November 1802 collections were still being made at the church door 'to answer the present emergencies of the poor'. It was a heroic effort by Council, Guildry, Trades, Kirk and private individuals, but it highlighted the town's terrible lack of income and capital resources.

No account of the years to 1830 should omit the executions of John Baird and Andrew Hardie, which occurred in 1820. They followed the so-called 'Radical War' or 'Bonnymuir Rebellion' of that year. Following the end of the Napoleonic Wars in 1815, there was a period of sporadic unrest and protest all over Britain, caused variously by unemployment from industrial and rural mechanisation, hunger from the Corn Laws, complaints that only 2% of people in Britain could vote, attempts to form trade unions, and cries for more democracy from radical politicians such as William Cobbett. With memories of the French Revolution and its horrors still fresh, this working-class unrest was vigorously suppressed by Prime Minister Lord Liverpool and the Tory government. Civil liberties were suspended, emergency laws were introduced, *agents provocateurs* were used by the government to infiltrate working-class organisations and, when necessary (in the days before police), troops were used to break up meetings and demonstrations.

Some of this spread to Scotland, especially among radical weavers in the west. Various plots and plans for risings against the government were hatched and broken by timely arrests. In April, however, posters appeared in Glasgow urging people to support a national strike and form a new revolutionary government. At the same time hundreds of weavers went on strike. The government responded quickly; important Glasgow buildings were sandbagged and guarded, and the cavalry was called in to disperse hundreds of demonstrators in the city.

The incident might have ended there, except that on the same day a group of about fifty radicals set off towards Falkirk, expecting to join up with Stirlingshire supporters and raid the Carron Iron Works for guns. This party was intercepted by a detachment of Hussars and Stirlingshire Yeomanry troopers on a moor just outside Bonnybridge. A short skirmish followed during which the radicals were routed and scattered. Forty-seven were subsequently caught and after trial three were sentenced to death for treason. James Wilson was hanged and then beheaded at Glasgow. Baird and Hardie were kept at Stirling, the county town for Bonnybridge where the fight had occurred.

Trial of the two began on 13th July in the Stirling tolbooth. That day the *Stirling Journal* brought out its first edition, which included an announcement that it was prohibited from carrying any account of the court's proceedings. Despite an impressive defence by the eminent Whig lawyer Francis Jeffrey, who charged no fee, the two men were inevitably found guilty of sedition and sentenced to death. With the government in determined mood, and lest there be any attempt to rescue them from the tolbooth, the two condemned men were put in irons at the castle. Hanging was fixed for September 8th at two o'clock.

Several newspapers reported the execution. According to the *Courier*, 'This day at one o'clock, the Sheriff's Depute and Substitute of the county of Stirling, accompanied by the Magistrates, and preceded by the Town and Sheriff's Officers, went in procession from the Town-house to the Castle, to receive the prisoners at the Castle gate. They were met by the Lieutenant-Governor, General Graham, when the Sheriff demanded the two prisoners, Hardie and Baird. The gates were thrown open and a strong party of the 13th [Regiment of Foot] . . . marched out and formed two lines, one on each side of the road. A squadron of the 7th Dragoon Guards were already drawn up outside the Castle gate, and when the prisoners arrived, formed outside the infantry, and also in front and rear of the procession. The prisoners, who were decently dressed in black clothes, with weepers and crepe, attended by the three Ministers of the Established Church, now came out of the Castle, and mounted the hurdle with a firm and undaunted mein'.

Waiting in the same cart was a black-masked executioner, with an axe resting on his thigh. He sat facing forward over the horses; Baird and Hardie faced backwards. The procession then returned slowly to Broad Street where a scaffold waited. Here the troops formed three sides of a square, while the prisoners were escorted into the tolbooth by the churchmen. For an hour they said prayers and read psalms. Meanwhile the post arrived and brought no last-minute reprieve. According to the *Courier*, 'the executioner was then called in to pinion the prisoners [their irons had been taken off when they left the Castle]. This they submitted to, almost with cheerfulness, and declaring they were now ready to proceed to the scaffold. The scaffold was prepared with all the insignia of death. On each side were placed the coffins with the block for decapitation; the floor was covered with sawdust'.

Broad Street and the tolbooth (with steeple) to the left. The mercat cross was removed in 1792 and not replaced until 1891. The execution of Baird and Hardie took place in the foreground in 1820. *Photo:* Stirling District Libraries.

By the time they emerged from the courtroom some spectators had gathered but all newspapers agreed that the crowd numbered no more than two thousand and was rather small. The *Times* said, 'To the credit of the humanity of the inhabitants of this place, very few attended the execution. The crowd seemed almost entirely composed of people from the country, this being the market-day. Females of any respectability there seemed none; and scarcely any spectators occupied the neighbouring windows'. The *Courier* reported that 'women and children were walking freely within six yards of the cavalry'—in other words, the ring of people was not very deep.

Both prisoners were allowed to address the crowd, but there were no last-minute defiant battlecries. According to the *Times*, Baird said, 'Oh! I entreat of you, notice your Bibles, and conduct yourself soberly; mind religion at all times: but be not regardless of justice and reason on every subject'. The *Courier* reported that Hardie 'requested the crowd not to go to public-houses to drink to the memory of Baird and Hardie, but to go home and think of God, and mend their lives. He then said "I die a martyr to the cause of truth and justice". The crowd gave a faint cheer, and immediately, as if in a panic, they fled towards the cross streets and closes'.

Then the executioner pulled a black bag over Baird's head and placed the noose around his neck. Hardie knelt in prayer by his coffin and sang one verse of Hymn 5 before a cap and noose went over his head too. The two men held hands and prayed for a moment; then Hardie dropped a signal and 'they were immediately thrown off and died without a struggle. Baird kept his copy of the New Testament in his hand, and it afterwards fell on the street'. The bodies were left to hang for half an hour to be sure they were dead, then the Sheriff's Officers held the legs while the executioner cut each one down.

The bodies were placed on top of their coffins face down over a chopping block. Clothing at the necks was then pulled back for decapitation. To a chorus of hisses, boos and cries of 'murder!', the man in the black mask 'felt the neck of Hardie's corpse with his right hand, raised his ponderous hatchet, hesitated, lowered it, adjusted the crepe on his face, and raised it again, and after two powerful strokes, a third slight touch was still necessary to sever some of the adhering fibres and skin. He then held up the head in the right hand to the shuddering spectators, and exclaimed "this is the head of a traitor." He next turned round to the corpse of Baird, and took his aim apparently with less trepidation: the first stroke of the axe cut the neck slightly and stuck fast in the wood, but the second severed the head from the body. He then held it up also, streaming with blood, and made the same proclamation "this is the head of a traitor," and retired. The bodies were taken inside the jail and the crowd instantly dispersed'. Although several public hangings followed over the years, Baird and Hardie were the last people to suffer a beheading at Stirling. It was a sad business.

In November 1826 crowds gathered to watch Stirling's first gas lamp being lit, 'a perfect success in every way . . .' which '. . . rather astonished those who knew nothing about it, and quite delighted those who did'. Four years later, however, much the same people gathered again to watch Stirling's last public whippings. Two

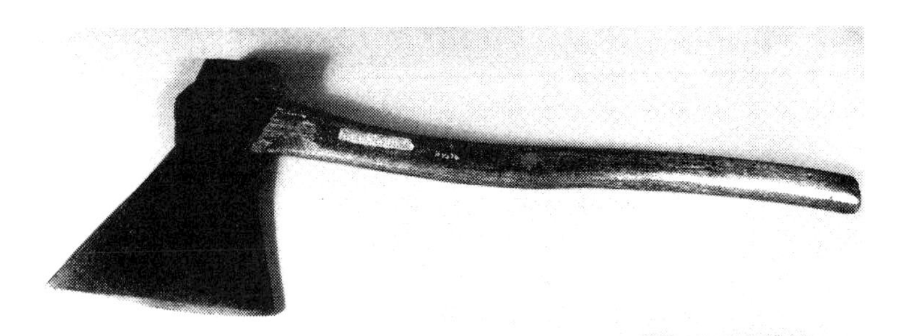

This axe was used to decapitate the bodies of Baird and Hardie on 8 September 1820. It was the last time an axe was used in Stirling.
Photo: The Collections of the Smith Art Gallery and Museum, Stirling.

smirking young thugs called McKenzie and Ord had been found guilty of an 'atrocious assault' on Alexander Baird, and later on William Ward, Sergeant of the Town Guard. At 2 o'clock on Friday 2nd July 1830 the two were brought out of the tolbooth and tied to a cart in Broad Street. A large crowd of four to five thousand people had to be kept back by a body of one hundred special constables, who formed a square round the cart. The two men were each given twelve lashes in Broad Street, another twelve in Baker Street at the corner with Bank Street, and yet another twelve in front of the Athenaeum at the top of King Street. Stirling may have had gas lighting, but just under the surface it was still a burgh little changed from the old days.

CHAPTER 11

Early Victorian Stirling 1830–1870

On 5th July 1838 the coronation of Queen Victoria was celebrated at Stirling. To the booming of cannons, a procession set off from the Castle esplanade through the town to King Street, where a foundation stone was laid to mark the start of work on the town's new Corn Exchange. That evening, while celebratory dinners were held at various hotels and inns, ordinary people caroused round bonfires in Broad Street and King Street.

Just five years later, the young Queen made a ceremonial tour round Scotland, and on 13th September she reached Stirling by way of Dunblane and Bridge of Allan. Lauder's *Memorial of the Royal Progress in Scotland*, and even Drysdale's description of the visit, are both too long to quote but it has been well summarised by Tom Lannon:

'On reaching the bridge at Stirling, the horses of the royal coach were changed, and the entourage was joined by several hundred men belonging to the local militia to escort Her Majesty through the town . . .

'At the bridge, which was spanned by a large floral arch bearing the word 'Welcome', Provost George Galbraith read out the address to the Queen on behalf of the town, after which the Burgh Keys were presented to Her Majesty and Albert, the Prince Consort, was presented with the Freedom of the Burgh. The assembled cavalcade then made its way . . . up Upper Bridge Street and snaked up St Mary's Wynd and Broad Street to the Castle, passing crowds of flag-wavers and onlookers standing in the streets and perched at windows and vantage points along the way.

'After being greeted by a military band and a guard of honour, the Queen went on an inspection of the Castle, which was adorned with crimson cloth and red carpets. On leaving the Castle after their visit the royal company went by carriage down Baker Street towards the Port Street exit from the town and proceeded towards Falkirk.

'On the Queen's departure at about 2 p.m., an orgy of merry-making erupted in the town. At the Bowling Green beside the Guildhall about four hundred of the 'poor people' of the town were each given a free pie and a draught of beer to wash it down. Then an ox which had been roasted during the morning in the adjacent valley was carted in and shared out among all present, the day being concluded with several dinners, dances and all-round revelries.'

What sort of place had Stirling become by the Queen's visit in 1842? In just a few years the town had greatly changed. According to the census of 1841 its population was now 8868—a modest increase. But in attitudes and appearance the town was changing more quickly. Three moments from around 1832 particularly moved Stirling forward into Victorian times.

The first came in May 1833 when the 'new' road bridge was opened. In 1806, with turnpike roads now developing around Stirling, the town had petitioned the government for £7000 to widen the old bridge, which was too narrow for coaches to pass; fortunately, in retrospect, this appeal came to nothing and the historic old bridge survived unscathed. In 1821 Thomas Telford was consulted and, scorning the town's cut-price schemes for various inferior bridges, recommended a proper stone bridge approximately where it was eventually built. His outline of roads to link with this bridge was too controversial, however. He wanted to extend Allan Park across Dumbarton Road and King Street as the main line of approach—this was known as the 'high road' to a host of objectors, whose 'low road' alternative went by what is now Murray Place. Telford's scheme was shelved.

At this point Robert Stevenson, a civil engineer best known for having built the Bell Rock lighthouse, was working to deepen the fords on the River Forth. Having recently completed a fine stone bridge at Annan, and being currently engaged in designing the Hutcheson Bridge in Glasgow, he was invited to plan a new bridge for Stirling. The result was the excellent road bridge which stands today, with a more straightforward approach by what is now Wallace Street, and also by Union Street. The actual work was done by a contractor called Mathieson, although Stevenson regularly visited—indeed his 16-year-old son David helped dress many of the stone blocks.

The foundation stone was laid on 8th September 1831 (by coincidence King William IV's coronation day), 'by Mr Murray of

Polmaise [after whom Murray Place was later named] . . . in the view of thousands of spectators and under a discharge of twenty-one 12 pounders from the seven gun battery of the Castle', as the papers reported. Work went more slowly than expected, but by April 1832 the first arch was completed. 'When the key stone was fixed in its place, three hearty cheers were given by the workmen, who were afterwards regaled with whisky and the music of the bagpipe in honour of the occasion', as the *Stirling Journal* described. By now a wooden framework of scaffolding stretched across the river, and in May the second arch was completed. 'Altogether the work is getting on swimmingly', the papers said. As work progressed, the fine dressed stonework became more apparent: '. . . the forming and polishing of the cornice . . . is moulded to a mathematical precision merely by the common hammer, from huge blocks of granite, some of which exceed five feet in length'.

In May 1833 the bridge, 'light, easy and graceful, and yet [which] bears the marked impress of solidity and strength' as the *Stirling Journal* commented, was at last finished. There was no opening ceremony—traffic simply started using it. A few days later, however, Stevenson made a final examination of the work and 'complimented the contractor in the most gratifying terms, on the superior manner in which he had implemented his agreement'.

The opening of this bridge had a great effect on Stirling's development. By now it was obvious that Cowane Street had to be connected somehow to King Street. In March 1833 plans were drawn up 'making a thoroughfare thro' the Town from Port Street by the Mill Lane and foot of Friars Wynd to Cowane Street', as the Patrons of Allan's Mortification minuted. This would cost £6000 for which the Town Council required the authorisation of the Cowane, Spittal and Allan trustees, since their funds would act as security and the road would also pass through Cowane property. The trustees agreed, but insisted that the new street should cross the bottom end of King Street—and so Murray Place was born.

By that one act, even more than by demolishing the Barras Yett fifty years earlier, the emphasis of Stirling slipped away from Broad Street to the lower parts of the burgh. Traffic could now enter Port Street and move straight through the town by Murray Place and Wallace Street to the new bridge, bypassing the old town altogether. Doctors, lawyers, bankers, and other professional people began to drift away from the top of the town towards Allan Park, while shopkeepers, dressmakers, corn merchants and the more skilled craftsmen looked to the new terraced houses of Murray Place, Cowane Street and Wallace Street. Finlay McKichan has shown how in 1851 'James Burden, a town councillor and master brewer, still lived in St Mary's Wynd . . . but this was becoming more and more unusual for a man of his standing. In 1851 we find that twenty-two per cent of the householders in that street owned their own businesses, were professional men or lived off landed property, capital or pensions. By 1881 only eight per cent were in these categories'.

The second great change to Stirling came in 1832 with a cholera epidemic. It is hard to imagine now the terror which plagues must have had in the past—and cholera, an unexplained but deadly illness which struck at rich and poor alike with dreadful suddenness, *was* a kind of plague. At least 10,000 people are reckoned to have died during its first outbreak in Scotland, but it returned in 1848 and 1853 to kill again before the connection with germs in water was properly understood. Meanwhile, as I.M.M. MacPhail has described 'during cholera epidemics, barrels of burning tar were set in the middle of the streets as disinfectants (under the impression that the disease came from the air) and the smoke and lurid glare made a weird impression on spectators'.

While affluent people could afford a doctor, the only hope for poorer folk was the public Dispensary, which had opened in 1831. As Tom Lannon has written, this 'consisted of one doctor [W.H. Forrest] who could enlist the help of three specialist physicians. Individual subscriptions of five shillings per annum plus a special subscription for group membership from Kirk Sessions provided the funds out of which came the doctor's salary and the costs of medicines and appliances. The doctor was in attendance three days a week, during which time he attended to all types of complaints including dental, although because of the relative absence of sugar from diets, bad teeth were mercifully rare'.

Cholera first appeared in 1831 in northern England and by the end of the year had spread to Edinburgh. The town council's Board of Health sent doctors John Runceman and William Forrest to find out what precautions should be taken at Stirling. Having visited Tranent, Musselburgh and Edinburgh itself, the disease, it seemed to them, 'generally prevailed in crowded, ill ventilated and dirty parts of the town'. Their advice was therefore to the point. All tramps and others likely to harbour disease were to be thrown out of town; at Edinburgh 'intercourse betwixt towns, and more especially infected towns, has been prohibited, at least as far as vagrants and beggars are concerned; and in Edinburgh persons of the lower orders who have been long in contact with the disease are, under a warrant from the Sheriff, confined in Queensberry House lately fitted up as a Cholera Hospital, until they shall have been subjected to a suitable quarantine'. Food and clothing was also to be issued to the poor 'for the purpose of invigorating their constitutions and enabling them to withstand the disease'. Above all, the two doctors urgently recommended the creation of cholera hospitals for different parts of the town—'their erection should not be delayed a day longer' since 'no medical practitioner, however energetic, can bestow that time and attention which this dreadful disease demands in the dwellings of the poor'.

As a result of this advice subscriptions were collected to provide a soup kitchen, food and clothes for the poor, and an emergency Cholera Hospital at the Guildhall—not so different from the burgh's response in previous centuries when struck by plague. The town was also divided into eleven districts, each controlled by a committee of six prominent citizens plus a churchman and a doctor. These emergency committees were to make daily visits to the homes in their areas, inspecting lanes and closes to have rubbish, ashes, dung and filth removed, reporting any sickness found, chasing off any vagrants found hanging about, and urging wealthy inhabitants to contribute food and clothing to the poor—but definitely not to beggars. Dr Forrest himself worked in the Castlehill area, where he ordered lodging houses to be closed and had 'all the nuisances on the public streets . . . removed. Every house in this quarter too, was, with a single exception, whitewashed, both outside and inside, and I believe with the happiest results'.

For a time nothing happened, and it seemed that Stirling might escape the cholera. Subscriptions dwindled and the soup kitchen was closed—next day the first of ninety-six cases was reported to the Board of Health. Fifty-nine Stirling people died.

Thus began a much greater concern for public hygiene in the burgh. There is no doubt that it was a stinking, filthy place; when Robert Southey visited Stirling in 1819 he wrote of 'the general want of cleanliness, and a total indifference to any appearance of it'. In 1834 there was such an outcry about blood from the slaughterhouse in St John Street running downhill through the town that the council was forced to build a cesspool—it helped, but years later waste was still trickling down the street. In 1841 Dr Forrest described how 'the filth of the gaols, containing on average sixty-five prisoners, is floated down the public streets every second or third day, and emits, during the whole of its progress down Broad Street, Bow, Baker Street, and King Street . . . the most offensive and disgusting odour'. He described how 'two drains from the castle convey the whole filth of it into an open field, where it spreads itself over the surface, and pollutes the atmosphere to a very great extent'. There was, indeed, much to do.

Although germs were still unknown, the connection between filth and disease was accepted. But there were many problems to tackle and each cost money, in a burgh where the only income was still the common good fund. A special Cholera Act was passed by the council whereby wealthy inhabitants were assessed or taxed to cover the cost of that particular emergency; since cholera had attacked all classes of society, this was generally accepted without too much grumbling, but most other hygiene problems seemed to stem from the filth and squalor of Stirling's poorer folk and the rich were much more reluctant to be taxed for these. In 1837, for example, a hundred people died in one week during an outbreak of influenza, but there was not the same widespread concern. A typhus epidemic that year was similarly seen as a working-class disease. In 1842 the local minister described in the *New Statistical Account* how typhus, scarlet fever, measles, whooping cough, small-pox, consumption (TB) and other diseases frequently prevailed 'chiefly among the poor'. Nevertheless, thanks to a ceaseless propaganda campaign against filth and disease by Dr Forrest especially, minds were changed and progress was made.

Between 1834 and 1841, for example, most of the older streets at the top of the town were finally paved and guttered. Residents paid a proportion for this and the rest came out of the common good fund. In 1834 improvements were also proposed for the Touch water supply—unfortunately the £3,000–£5,000 proposal would have required a public subscription and in the end only one more stream was diverted to swell the flow. The problem of insufficient water could only be solved in the long run by a permanent water rate on proprietors, but for years there was resistance to compulsory rating until, following a series of bitter council wrangles, the Stirling Waterworks Act was passed in 1848. Eventually street-cleaning, sewerage, hospitals and the like followed, but it is doubtful if they would have appeared so readily in a town of reluctant ratepayers had it not been for the crusading Dr Forrest and the cholera outbreak of 1832.

The third great push which Stirling experienced during the early 1830s was the passing of the Reform Act in 1832. This increased the number of voters in parliamentary and local elections and eventually paved the way for improvements in local services. Stirling folk were never slow when it came to politics; the burgh records are littered with examples of demonstrations and riots in the streets over all sorts of issues. Andrew Muirhead has described the events of 1734, for example, when Provost Littlejohn and his supporters were voted out of office and promptly formed a rival town council. This led ultimately to scores of armed people rioting and fighting in Broad Street, with townsfolk and soldiers from the Castle garrison joining in. Rioters included the county MP, the Sheriff of Stirlingshire, several local landowners, an advocate, some officers from the Castle, the Comptroller of Customs from Alloa, ex-provost Littlejohn and a Justice of the Peace (who actually ended up in a tolbooth cell). Drysdale described a similar scene: 'A great political battle was fought in 1774, and another in 1784, the Council being then divided, as it generally is, into two parties. The more powerful distinguished themselves by the name of "The Royal Twelve", the number they consisted of; and the mob, not to be behind, honoured the minority with the title of "The Holy Nine", huzzaing them in their processions'.

The French Revolution of 1789 sparked off the first serious demands for 'reform' but these cries were submerged by the events of the Napoleonic War and did not really reappear until 1815 when peace returned. For a time the Tory government firmly resisted calls for any kind of reform (as the executions of Baird and Hardie in 1820 were to show). Looking back today, the demands were very mild—the right to vote (only one-fiftieth of the population could vote), to form trade unions, to have fairer town councils and fairer taxation—but the government stood firm. Eventually the old Tories died or retired, however, and were replaced by others more willing to make concessions.

In 1828 the Stirling council was split ten/ten on the issue of reforming local councils; the Provost sided with the reformers and the opposition was thus voted out. As Drysdale says, 'There was great rejoicing in the burgh over the defeat of the anti-reformers, the bells being rung and a procession taking place, in which a pole was carried with a flesher's apron fixed half-mast high, the fleshers at that time being the predominant incorporation of the Seven Trades, and their deacon the leader of the anti-reform party'. Throughout history Stirling folk have often sided against the 'establishment', be it to support William Wallace, James Guthrie, Bonnie Prince Charlie or Robert Burns.

In fact, the beginnings of the reform they supported were not far off. In 1830 the Tories lost a general election to the Whigs (better known now as the Liberals) and the Reform Act followed in 1832. This did not do much by itself—middle-class people who owned or rented property worth £10 a year gained the vote and now one twenty-fourth of the population had a say, but it was a start. As a result of this Act the number of voters in Stirling stood at 362. Local people rejoiced, as Tom Lannon describes: 'On receiving the news of the passing of the Reform Act, the magistrates of Stirling ordered a general celebration in the town. Bonfires were lit in Broad Street, firework displays were held, and shops and houses were lit up till late at night. In Dunblane, an effigy of the Duke of Wellington, an obstinate opponent of reform, was dragged through the village on a donkey, and burned in front of a cheering mob'.

Having taken the first step, the Whigs then reformed local government in 1833 by empowering the same £10 householders to elect town councils. This greatly changed the type of people entitled to vote by including the new middle-class bankers and doctors and industrialists of the nineteenth century; from then on councillors had to think much more about the electorate. In an 1836 local election, for example, Dr Forrest caused the defeat of Bailie Robert Smith by emphasising Smith's opposition to a plan for improving the town's water supply. Slowly, though it took years to break down public hostility to municipal rates, improvements were gradually introduced by the new-style councils. In 1848 a new water scheme was finally accepted. During the 1850s sewers were laid in most main streets. In 1857 the first proper police force was established; this consisted of a superintendent, a sergeant, seven night and four day constables. On the other hand, local ratepayers still refused to be assessed for pavements and in many parts of town these did not exist.

One consequence of these changes affected the Guildry. Merchants had always enjoyed a two-thirds majority representation on the town council, but this was ended in 1833. The Dean of Guild Court continued to control some aspects of town planning and building, but from 1833 the old merchant dominance of Stirling's life was ended. This was followed by the Burgh Trading Act of 1846 which swept away all the traditional privileges of the Guildry. From then on anyone could open a shop or follow a business in the town, whether they were members of the Guildry or not. Quality controls, the fixing of prices or trading hours, the details of apprenticeships and so on were all taken out of Guildry hands. All that remained was the right, if desired, to educate and care for needy brethren and their families, and to recall (as the Guildry still does) a long and steady service to the burgh stretching back as far as can be traced into history.

Although the Reform Act did not yet give ordinary people the right to vote, they always took an active part in elections. In 1837, for example, the crowd supported the sitting MP, Lord Dalmeny against Mr Forbes of Callendar. When supporters of Forbes arrived at the St Ninians toll-bar on their way to vote they were stopped by a mob and were forced to take refuge in a nearby house. Eventually they escaped through a back window but were again abused and even stoned by people in Baker Street and Broad Street. At Cambusbarron in 1837 a local weaver called John Henderson threatened 'to go to London to swear that the value of the property of several determined reformers in the village was not of the requisite value to entitle them to vote . . .' As a result Henderson's effigy, and that of his wife, were burned at Cambusbarron Cross.

In 1842, during Queen Victoria's procession through the town, a local weaver was pushed by the surging crowd against the carriage of Sir Robert Peel, the Prime Minister. Taking the opportunity while it briefly lasted, this man urged Peel to end the detested Corn Laws, or working people, as well as manufacturers, would be entirely ruined: '. . . my pockets are now, and have been for months, empty; my meal-barrel at home is also empty, as well as the cupboard; my house is also beginning to get empty, and when that is finished, my good clothes must follow; and then, neither I nor many others will have a coat to go to church or to honour the Queen when she appears among us . . .'

Not surprisingly Stirling folk supported the Anti-Corn Law

League. The leading organisers of this movement were Richard Cobden and John Bright. On 17th June 1843 a crowd of no less than 1500 people gathered in the Corn Exchange Hall to hear Cobden and Bright make speeches against the government's policy of high bread prices. Afterwards Cobden was given the Freedom of the Burgh by Provost Galbraith. In 1846 when famine struck Ireland, the burgh petitioned Queen Victoria to dismiss Peel as Prime Minister—local people could see for themselves the starving Irish who came to town for work and food. Soon afterwards the government repealed the Corn Laws. Perhaps Stirling had a say in forcing Peel to that decision.

Political activity went on. By the 1840s the Chartists were calling for the six famous demands of their People's Charter, including a vote for every man and the introduction of secret balloting. In Scotland their strength lay mainly in the weaving towns of the west—Paisley was a hotbed of Chartist support, for example. Once again local people joined in. A huge Chartist rally was called for April 29th 1848 to support a petition being sent to parliament (two previous petitions had failed). Contingents marched in from Alloa and the hillfoots by Causewayhead and through Stirling to a mass meeting at Bannockburn. Some Chartists had a reputation for violence, but the militia and special constables held in readiness by the town council for expected trouble were never used. In the end this Chartist campaign failed but, undaunted, on 8th May 1848 a packed public meeting in the tolbooth courthouse again supported the Chartists' aims. A motion demanding votes for every man was unanimously passed and a petition was sent to local MP John Benjamin Smith.

In the general election of 1852 the non-electors of Stirling published the names of all those who voted for the two candidates. For some this may have been embarrassing, but it was done to highlight the facts of public elections and to demand, yet again, a move to secret voting. Along with the list of names, the Stirling Non-Electors Committee also published a statement which included the complaint that 'a great bulk of the intelligent and industrious part of the population of this country are unjustly deprived of their inherent right to exercise the suffrage in sending members to the Commons House of Parliament, while, at the same time we are compelled to support the State by the payment of a large quota of the general taxation . . .'

In 1867 the Second Reform Act gave the vote to all householders paying rates; this included many poorer people and increased the number of Stirling voters from 1272 to 4356. Next year, in a general election, these people chose a young radical Liberal candidate called Henry Campbell who stood for 'land reform, universal suffrage, religious equality, and national compulsory education'. Stirling folk approved—he remained their Member of Parliament until his death in 1908. In 1894 he became Sir Henry Campbell-Bannerman, and in the crushing Liberal election victory of 1906 he became Prime Minister. For a fairly small town, Stirling had a pretty big political voice.

By 1861 Stirling had grown into a small but solid Victorian town of 11,477 people. This contrasts markedly with a population of 8868 in 1841 but the principal reason for this growth is not difficult to find—the railways came to Stirling. A line already ran from Edinburgh to Glasgow and for a time regular stage coaches from Stirling connected with the stations at Falkirk for Edinburgh, and Castlecary for Glasgow. On 1st March 1848, however, the Scottish Central Railway opened a line from Glasgow to Stirling, followed by a continuation to Perth on 22nd May. Other lines soon followed: the Stirling and Dunfermline Railway in 1852, and the Forth and Clyde Railway to Buchlyvie and Balloch in 1856. By then you could travel to Glasgow in one hour, Edinburgh in one hour twenty minutes, and London in thirteen hours, sometimes in just ten.

Construction of the Scottish Central Line took nearly three years from the start of work in July 1845. The foundation stone for a wooden railway bridge on stone piers across the Forth was laid in July 1846 (this was replaced with an iron-girder bridge in 1863, and by a stronger bridge again in 1906). The period of construction work was a short but traumatic time for local people. Swarms of navvies, many of them English and Irish, invaded the area; they worked hard and were paid well but the result was an outbreak of drunkenness, violence and thefts all around Stirling.

The *Stirling Journal and Advertiser* carried details of the court cases which followed: '. . . all employed on the Scottish Central Railway in or near Dunblane, were charged with a serious riot and breach of the peace in Dunblane. All the parties pleaded guilty. Cameron, Hardie and Jackson were sentenced to pay a fine of £11 1s 6d each or suffer thirty days' imprisonment . . . Neil McCallum, railway labourer, charged with breach of the peace in Dunblane . . . John

Stott, miner on the Scottish Central Railway, accused of a rather serious assault upon an Irish railway labourer . . . John Mulligan, railway labourer, charged with theft from the shop of Mr John Monteith, merchant in Dunblane, found guilty and sentenced to sixty days imprisonment . . . Thomas Sheridan, railway labourer, charged with falsehood, fraud and imposition . . . during the evening [Dunblane] was a complete scene of drunkenness and rioting, which continued through the course of the night and the whole of Tuesday' . . . and so it went on.

The work was also dangerous, and numerous accidents were reported by the *Stirling Observer*. A sturdy oak tree at Lecropt School near Bridge of Allan 'required to be removed, and just when the workmen expected that it was to fall southwards, it unexpectedly swung round and fell . . . upon one of the huts erected for the accommodation of labourers, and crushed the frail fabric with its tremendous fall'. Four people inside the hut miraculously escaped without serious injury, but other incidents were more serious: '. . . attempting to get on the front of one of the large waggons, lost his footing and fell, and both of them went over one of his legs, crushing it in a shocking manner . . . James Whyte instantly bereft of life when a beam fell and crushed him to death . . . in the act of charging a shot when [he] observed something wrong with the fuzee, and while endeavouring to extinguish it, the charge went off and killed him on the spot . . . He was interred in Dunblane church-yard upon Monday last, when upwards of 700 labourers [all those working between Bridge of Allan and Kinbuck] attended the funeral . . .'

For a time the older stage coach companies tried to compete with the railways, claiming to be faster, cheaper and more convenient, or running regular connections to the Forth and Clyde Canal passenger boats. People in outlying villages such as St Ninians were especially likely to take a coach rather than travel into Stirling for a train. James Grant was particularly determined to take on the railways, but every time he changed his timetables or fares, the railways changed theirs too, and eventually he was beaten.

This had two results for Stirling. With Glasgow now just an hour away by train, wealthy city businessmen began to live in the more scenic surrounds of Stirling and commuted to work. All through the 1860s and 1870s their expensive houses spread across the old burgh croftlands, forming the beginnings of Abercrombie Place,

This is said to be the first passenger train from Stirling to Oban, taken about 1880. The Glasgow—Perth railway reached Stirling in 1848, and links soon followed to Alloa in 1852 and Loch Lomond in 1856.
Photo: The Collections of the Smith Art Gallery and Museum, Stirling.

Clarendon Place, Victoria Place and Queen's Road. As a road and rail gateway to the Highlands, the town also developed into a tourist and touring centre. Hotels multiplied—by 1868 there were eight in Stirling, namely the Royal, the Golden Lion, the Railway and Commercial, the Queen's, the Corn Exchange, the Star, the Eagle, and the Castle (and two more temperance hotels). There were also sixty lodging houses, and many businesses to cater for tourist interests such as carriage hirers, fishing tackle shops and toy shops. Stage coach companies, forced out of competition by the railways, turned instead to the tourist trade, and soon the newspapers were full of adverts for trips to the Trossachs, Loch Lomond, Dunkeld, Blair Atholl and the like.

Many people also came to 'take the waters' at Blairlogie and especially Bridge of Allan. This began slowly, for Bridge of Allan was some distance from Stirling and people had to take a coach. By 1842, however, when Queen Victoria passed through on her way to Stirling, the beginnings of the present Royal Hotel were under construction—workmen waved from the scaffolding as the Queen drove past. In 1848 the railway brought Stirling much closer; some trains took only six minutes, and with hotel coaches waiting for passengers at the station the village began to grow rapidly.

Major John Alexander Henderson, the local Laird of Westerton, did much to encourage progress, and this continued under Sir

James Edward Alexander in 1858. Ella Maclean, in her history of Bridge of Allan, reckoned that by 1855 an estimated 30,000 visitors were coming annually to a community of only 1600 people. The result was a mushrooming of fine residences and lodging houses. Charles Roger in a local guide wrote in 1851: 'Such has been the rapidity with which handsome houses and villas have since sprung up at this rising spa, that the visitor could scarcely credit the recentness of its origin. Handsome and commodious houses are annually reared . . . Such is the demand for house accommodation that no sooner is the building of a new structure commenced than offers are made to take it in lease, at least as a summer residence, on the fabric being finished'. Inevitably the old communities, the various mills of Airthrey, and farm hamlets with names like Keirfield, Lecropt, West Airthrey or Pathfoot, were swallowed into the growing community. By 1864 Alexander Smith called it 'the most fashionable of Scottish Spas'—an 1865–6 local street directory listed five hotels and one hundred and twenty-six lodging houses! In 1867 Charles Dickens came to recuperate from the exertion of public readings in Glasgow—an amazing growth in just a few years.

Among those who came was Robert Louis Stevenson, brought several times as a sickly boy by his parents. Rather than travel by train to the more convenient station, the family traditionally came by coach from Stirling, across the bridge built by the lad's grandfather Robert Stevenson—who also, incidentally, engineered the underground tunnels and pipes which supplied the spa's mineral water. RLS's name still survives scratched onto a window at Mine Cottage, where the family lodged in 1860. Like most other visitors to the spa, the Stevensons would have strolled along delightful wooded or riverside paths, or taken a trip to Doune or Rumbling Bridge following Charles Roger's suggested tours. It was indeed a pleasant way to pass the time for those with the money to afford it.

Charles Roger had another important influence on the locality, for he was the driving force behind the construction of the Wallace Monument, designed by J.T. Rochead. The ceremonial laying of the foundation stone was described by William Drysdale:

> On Monday, 24th June, 1861, Scotland at last made effort to atone for neglect of the memory of the patriot, Sir William Wallace, and if numbers and enthusiasm could make up in any manner for that neglect, the effort proved a decided success, for never had gathering

> so vast been seen in Stirling. From early morning trains arrived from all parts, with municipal bodies, Volunteers, and about 200 lodges of Masons, Oddfellows, Crispins, and others. 40 bands of music and pipers innumerable discoursed martial and patriotic airs, "Scots Wha Ha'e", "God Save the Queen", and the "Masons' Anthem" being the favourites. Various estimates were made of the numbers present, one being placed as high as one hundred thousand, the procession itself extending fully two miles. Conspicuous in the line were 30 companies of Volunteers, representing as many regiments . . . the various Artillery and Rifle Volunteers, Curling Clubs, Gardeners' lodges, and Oddfellows' and St Crispin lodges . . . the ancient Society of Omnium Gatherum, the master and pupils of Allan's and Cunningham's Mortifications, the Stirling Cadet Corps, the Seven Incorporated Trades, with the "Blue Blanket" [their banner], the Convener Court, the Guildry Officer carrying the Stirling Jug, the members of the Guildry, the Town Officials, the Town Chamberlain, bearing on a cushion the silver keys of the burgh.

The procession from the King's Park to the Abbey Craig must have been an impressive and stirring sight. Huge crowds, especially

The Allan Water Hotel, Bridge of Allan, built in 1864 as the Ochil Park Hydropathic Institution and now converted to private flats. It was the centre of the village's fame as a spa, where visitors came to drink the mineral waters. *Photo:* The Dr W.H. Welsh Educational and Historical Trust.

at Causewayhead, almost blocked the way—it took four hundred soldiers and one hundred and fifty policemen to maintain order. With cannons firing, bells ringing, battle honours flying, and the great battle-swords of Wallace, Bruce, Black Douglas and the Laird of Lundin (included because it was said to have been used at the Battle of Stirling Bridge) all carried reverently by bearers, it took two hours for the leading dignitaries, headed by Lieutenant-General Sir James Maxwell Wallace, K.C.B., to reach the site of the monument. The foundation stone was laid by the Duke of Atholl, whereupon a Union flag was hoisted and from the Castle twenty-one guns fired in salute.

There was, of course, a darker side to Victorian life. Any visitor of the 1850s or 1860s who, on a stroll up to Stirling Castle, ventured into the closes of Baker Street or Broad Street would have found a dingy world of poverty, overcrowding, public houses and disease. In 1842 Dr Forrest described how 'the closes where the poor dwell, and where accumulations of filth abound, are utterly neglected by the scavengers [street cleaners]. In some situations the ventilation around the residences is good, but in many others, and especially in the closes, it is very bad, and in my opinion, quite hopeless'. By

Henderson Street, Bridge of Allan—the village's main thoroughfare. The Royal Hotel, built in 1842 and where Dickens stayed in 1867, is on the right, and beyond is the Trinity U.P. Church (1898–1948). There were several churches to cater for the different denominations of visitors to the spa. Note also the tram lines linking to Stirling, and Philps' Tartan Bus which collected visitors from the railway station.
Photo: Dr W.H. Welsh Educational and Historical Trust.

1860 most main streets had proper sewers but these did not yet extend into closes or wynds.

As a result there was also disease. In 1841 Dr Forrest published a table which, though compiled from inexact statistics by today's standards, clearly showed that sickness was most common in the poorest parts of town, where folk could not afford a doctor and lived in the worst housing. Easily the worst was St Mary's Wynd, then a narrow, overcrowded vennel of 651 people, where there were seventy-five cases of fever that year. Next in order of 'fever cases per head of street population' came St John Street, Broad Street and Bow, Spittal Street, Castlehill and Baker Street—all at the increasingly run-down top of the town.

In Stirling drink was regularly associated with this scene of poverty. In 1841 the local minister wrote, 'The effect produced by the great number of low tippling houses, and the facility with which almost the smallest pittance in the hand of a poor person can be exchanged for ardent spirits at a grocer's shop, in increasing the number of the destitute and sinking them to deeper wretchedness, has been for a long period forcing itself upon the notice of every real friend to the moral welfare of the poor'. According to a street directory of 1868–9, there were sixty-five public houses in Stirling. These included seven in Broad Street, seven in St Mary's Wynd, and twelve in Baker Street. A similar directory for 1865–6 lists fifty-two 'vintners and spirit dealers'.

Prostitution was also common, perhaps more so than in some towns where there was no military garrison. In 1848 some prostitutes were literally 'drummed out' of the town, in a ceremony unchanged for centuries. The women, with aprons over their heads in shame, were led in solemn procession from Broad Street by the Provost, Bailies, High Constables and town drummer playing long rolls on his drum. At Melville Terrace which stood outside the old burgh, the women were formally ordered to 'flit', but Drysdale reports that before the Provost and magistrates had even returned to Broad Street the 'mournful maidens were leaping over the upturned earth where workmen were engaged in laying water pipes, screaming and laughing in the forefront'.

Stirling was never a truly industrial town, with the pollution and back-to-back slums associated with factories and mills. As the county town serving a mainly rural area it tended to produce smaller businesses—coopers, small foundries, curers, tanners and cutters of leather, no less than thirty-four dairies in 1868, two 'reaping machine and farming implement makers' in 1865, and even a cattle food manufacturer. There were also more general small industries—rope works, brass foundries, brewers, chemical manufacturers, at least three aerated water manufacturers (including a lemonade works opened in 1825), three brick and tile makers, an umbrella maker, a gunsmith and cutler, a vinegar works (which gave off dreadful smells) and two coach builders. William Kinross's coachworks in Port Street even made the Queen's coaches, as well as many of the railway carriages used on local lines, and employed around one hundred people. Details of the working conditions in such places are not easy to find. Few were subject to any kind of government regulation or inspection and only made it into the papers when serious accidents occurred; day-to-day life has gone relatively unrecorded.

Inspectors *did* visit the local woollen mills, however, especially in 1832 prior to the Factory Act of 1833 which regulated the employment of children in the textile industry. In 1832 the small water-powered Milton Old Mill at Bannockburn made woollen yarns; 'the machinery is not boxed [i.e. protected] and there is very little room to pass between . . . the quantity of whale oil used [for lubrication] produces a very offensive smell. The workers are of necessity very dirty', the inspector noted. He also met Jane Reid, one of twelve little children employed at this mill. She worked from 6 am to 8 pm with two hours for meals. 'I like being at the mill fine,' she said when questioned. 'I can't say I'm very tired. I get licked by some whiles but not much—just a skelp or so on the lug to keep me at work. I earn 2s 9d per week.' At Smith's Woollen Mills in Cowane Street the inspector found that about half the fifty workers were children from eight to fifteen years of age. Here he met William Carr, aged ten. When questioned he said, 'I get sleepy in the evening and my feet get sore. Sometimes I have a cough, but I like the work well enough. I receive ten shillings a month which I give to my mother, but she allows me twopence or so. I have never been to school since I started work. None of the young ones go to school. I cannot write'.

By the time of the *New Statistical Account* of 1841 (published in 1842) the local textile industry had grown. 'Since 1832 the woollen manufacture has more than doubled. That of cotton has fallen off, and is now inconsiderable . . . There are three mills for spinning wool. In these, there are 140 hands employed. They work six days of the week; during five of which they work eleven hours, and on Saturday nine. There are not less than 280 looms employed by Stirling manufacturers in the weaving of wool into tartan pieces, shawls etc., there being now little carpet weaving. They give employment to about 650 weavers, winders etc.' These people worked fourteen hours a day, six days a week.

By 1868 the textile industry had developed still further; all mills

Hangman's Close which linked St John Street (where the Hangman's house was) to Broad Street. It was one of many dark, foul-smelling, overcrowded closes in the old part of Stirling. *Photo:* The Collections of the Smith Art Gallery and Museums, Stirling.

were, for example, now steam-powered. The largest factories were the Parkvale and Hayford Mills near Cambusbarron which employed 950 people, of whom 590 were women paid between 8s and 13s 6d per week (men, who admittedly had different jobs, earned from 18s to 35s a week). These mills, owned by Robert Smith and Sons, specialised in the making of wincey, a mixture of wool and cotton, which they obtained from Lancashire, and for which the firm won several prizes at international exhibitions. Other factories included the Forthvale spinning mills which employed sixty-five people, mostly women, and William Wilson and Sons at Bannockburn which wove carpets, tweeds and tartans and employed over 500 people. The carpet makers J. and J. Wilson of Bannockburn also employed around 180 people, making the textile industry easily the most important local employer.

For a time St Ninians was a centre of the nailmaking business. This was a particularly hard and pitiful employment, mostly for little boys. At Camelon, near Falkirk, where there was a much bigger nail business arising from the local iron works, these boys were normally obtained from Edinburgh orphanages. They were bound to masters for six years, during which they worked an average of fifteen hours a day, six days a week, normally making between 1000 and 1500 nails a day, depending on the size. Typically this meant at least two hundred before breakfast, another four or five hundred by lunch, and the rest before being given tea—this applied even to boys of six or seven years of age. Older boys were sometimes paid up to seven shillings a week, but from this five shillings and sixpence was deducted for board and lodgings, and tenpence for use of tools, coals, and the doctor. Most boys' legs and ankles became deformed from standing so much, and almost every one seen by an inspector wore only rags—some said they had not received new clothes for years.

Compared to this, the St Ninians boys were better off. Of 182 nailmakers at Whins of Milton in 1842, only fifty-one were aged under thirteen. Most worked for their fathers and conditions were better. Nevertheless, when 11-year-old John Duncan was questioned by an inspector he admitted that he worked from 6 am to about 7 or 8 pm, making an average of 800 nails per day, 'but I could make 1000 if forced'. Fortunately machines reduced the nailmaking trade during the 1850s, and though specialists continued to make horseshoe nails at Camelon into this century, the hand-made nail business at Whins of Milton disappeared. Thereafter, only a machine-powered workshop continued the nail-making industry at St. Ninians.

None of this nineteenth-century industry, dependent on steam power, could have survived without the local coalmines, and here too the inspectors of the 1840s found widespread child labour. In 1842 the Auchenbowie Mine employed fifty-six people, of whom eleven were classified as children (i.e. aged under thirteen). The Bannockburn Mine had three hundred workers, of whom forty-two were children (plus another forty-eight 'young adults' aged from thirteen to eighteen). The Plean Muir pit employed ninety-three, with fourteen children and twenty-one young adults. John Allan, for example, was a 12-year-old coalface hewer helping his father at Plean when he was interviewed. He had worked from the age of ten, between twelve and thirteen hours a day, struggling through flooded tunnels which, by the time of the interview, had water rising to above the knees.

Not surprisingly, there was much poverty in Stirling—there always had been, for while merchants and craftsmen had strutted the streets in their finery, others had begged or stolen to survive. For more than two centuries care of the poor in Scotland had fallen mainly upon Kirk Sessions, which disbursed Sunday collection moneys as best they could. In Stirling, however, this burden was greatly eased by other sources of income. According to the Reverend James Sommerville in the *Old Statistical Account* of 1791, the Kirk supported fifty-six 'pensioners' at sixpence per week, and gave out another £40–£50 a year to the 'incidental poor' but, by comparison, over one hundred pensioners were supported at a rate of 1s 6d—2s 6d a week by the patrons of John Cowane's money (though Cowane's Hospital was no longer used and was now the Guildhall). In addition, Robert Spittal's bequest supported another forty-four, who received 1s 2d—1s 4d a week, and John Allan's mortification, left by a Stirling lawyer in 1725, provided maintenance, clothing and education for fourteen 'children of decayed tradesmen' and another eight needy Allan descendants. Above all this, the Guildry paid the education costs for children of their most needy brethren.

When added to the 'indigent squanderers' and the 'negligent and unindustrious', the total number of people receiving aid in Stirling was estimated at about one-twelfth of the entire population.

The local minister had little doubt that the problem lay with Drink and Highlanders. Stirling was so full of ale houses that 'the fathers soon die, worn out with intemperance. They leave their families beggared, unprincipled, debauched. These families are the nurseries of beggars. Nearly one half of the paupers in Stirling itself spring from these nurseries'. To make matters worse, knowing that the town was fortunate to have the Cowane and Spittal bequests, folk came from the Highlands whenever famine or hardship struck in the north; 'the greater number of poor on the Stirling pension lists are obviously of Gaelic extraction. Their names are almost all Gaelic names', wrote the minister.

Distinctions were made between the 'deserving poor' and those whom the charity-givers suspected were just lazy or would simply spend money on drink. The *New Statistical Account* of 1841 mentions how 'pawnbroking is carried on to a great extent; and, instead of proving any effectual relief to the poor, aggravates the evil . . . The same class of persons, who avail themselves of this delusive remedy, are in too many instances already demoralized by the use of ardent spirits; and it rapidly accelerates their downward progress'.

The fact is, however, that there *were* many poor people, and the problem was getting worse. By 1841 the 'Spittal poor' had risen from forty-four in 1791 to seventy-four; the Cowane numbers had jumped from about one hundred to over one hundred and fifty; the needy Allan schoolboys had increased from fourteen to twenty-three, and a new bequest from Alexander Cunningham, a local merchant who died in 1809, now additionally provided maintenance and education for twenty boys. And still it got worse. A glance at 1851 Census returns for the top of the town area in Stirling shows a great influx of Irish, perhaps working on the railways but more likely victims of the potato famines. Similarly, by the 1850s local newspapers were complaining of overcrowding at the top of the town, and were demanding that proper housing be built for Stirling's working classes.

Public attitudes to poverty and poor relief were slowly changing. By the 1840s there had been so many splits away from the Church of Scotland that the income from Sunday collections was seriously reduced, while the problem of poverty was clearly getting worse. In 1844 the local Kirk Session could no longer cope, and gave up. Following the Poor Law Amendment (Scotland) Act of 1845, parochial boards were set up to organise poor relief, and in 1846 a Poor Rate of 1s 3d in the pound was levied in Stirling with little protest from ratepayers.

This was soon put to good use. In 1857 a proper Poorhouse was erected in Union Street (part of which survives as Orchard Hospital today). This provided accommodation for two hundred paupers, and included a hospital and lunatic asylum, though the Cowane and Spittal hospital funds also continued to support scores of paupers for many years yet. The first names to be listed as entrants to the Poorhouse were James Malcolm, four years old, and Thomas Malcolm, two years old, classified as 'deserted' when their father was enlisted into the army; they were admitted in April 1857. Lists of adult paupers are missing until 1865, when the first recorded name was that of 88-year-old Michael Hainachan, once an Irish labourer but now wholly disabled. He came 'off the roll' (presumably died) in September 1877.

In 1856 the old Ragged or Industrial School for poor children moved out of its overcrowded accommodation above the Corn Exchange Inn to a purpose-built school in Spittal Street. Even now, however, the school still depended on some charity; it was proposed to keep two pigs in a back yard, but the *Stirling Observer* had to ask local farmers to donate the necessary pigs. The paper also added, 'The cost of the erection will be about £700, a large proportion of which is still unpaid. We trust the philanthropic and benevolent portion of the public will come forward with liberal subscriptions and wipe off the debt'. A nice story appeared in the paper in 1855 when it reported that the owners of the Stirling steamers organised a free trip to Granton for the Ragged School children, adding that the collector of shore dues at Stirling had 'declined to levy the exaction on the children', as had the authorities at Granton, who had allowed the party to stroll along the pier. Again, however, the paper added, 'many of the children (we would also hint to the benevolent) are at present in want of suitable clothing'.

Despite all this poverty, there was comparatively little crime in Stirling. There was some petty theft but few serious crimes occurred. Of the eight executions which were held after those of Baird and Hardie in 1820, one was for forgery, one for robbery, two for housebreaking and four for murder. The last was that of a violent and cantankerous farmer called Allan Mair (no known relation to this writer!) who, at the age of 84, battered his 85-year-old wife to death with a blunt instrument at Muiravonside, near

Polmont. He was brought to the county town for trial where, having been found plainly guilty on the evidence of several neighbours, he was sentenced to be hanged on 4th October 1843.

Quaking with fear and too nervous even to say prayers or hymns, the old man had to be carried in a chair to the scaffold in Broad Street. Here he asked to be allowed to speak to the crowd, insisting that he was innocent and going on for so long that people became impatient and shouted for the hangman to get on with it. Seeing this, the old man (according to one account) angrily 'hurled fire and brimstone, death and damnation, both temporal and eternal, upon all . . . who had any part in his apprehension, examination and trial . . .', in the middle of which the hangman was ordered to pull the bolt and Mair dropped to his death. The crowd cheered, but seconds later they were horrified to see the prisoner burst the bands which tied him and try to loosen the rope around his neck. According to Drysdale 'the hangman drew away the man's hand, pulled his legs, and amidst a guttural sound from his lips, and a yell from the excited crowd, Allan Mair's head fell to the side, and he was dead'.

Allan Mair is said to haunt the tolbooth cells, which are now part of a restaurant. Employees there claim that he regularly disturbs them.

The sight of a frail grey-haired old man being carried on a chair to his death finally turned the stomachs of Stirling's people however. Many of those in Broad Street had never witnessed a hanging and were appalled by what they saw. Happily it was the last public execution in the town—Victorian sensitivities saw to that.

CHAPTER 12

At the Turn of the Century 1870–1900

In 1871 Stirling had a population of 11,788 people; by 1901 this had risen to 18,609, for the town was still a growing place. Bit by bit the lands of the Spittal and Cowane hospitals were sold off and developed. All around the old burgh new housing areas spread over lands once known as Justinflats, Gallowfauld, Spittlemyre or Meikle Croft, sweeping away the past in a march of Victorian progress. By now the Bow was Bow Street, and in 1863 Friars Wynd became Friars Street. Thatched houses and rickety old cottages with outside stairs disappeared. Even the grand town houses of the nobility, such as the Earl of Linlithgow's lodging in the Back Row, were demolished. Now there was gas lighting and proper sewers, and so much water from the new Touch reservoirs that the Black Boy fountain could even waste it. Folk of just a generation earlier would never have imagined how the historic old burgh could change so much.

On the other hand, these changes had little effect on the lives of the poor. The Spittal or Allan hospital managers wanted the maximum possible price for the lands they were selling off. That meant low-density expensive housing in the King's Park area for the new upper middle classes; houses with fine gardens and purpose built by chartered architects such as Francis and William Mackison or, later, John Allan. According to Slater's *Commercial Directory of Scotland* for 1889 all but one of Stirling's fourteen doctors, for example, lived in the King's Park area. In 1885 a house called Ochil View, situated in the Southfield part of town, was advertised for sale in the *Stirling Saturday Observer.* It included three public rooms, five bedrooms (one with dressing room), ample servants' accommodation, stables and coach house and the upset price was £1900. Meanwhile, according to other newspaper adverts, the typical wage for a servant girl or cook in such a house was £20–£25 a year, plus board and lodgings. At the same time a shop girl ('must be smart and respectable') could expect only five shillings (25p) a week, while an advert for quarrymen offered 6½d per hour—less than £2 a week. The fine dwellings of Royal Gardens or Clarendon Place may have been only a few hundred feet away from Broad Street in distance, but at that time they were a world away in lifestyle.

The Cowane Hospital lands were mostly to the north of Stirling, but these too were gradually sold off to make way for Forth Crescent and the tenement housing around Wallace Street. These were homes for skilled working people—Wallace Street in 1872 contained salesmen, clerks, dressmakers, teachers, a photographer, a leather cutter, a bank accountant, a glazier, a coal agent, a grocer, several boarding houses and so on. As Bob McCutcheon has described in his *Stirling Observer 150 years on*, 'Housing in nineteenth century streets such as Bruce Street, George Street and the Wellgreen did cater for the skilled artisan who was on a reasonable wage but for the vast majority of the working class there was only the old housing at the Top of the Town. Here, as the middle classes moved out, the existing houses were sub-divided and any new building took place in the backlands off the streets. The area became a warren of closes where families lived in atrocious conditions. It was common for many of the houses to contain one family per room and sometimes there were also lodgers staying there'. By comparison to Wallace Street in 1872, St Mary's Wynd mostly contained labourers, hawkers, shoemakers, public houses, various provisions dealers, plumbers, tanners, brewers, bakers and tailors.

By the 1870s Stirling was well established—indeed into a second generation—as a Victorian town. A look at Stirling's two principal newspapers of the period, the *Observer* and the *Journal*, offers a kaleidoscope of impressions of Victorian everyday life. On the one hand there were adverts for such things as Tomlinson's Butter Powder ('Brings the butter quickly, removing all unpleasant flavours of Turnips, Lake, Marigolds, Wild Garlic, Sour Grass, Leeks, Dead Leaves etc.') or Keating's worm tablets for children, or those wonderful potions which could cure everything from hair loss to palpitations. On the other there were offers of cheap travel to Australia and news of the latest fighting in Afghanistan or South Africa. Somewhere in between came the comments and articles on such typical concerns as education, the churches, law and order, or vagrancy.

The problem of vagrants was one which exercised many people, and in 1888 a Stirlingshire Mendicity Society was established. According to the *Stirling Observer* its object was 'to endeavour to lessen the army of professional tramps with which Stirlingshire and the towns within its borders are infested . . . To overcome this the Mendicity Society has established throughout the county 30 relief stations for the supply of bread tickets, and 12 places where night lodgings are given to wayfarers of the class mentioned . . . the book of bread tickets, twelve in number, only costs sixpence, whilst ten lodging tickets can be purchased for half-a-crown'.

Crime was another serious concern. Some court cases reported in the press have a particularly familiar ring to them, such as that of John Parlain, a labourer in St Mary's Wynd who pleaded guilty to causing a disturbance in Bow Street. He was '. . . standing at a shop window at the top of Baker Street, and on being ordered to move on by Constable Ferguson he became outrageous and challenged him to a fight. He was then taken into custody, and resisted stoutly all the way to the Office. Unless something was done to put a stop to these loafers hanging about [said bailie Kinross], there would be no end of them, as they seemed to have taken possession of the place, and shopkeepers blamed the police for not doing their duty. A fine of 12s was imposed, the option being ten days' imprisonment'. There was also the case of Charles Young who, '. . . the worse of drink, had gone into a shop in King Street the previous evening and requested assistance, and on being refused, he snatched up an ink bottle and threw it at the shopkeeper, but it fortunately missed him and struck the wall. He also cursed and swore, and used the most abusive language. The Superintendent considered this was a case in which the highest penalty should be inflicted. Sentence of thirty days' imprisonment was passed'.

Prison in the 1880s meant a stint at the County Prison in St John Street. Overcrowding in the small Tolbooth prison had become so serious during the 1840s (with some prisoners even being sent to Edinburgh jails) that a purpose-built, fifty-one cell prison, paid for by the County Prison Board and the burghs of Stirling and Falkirk, was opened in 1847. During the 1880s this building was compulsorily bought by the government for use as a Military Prison or 'Detention Barracks'. In spite of strong protests from the Stirling town council and questions in the House of Lords by the Earl of Mar, it closed as a civilian prison in 1888, to be replaced by only ten new cells in the Tolbooth. The military prison was itself closed in 1935 but the building was restored during 1994–5.

In a town with over ninety public houses or licenced grocers, drink was believed to be a cause of much crime. A great deal was done to counteract this; a Temperance Society was formed at Stirling in 1831 and by 1837 it had nearly four hundred members sworn to abstain from intoxicating spirits and to drink only wine and beer in moderation. There were even two 'temperance hotels' (Dowdy's in King Street opened in 1841 and Carmichael's in Murray Place opened in 1845). For some this did not go far enough, so in 1838 a Total Abstinence Society was formed at Stirling, and within a year had 640 members. Many members were local workmen who then campaigned to have their workplaces made into alcohol-free premises; in one case a local excise officer 'took the pledge'!

There was also the work of the burgh licensing court. Headed, as it had been for centuries, by the bailies, this was the power which could grant or withhold the right to serve alcohol. The bailies were traditionally very lenient, but there are signs that by the late nineteenth century they were beginning to respond to the public's concern about the demon drink. In May 1885, for example, bailies Kinross and Forrest sat in judgement of an appeal by the owner of the Star Hotel to have his licence renewed. In granting this the bailies urged that '. . . great care should be exercised in supplying drink to persons coming from Bannockburn, and other short distances on Sundays, who could not get drink at home, so that those who came to Stirling for the express purpose of getting drink should be refused. While keeping in view the fact that the hotel-keepers had a duty to perform and a right to supply *bona-fide* travellers with a reasonable refreshment, bailie Kinross also pointed out that they were under a strict obligation to exercise this right with very great care, and in such a way that the inhabitants should not be annoyed'.

Much of the work against drink was undertaken by local churches, or by Drummond's 'Stirling Tract Enterprise', an extraordinary venture based at Stirling but which eventually spread across many countries. Peter Drummond was a seedsman who, in middle age, suddenly discovered an entirely new vocation as an evangelist. This began modestly in 1848 when, offended by those who spent their Sundays fruit-picking at Cambuskenneth, he printed 10,000 copies of a pamphlet urging greater respect for the

Sabbath. Within a month these were gone and two more editions, each of 100,000 copies, were just as quickly snapped up. As Drysdale writes, 'The success of this little effort took him by surprise . . . [but] he felt constrained to go forward—again in a direction to which local circumstances seemed providentially to point'. Pamphlets and tracts against theatregoing and then horseracing followed, as a result of which both activities sharply declined in Stirling. By now he had published no fewer than three *million* copies of various leaflets!

In later life Drummond issued new, bestselling pamphlets—the *British Messenger* (price one penny) in 1853, the *Gospel Trumpet* in 1857 (which, at a halfpenny, was selling 60,000 copies a month within a year of its launch), and *Good News* (illustrated) in 1862. In addition there were booklets for children and Sunday schools and the standard 'Stirling Tracts' (which alone sold well over fifty million copies). Peter Drummond died in 1877, but his work was carried on by trustees and continued to expand. Having moved to King Street premises in 1862, they had to move to a larger building (now the SSEB showroom) in Dumbarton Road in 1888, and this was again expanded in 1893. In 1898 celebrations marked the fiftieth anniversary of Drummond's first pamphlet—by that time the Stirling Tract Enterprise was publishing in ten foreign languages and had produced an estimated 470 million booklets, raising money to support a host of ventures from missionaries and Sunday schools to temperance societies. The organisation continued into the 1950s.

Drysdale admired Peter Drummond and wrote: '. . . [he] was in many respects a remarkable man. Of a warm and sympathetic nature, he was ever ready to extend what aid he could to young men, and not a few have reason to revere his memory on this ground. He was also genuinely simple, sincere, and kindly in his personal religion, and possessed of a rare energy, strong moral courage, and indomitable perseverance in his efforts to combat evil, in whatever form it presented itself'. Tom Lannon, on the other hand, wrote from a more recent standpoint: 'A staunch and fanatical propagator of authoritarian benevolence, killjoy Drummond . . . admirably typified the dominant Victorian ideals for "do-gooder" Christianity, stiff formality and cold exhibitionist charity.' Whatever the verdict, there is no doubt that Drummond had a considerable impact on Victorian Stirling.

Drummond was an elder of the Free Church in Cowane Street. At the time of his death there were sixteen churches in Stirling, a town of around 13,000 people. Stirling had always been at the centre of national religious controversies—John Knox preached in the Holy Rude Kirk at the Protestant coronation of the infant Roman Catholic king James VI, and James Guthrie of the Holy Rude was the first Presbyterian minister to be executed for his faith in Scotland. These diehard stalwarts would hardly have believed that just three hundred years later no fewer than seven different Christian denominations, including even the Roman Catholics, would have churches in Stirling.

Although local attitudes were vastly improved since 1656 and the acrimonious division of the Holy Rude kirk into rival congregations, the subsequent story of national splits and schisms in the Church of Scotland can be followed in Stirling. During the eighteenth century there is no doubt that the Kirk became 'softer' in attitude and doctrine. Ministers, appointed by lairds under the patronage system, did not always reflect the views of their flocks. The enforcement of strong Calvinism weakened; folk rarely went to the stool of repentance for crimes other than Sabbath-breaking, drunkenness or fornication. Some people saw this as a 'backsliding' from the old Covenanting ideals which ancestors had fought for, and eventually splits occurred.

One of the most important schisms happened at Stirling in 1733 when Ebenezer Erskine, recently appointed to the West Church (i.e. the western half of the walled-up Holy Rude kirk) led a breakaway group of four ministers to form the Associated Brethren, for which they were expelled from the General Assembly in 1740. Although many have seen him as narrow-minded (he opposed any toleration of the Episcopalian church, for example, and wanted to continue the persecution of witchcraft), Erskine was also a man of the people: 'I can find no warrant from the word of God to confer the spiritual privileges of His house upon the rich beyond the poor . . .', he said, and many followed his breakaway. They built a church in St John Street, replaced by the Erskine Marykirk in 1826, now the Youth Hostel. The West Church meanwhile stood empty from 1740 to 1817.

In 1748 these seceders from the Church split again in an argument over the wording of the burgess oath. Every merchant and craftsman had to take an oath of loyalty on becoming a burgess, but it included a promise to abide by 'the true religion presently professed within this realm, and authorised by the laws thereof . . .', which some interpreted as the Church of Scotland. As a result two churches formed—the Burghers who were willing to accept this oath, and the Anti-Burghers who refused to accept it. Towards the end of the eighteenth century both groups again split in an argument about how far the State could interfere in religious matters, such as the enforcement of church discipline. The outcome was the 'Auld Licht' and 'New Licht' splinter groups—four different sects from Erskine's original breakaway. For a small country of only about two million people, Scotland managed to inflict on itself a disproportionate number of religious arguments!

There were others in Stirling who also disapproved of the Church of Scotland's increasingly moderate views. Descendants of the diehard Covenanting tradition, they were originally called Cameronians or Dissenters but later settled down as the Reformed Presbyterians. Having met privately in each others' houses for almost a century, they finally obtained a minister in 1777 and opened a church in the Upper Craigs in 1786. They even organised a training school in the session-house for new ministers; students attended for four summer sessions of eight weeks, following which they were ordained. Between 1805 and 1819 some thirty-three young men, mostly from the west of Scotland or northern Ireland, studied there, many going on to become distinguished churchmen, theologians or professors in later life. One member of the congregation was Thomas Nelson, born at Throsk in 1780, who later became the well-known Edinburgh publisher.

Then there was the famous Disruption of 1843 which arose from an argument over who should appoint Church ministers—the congregation, or the local heritors (who may well have built the church). From a total of around 1200 parishes in Scotland, some 474 ministers believed so strongly that ordinary parishioners should have the final say that they broke away to form the Free Church. Most came from urban areas where the working-class Calvinist tradition was strongest; two-thirds of the congregations in Edinburgh, Glasgow and Dundee and all of those in Aberdeen followed their ministers in this split. In Stirling all four Church of Scotland ministers broke away—indeed the North Church congregation (which had only rejoined the established church in 1839, having been New Lichts before) now transferred even their church building in Spittal Square to the new Free Church.

In 1847 some of the various Erskine splinters re-formed to become the United Presbyterians—in Stirling this meant that the Erskine Marykirk, Viewfield, and later the Allan Park congregations, now belonged to the same sect. Nevertheless, taking into account the three Church of Scotland congregations, the two Free Churches, the Reformed Presbyterians in the Craigs, the Episcopal chapel in Barnton Street, the Baptist church in Murray Place, the Methodist chapel in Queen Street and the Congregational chapel in Murray Place, this meant that by the 1870s there was a bewildering variety of Christian churches in Stirling. If nothing else, it certainly reflected the town's strong tradition of religious dissent.

By 1838 there was even a Roman Catholic church, in Irvine Place. For years after the Reformation there had been no Catholics at all in Stirling—Webster's census of 1755 lists only eight in the whole county, and the *Old Statistical Account* of 1792, while enumerating seven different denominations in the town, still does not mention Catholics. Thereafter, however, Irish people began to drift in; by 1800 there were enough Irish weavers in Raploch to earn the area the nickname 'Little Ireland'. By the 1830s there were clearly enough (perhaps augmented by Highland folk) to form a congregation—the 1841 census lists dozens and dozens of Irish people, almost all living in the top of the town area of Broad Street, St Mary's Wynd, Bow and Baker Street. In 1838 Mrs Murray of Polmaise gifted land at Irvine Place for the construction of a church, and this continued in use until replaced by the present St Mary's in Upper Bridge Street in the 1900s. The previous church building became the new church hall, as it still is.

If Stirling folk took a strong interest in their various churches, this was closely matched by a concern for education. On 3rd August 1854 the foundation stone of a new High School was laid 'with full masonic ritual' by Sir A.C. Maitland of Sauchieburn, Provincial Grand Master Mason, on the site of the old Franciscan monastery in Spittal Street. As a mark of the importance of this event, great crowds came from all around, brass bands played, and there was a ceremonial civic parade from Allan Park up King Street to Spittal Square (thereafter known as Academy Road). The new High School was opened two years later and became the very heart of Stirling's education for over a century—but only after a long and bitter row in the town.

Stirling's Baptist Church—a local landmark in Murray Place with a spire visible for miles around. Built in 1851–53 as a Free Church, it later became the South Church, but was later abandoned. The building was rescued from decay by a magnificent restoration and opened for use again in 1989.
Photo: Whyler Photos for the Stirling Observer.

There had been a school in the town since the 1150s, run first by the Church and, after the Reformation, by the town council. They appointed and paid the teachers, set the fees, decided the syllabus and even the textbooks, provided the premises, granted the annual holidays and so on. Encouraged by the Kirk to master the '3 Rs', most local children attended from about the age of five, but beyond the age of about ten numbers quickly dropped off as youngsters were sent to work by their parents. A few, supported by the Cowane or Spittal funds, stayed on for a bit but most older children tended to come from wealthier homes.

In 1783 this Grammar School (which taught mostly Classical subjects) moved from a thatched hovel in Castlehill to a new building at the foot of the Castle Esplanade, now the Castle Hotel, where it remained until 1854 (the building then became a military store). By the 1780s the council was also running two other schools—the English School which opened in 1740 and concentrated on reading and writing, and a school for writing and arithmetic opened in 1747. These three were collectively known as the Burgh Schools. There was also Allan's School for the sons of destitute craftsmen—in 1797 this moved from a site opposite Mar's Wark to a new building in Spittal Street, where a replacement school erected in 1888 still stands. Under Peter MacDougall the Writing and Mathematical School had a particularly good reputation; as Bob McCutcheon says, MacDougall's teaching of writing 'was of such quality that one of his pupils, Alexander Forrester, who was thought to be the "finest penman of the century", was asked to write on the walls of the Guildhall in London in order to ensure that examples of his penmanship survived for posterity'. The 'prestige' establishment was always the Grammar School, however, and particularly thanks to Dr David Doig who was Rector from 1760 to 1800. Though best remembered for his dinner with Robert Burns in 1787, he was also a friend of local educated men such as Lord Kames and Ramsay of Ochtertyre, and a great linguist, having 'made himself master of Hebrew, Arabic and other Oriental languages'.

During the nineteenth century the Grammar School's fine reputation was lost, thanks to the appointment of Dr George Monro as Rector in 1820. He was an excellent scholar but a dreadful teacher; under his guidance pupil numbers fell from ninety-seven in 1824 to just eighteen in 1830. In 1826 his assistant teacher even left with many pupils to start a rival school known as the Classical and Mathematical Academy at the Guildhall. Although the town council tried to stand by its own school and rector, such was the pressure from articulate parents that it was also persuaded secretly to donate £15 to the new school and give the Guildhall premises rent-free.

Monro retaliated. His brother Colin was proprietor of the *Stirling Journal* and threatened not only to publicise the £15 but, as Tom Lannon puts it, to 'blow the whistle about other discrepancies and maladministration'. Monro was kept on, but in the end parental choice had its way; so many pupils were sent to the Guildhall that in 1840 it was officially recognised by the council as an Academy. Indeed larger accommodation was soon clearly needed.

By 1845 a town council committee had plans ready for the construction of a proper new school—the only problem was money. For six years the plan stayed on the shelf for lack of funds; many parents would not make donations for fear that Monro would become the new rector. Then in 1852 Colonel H.T. Tennant, a native of Stirling then living in Middlesex, offered the town £1000 towards the construction of a new school, provided that a firm decision was made by the end of that year. He also suggested that it should be on the site of the old Greyfriars' monastery where the insanitary slaughterhouse then stood. This was the push which the town needed; by September the council had agreed to build and had donated another £1000. Public subscriptions followed and the foundation stone was laid in 1854. In May 1856 four classrooms were ready and the school was partially opened for lessons (at 7s 6d per quarter, which only reasonably affluent people could afford). At the outset there were four departments—English (which included reading, writing, geography and history), Commercial (including arithmetic and book-keeping), Modern Languages (French, German and Italian) and Classics (which included Latin, Greek, natural philosophy and astronomy). Teachers were paid £60 a year plus part of the income from fees, for which they taught lessons and ran their own departments; to begin with there was no Rector.

The High School quickly went from strength to strength; there were 373 pupils on the roll by 1863. From the beginning there was not enough money to fulfil the original grand plans, but a Spittal Street wing, complete with an observatory which still works, was

A Victorian primary school class, possibly at the Whinwell Home, and a far cry from the new High School which opened at Spittal Street in 1856.
Photo: The Collections of the Smith Art Gallery and Museum, Stirling.

opened in 1889. That year the staff stood at one Rector, two English teachers, one maths and 'senior arithmetic' teacher one writing, book-keeping and 'junior arithmetic' teacher, one modern languages teacher, two art teachers, one natural science teacher, one music teacher, one gymnastics teacher and the janitor (an ex-army sergeant who doubled up as gym teacher when required). With the 1872 Education (Scotland) Act having designated the building a 'higher class' public school (one of only thirteen in Scotland), it was taken out of well-meaning but amateur town council care and placed under the control of a proper School Board. Thereafter it

The typically Victorian interior of Miss Croft's house. She was a local piano teacher.
Photo: The Collections of the Smith Art Gallery and Museum, Stirling.

was more professionally run, with government school inspections, nationally standardised subjects and examinations and properly qualified teachers.

Stirling would not have been a typical Victorian town had it not also been full of other small schools and private establishments. Allan's School has already been mentioned, but there were quite a few more. By the 1880s the Ragged or Industrial School (Chapter 11) had been divided into a girls' school in Spittal Street and a boys' school in Baker Street. There was a Roman Catholic school in Irvine Place and an Episcopal one in St Mary's Wynd. There was also the 'Territorial' school in Cowane Street (now the Cowane Centre), a primary school in the Craigs and another for infants in Murray Place. There was also a one-teacher school at Raploch and the Abbey school at Cambuskenneth. Then there was the remarkable Stirling School of Arts, an evening school founded in 1825 by around two hundred enthusiasts 'to instruct the members in principles of mechanical philosophy and these other branches of science which are of essential service to the arts of life'. By 1872 it was listed as 'in connection with South Kensington' and was under the

Part of the Arcade, an elegant covered shopping street opened in 1881 and now restored. The upstairs building on the right was a cinema for some time. *Photo:* Craig Mair.

art tuition of Leonard Baker, who was also an art teacher at the High School.

There were also several private schools. These varied much in quality and some did not last long, but among the better known was 'Mrs & Misses Burton, from London' and their 'Private Establishment for Young Ladies' located at 13 Allan Park. This was listed in a street directory for 1865 and was still going strong in 1889.

Some of these schools (there were five for young ladies in 1865, for example) advertised special attractions such as servants at dinner for the pupils, 'vigilant superintendence' and 'steady progress' in lessons, or special classes in manners and deportment, rather than any great emphasis on academic study, but the usual curriculum included English, 'commercial education', Latin, French, German, Piano and Religious Instruction.

In 1882 the Arcade was opened, offering not just a short cut from the top of King Street to Murray Place, but also an elegant covered shopping area. Stirling never had a particular shopping area like Sauchiehall Street or Princes Street but during the nineteenth century its shops certainly changed out of all recognition from the traditional barrel-roofed pends, hidden and dingy under tall houses in the old parts of town. A century earlier most day-to-day needs were still bought at stalls in the various markets at the top of the town—the Fleshmarket in Spittal Square or the Butter and Poultry market in Jail Wynd, where country women sold their chickens, cheese and fresh butter and there was a weigh-house to make sure no-one was cheated. Most selling went on in Broad Street: 'On the right hand side . . . stood carts with potatoes; on the left, carts with fruit, vegetables, tinware, and boxes of young pigs; while at the upper part, near the Court House, was ranged a large number of fleshers' carts. Fish was also sold here'.

Victorian shopping was quite different. By the 1870s there were still markets and fairs, but these were now mostly for selling cattle and horses; Stirling had fair days in February, March, April, two in May and another in October. In addition Bannockburn's cattle and horse fair was in June and Bridge of Allan had animal fairs in April and October. But for ordinary shopping needs people went to the kind of shops which would still be recognisable today. The first plate-glass shop windows appeared around 1845; one of the first was for an ironmonger's shop in King Street and cost £35, while two more at £30 each went into Mr Wright's shop in Port Street. By the 1870s Murray Place offered over a dozen different kinds of shops, including three jewellers, two grocers, hat shops, shoe shops, a baker, a toy and umbrella shop, and so on. If anything, the choice in King Street was even greater; there were at least twenty different kinds of shops ranging from grocers, tailors, hairdressers and ironmongers to stationers, a china shop, a gunsmith and cutler, and two chemists (or druggists, as they called themselves). There

For many years Graham and Morton was a household name in Stirling. Not only did they sell furniture—they also helped with moving house.
Photo: The Collections of the Smith Art Gallery and Museum, Stirling.

were also banks, coffee shops, hatters, drapers, saddlers, greengrocers, hosiery and glove shops, photographic studios . . . the list could go on and on.

The prices of goods are of interest. A glance at any local newspaper shows that competition and advertising were as keen and cut-throat in the nineteenth century as they are today. Retailers could take advantage of mass production, cheap labour, and cheap imports from the British Empire, to offer never-to-be-repeated bargains and/or grand sales. Nineteenth-century prices seem a world away from those of today. In 1831 tea cost 4s 8d (23p) per pound, but this actually fell as tea imports grew. By 1869 tea was down to around two shillings a pound, and by 1885 it ranged from about 1s 6d to 2s 8d a pound. Other typical food prices in 1885 included bread at 6½d a loaf, Robertson's marmalade at 3½d a pound, green peas at 4½d a tin, roast beef at 9½d for a two-pound tin, tinned salmon at 5½d, coffee at 1s a pound, and malt whisky at 3s 4d a bottle or 19s a gallon. Beer cost 2d a pint.

Moving away from food, in 1885 you could buy a gent's 'respectable walking or business suit' at about £2, men's shirts from 1s to 3s, ladies' kid leather button-boots at 10s, children's boots from 5s to about 13s, or a waterproof tweed coat from about 10s. If you were furnishing a house, sitting-room suites (nine items, all leather-covered) started at about £9, brass beds cost from £8 upwards, dining-room suites in oak, mahogany or walnut started at around £17, chenille curtains were from 10s to £10 a pair, bedroom-quality carpets could be bought for about 2s 9d a yard (sitting-room quality was 3s 6d a yard) and sofas were from £2–£4 each. Other odds and ends of everyday life included Pears unscented soap 6d, pen nibs from around one shilling per gross, envelopes from around one shilling per dozen, Beecham's pills ('the most violent cough will in a short time be removed . . .') 1s 1½d per box, and Barrow Evans' hair restorer one shilling a bottle.

Some shop adverts were wonderful. There was James McCallum, 'ginger beer brewer and aerated water manufacturer' at 65½ Port Street, who sold 'The most Famed BURTON BITTER PALE ALES, The most Celebrated BLACKFORD SWEET ALES, and First-class LONDON PORTER, from the Old-established Houses'. And Robert Marshall's 'Hat and Cap Warehouse' at 35 King Street, with its 'portmanteaus, ladies' bags, travelling bags, caps and scotch bonnets in endless variety', or Alexander Baird's 'Toy and Fancy Bazaar' in Murray Place, which stocked everything from umbrellas and sun shades to baskets, desks, writing cases, ink stands, camp stools and croquet sets. In 1868 Meiklejohn's millinery shop in Baker Street begged ladies to note that it had now 'made such arrangements as to be enabled to add DRESSMAKING and STRAW-HAT MAKING to the business; and would assure those Ladies who may favour either of the Departments with their patronage, that every attention will be given to their orders'. Not to be outdone Gavin the Drapers at 22½ Murray Place 'in requesting a continuance of the liberal support he has received since commencing business, begs to assure his friends and the public that they may depend on having, as hitherto, a good article at a moderate price . . .' Meanwhile James Cowbrough and Co., Family Grocers and Wine Merchants, begged to 'call the attention of the Inhabitants and Visitors to their carefully selected Stock of GENERAL GROCERIES, including TEA and COFFEE of the finest description, and every article in the trade of the best quality'. And so it went on, and on.

Although part of Victorian life was certainly a picture of hardship, overcrowding, bad health and poverty, the fact is that most people could enjoy themselves, and even go shopping, sometimes.

D. & J. MacEwen's shop stood where Littlewood's store now is, and opened in 1904.
Photo: Central Region Archives Department.

The interior of D. & J. MacEwen's shop in 1904. The firm also had large warehousing space behind and below the shop. Some remnants of the delivery cart and stabling block can still be seen in Dumbarton Road.
Photo: Central Region Archives Department.

One highlight of the year was the Hiring Fair when farm workers and servants came into town to sign up with someone for another year. In Stirling there were traditionally (and unusually) two such occasions—the May or Feeing Fair when farmers hired people for shearing or the harvest, and the October Hiring Market, known all over Scotland as 'Peter Mackie's Fair', when country servants and ploughmen were hired. These were days of great fun and merry-making, with merry-go-rounds and hobby-horses, twopenny pies and pints of beer, and dancing in the Corn Exchange Hall. Sometimes a recruiting sergeant from the Castle would be there to entice a few recruits into the army, and the police would keep an eye on drunks and pickpockets, but for most it was just great fun.

One consequence of more pay and better hours was that folk had the time to enjoy leisure interests. Stirling could offer a wide variety of sports and other pursuits. In 1805 a racetrack was laid on the King's Park and for a time horseracing was very popular; prizes included the Milton Trade Cup paid for by working men at Whins of Milton, and a gold cup donated by William Ramsay of Barnton, the main promoter of local racing. On the day before a race meeting, King Street was full of sideshows, boxing booths and sweetsellers, while on race days betting was in full swing. Horseracing was at a peak from around 1837 (a grandstand was built in 1841) to its end in 1854, when Peter Drummond and the Stirling Tract Enterprise, strongly supported by the *Stirling Observer* with accounts of the gamblers, thieves, pickpockets and vagabonds attracted to Stirling's races, succeeded in having the meetings ended. For years the grandstand survived, neglected and vandalised, until it was burned down in 1871. So ended centuries of a horseracing tradition at Stirling.

There were, of course, many alternative pleasures for people to enjoy. Sports clubs mushroomed—by the 1870s the King's Park football club, the Stirling County and Stirling Town rugby clubs, Stirling County cricket club, Stirling golf club and the Stirling bowling club were all in existence. Tennis was also popular and the Scottish Lawn Tennis Association championships were later held several times at Bridge of Allan. Skating and curling were regular favourites; Ella MacLean has described how 'thousands of skaters walked to Airthrey . . . [where] successful fancy dress carnivals were held on the loch; 3000 people were present at one of these carnivals on January 30, 1899, all in gay, handsome costumes. Each carried a Japanese lantern, and the loch was festooned with lights. Bands of music and a refreshment tent added to the pleasure of the skaters'.

There were also many non-sporting interests which people could pursue. Pleasure steamers made regular trips down the Forth; on 16th May 1885, for example, the new saloon steamer *Stirling Castle* marked the Queen's birthday with a day-trip to Leith at two shillings for a return ticket. By the 1890s you could see silent films in the Arcade Theatre or go roller skating at the Olympic rink (now lost under the Thistle Centre). For those looking for something more serious there were the MacFarlane Free Library (originally in King Street) and the Stirling Subscription Library and Reading Room in Murray Place. The Smith art gallery and museum opened in 1874, paid for by a bequest from Thomas Smith of Glassingall, and was an immediate success. The Albert Halls opened in October 1883 with a performance of Handel's *Messiah*, and soon choral and operatic societies followed; serious concerts were not popular, however, and usually flopped, or as Lannon puts it, 'Stirling did not possess much of a musical ear in the 19th century'. In addition there was a Natural History and Archaeological Society (whose printed papers and proceedings have been a rich source of information for local historians ever since), plus successful Astronomical, Agricultural, Horticultural and Art societies. The Y.M.C.A. had a hall at Allan Park which included a reading room and gymnasium and was also very popular. So there was plenty for Stirling folk to do.

By the end of the century the town had dramatically changed from the neglected backwater it had been in 1800. Among improvements not already mentioned, the town's first infirmary opened in Spittal Street in 1874 and was allowed by Queen Victoria to call itself the 'Royal Infirmary of Stirling'. On 27th July 1874 the first horse-drawn tramway opened in Stirling; the line started at the foot of King Street and went by way of Murray Place, Barnton Street, Wallace Street, the 'new' bridge and Causewayhead to Bridge of Allan, where it terminated in Henderson Street at the bottom of Well Road. The journey normally took twenty-five minutes and the fare was 4d inside and 3d outside. The first telephones appeared in 1889, and in 1896 the first motor car was seen in a Stirling street.

On Saturday 23rd May 1891 the Mercat Cross, which had been

Curling was a popular sport in Victorian Stirling. By 1900 there were at least three sets of curling ponds around the town, as well as Airthrey Loch.
Photo: The Collections of the Smith Art Gallery and Museum, Stirling.

Stirling Golf Club already existed by 1870 but the first local golfer may well have been King James IV, whose accounts mention golf clubs and balls in 1503. Stirling's provost was certainly assaulted with a golf club in 1613, while in 1621 David Hairt was fined for golfing on a Sunday. The present King's Park golf course opened in June 1912.
Photo: The Collections of the Smith Art Gallery and Museum, Stirling.

The 'toast rack' horse-drawn summer tram which ran from St Ninians to Bridge of Allan. It is shown here at the passing loop on Causewayhead Road, where the present Esso filling station is. The Wallace Monument stands in the background. *Photo:* Dr W.H. Welsh Educational and Historical Trust.

removed from Broad Street during the eighteenth century, was re-inaugurated. In a great procession which started at the Black Boy fountain, Provost Yellowlees led a march of town councillors, Guild brethren, tradesmen with their 'Blue Blanket' banner and ordinary citizens up through the town to Broad Street. Here, following speeches and cheers from the crowd, the restored Mercat Cross (only the heraldic top was original) was unveiled. It was a great day for Old Stirling. But then on 28th March 1900 a switch was pulled and the first electric power came to the town, as if to confirm that a new century had dawned.

CHAPTER 13

Stirling at War 1900–1950

Outside Stirling Castle stand two statues. One is of King Robert the Bruce, watching over the scene of his victory at Bannockburn. The other is of a kilted soldier from the 1st Battalion (Princess Louise's), the Argyll and Sutherland Highlanders, and commemorates the 149 men of the regiment who fell in the South African war from October 1899 to 1902. It is a striking figure—and rightly so, for there can be few units in the British Army with such a distinctive and colourful history as the regiment known to every Stirling local simply as 'the Argylls'.

The regiment was created in 1881 when the older 98th (later renumbered the 91st) Argyll Highlanders and 93rd Sutherland Highlanders were combined into one unit by Viscount Cardwell's army reforms. The Argylls became the 1st Battalion while the Sutherlands formed the 2nd Battalion of the amalgamated regiment. The kilts were those of the old 93rd, but with the Seaforth Highlanders now being given Sutherland as a recruiting area, the new regiment was allocated the counties of Argyll, Stirling, Clackmannan, Kinross, Dumbarton and Renfrew, and was given Stirling Castle as its headquarters.

Both older regiments were born during the Napoleonic period. Of the two, the 93rd especially won a great reputation for dash and gallantry; they are perhaps best remembered for their famous 'Thin Red Line' during the Battle of Balaklava in 1854, when they formed a line only two deep to withstand a Russian cavalry charge during the Crimean War. Later, with bagpipes playing, they marched to the relief of Lucknow in 1857 during the Indian Mutiny. This first required an assault on the formidable Sikanderbargh fortress, during which the regiment won no fewer than seven VCs. By comparison the 91st saw little action and had virtually no battle honours. This changed in the 1890s when it was the 1st Battalion which was sent to fight in the Boer War—it is their losses at the Modder River and Magersfontein which the kilted statue outside Stirling Castle now recalls.

Stirling has always had a taste for military service and tradition. Until the formation of the Argyll and Sutherland Highlanders in 1881, the local unit was the 75th Stirlingshire Regiment, originally raised by the East India Company in 1787. It disappeared in 1881 to become the 1st Battalion of the Gordon Highlanders, but its 94-year history included service in Cape Province, the Far East and India. A red granite memorial cross on the Castle esplanade commemorates the regiment's heavy losses during the Indian Mutiny, when ten officers, twenty-two non-commissioned officers, three drummers and 216 privates were killed.

Wars were keenly followed at Stirling. The declaration of war against Russia in 1854 was announced publicly by the bellman at the tolbooth (there was no mercat cross then in Broad Street), and subsequent victories were similarly announced and greeted with cheering. Two Russian cannon were later brought from Sebastopol and mounted beside the Guildhall bowling green in 1857. In 1900 a new generation cheered the news from South Africa that first Ladysmith, and then Mafeking, had been relieved from sieges. The news from Ladysmith in particular saw a flood of rejoicing sweep through the town. Within minutes the town and church bells were rung and cannon were fired from the Castle. Soon bunting and flags appeared in every street and local schoolchildren were given a half-day holiday. Shops also closed early so that shop assistants could hurry home to celebrate. That evening Graham and Morton Ltd. draped the King Street steeple with electric lights which attracted a huge crowd. Later the Stirling Band played and there were fireworks and a huge bonfire on the Gowan Hill. 'Mafeking night' was not quite so spectacular because the news was not believed at first. However, when it became clear that other towns were celebrating, the railwaymen let off fog signals and placed 'Mafeking' destination boards on their trains. Then the town joined in with bunting, flags and fireworks, while on the King's Park the local Volunteers, Fire Brigade and Boys' Brigade staged a march-past.

This rejoicing was not simply a jingoistic Victorian enthusiasm for the Empire. There was a long military tradition in the area going back to the old Fencibles (by now the Fife and Stirling Yeomanry) and the local Militia. The Militia was now gone, but many Stirling men were keen Volunteers; there were both artillery and rifle units, and local newspapers regularly carried reports of their various manoeuvres and parades. Later, these became Territorial battalions in the army.

It is doubtful if many local people at the time would have anticipated the later connection with warfare, but on 28th July 1909 the first aeroplane was seen at Stirling. It was a biplane with two ten-foot propellers, chain-driven by a four-cylinder Humber car engine; the first flight was just eighty feet in distance, at a height of twelve feet off the ground. It may not have been much, but this was the start of a remarkable career for three brothers—Harold, Frank and Archibald Barnwell.

Originally from Balfron and educated at Fettes College in Edinburgh, the Barnwells had already experimented with gliders in 1905, and had even fitted one with a Peugeot motor cycle engine. In 1907 Harold travelled to America and met the famous Wright brothers, who had made the world's first powered flight in 1903 at Kittyhawk, North Carolina. Perhaps spurred on by this, the Barnwells moved to the Grampian Motor and Engineering Works at Causewayhead where they built a hangar and had the facilities to work on engines. In 1908 they built a monoplane but it was underpowered and never flew. In 1909 came the successful biplane, and the Barnwell story now really took off.

The biplane made several short flights before it was replaced by a better monoplane in 1910. In January 1911 it flew six hundred yards at a height of fifty feet. On 30th January it flew one mile in a time of one minute, two and three-fifths seconds, for which Harold Barnwell received the J.R.K. Law prize of £50 for the first all-Scottish plane to fly at least half a mile. The plane flew several more times that year, including a flight from Blairdrummond of five miles at a height of two hundred feet. It was also shown at the Glasgow International Exhibition of 1911.

These achievements, made from just a big wooden shed at Causewayhead, launched the Barnwell brothers on greater things. Harold joined the Vickers aircraft company as an instructor and later test pilot, and was killed while flying a prototype Vickers FB26 in 1917. Frank joined the Bristol aircraft company as a designer and went on to develop such famous planes as the Bristol Scout, the Bristol Fighter and later the Bulldog. He died in a flying accident in 1938, but his designs for the Blenheim and Beaufort bombers went on to become famous in the Second World War.

Having first seen an aeroplane in 1909, Stirling was then caught up in 'air race fever' when the *Daily Mail* staged its first thousand-mile Round Britain Air Race in 1911, for an enormous prize of £10,000. This involved short hops from London up the east coast to the King's Park at Stirling, and then down the west coast back to London. On Tuesday 25th July 1911 the big day came. Tom Lannon has described the scene: 'Spectacularly, the landing area was cordoned off by a rope, and flares and landing-lights marked out the area for the guidance of the pilots and the safety of the onlookers. By 3.45 am when the first plane landed [from Turnhouse airfield, Edinburgh], there were about 8000 people present. The first arrival was a Bleriot monoplane piloted by French Naval officer André Beaumont [perhaps a pseudonym], who was presented with a souvenir in the form of a suitably inscribed inkstand. The second, Jules Vedrines, came in at 5.00, and the third, James Valentine, came in at 8.20. Beaumont took off, heading for Paisley at 7.25, followed five minutes later by Vedrines. Valentine took off at 9.15 but was forced to land with mechanical trouble at Castlecary, and afterwards flew back to Stirling for repairs'.

These were heady times, when Stirling seemed to be on the national map. Buffalo Bill's famous American Wild West circus came to town in September 1904, for example, but there were other, more famous, connections. Until his death in 1908, Henry Campbell-Bannerman was not only the local MP but also the nation's Prime Minister. Herbert Asquith, another Prime Minister, visited the town in 1913. Then in June 1914 thousands of people came from all over the world to mark the six-hundredth anniversary of the Battle of Bannockburn, an event celebrated with all the pageantry, pipe bands, choirs and honoured guests the town could muster.

On Saturday 11th July 1914, soon after their coronation, King George V and Queen Mary made a visit to Stirling and again the town put on a big show. The King laid the foundation stone of the new Municipal Buildings—by pressing a button at the County Buildings, which worked a remote control switch at the Corn Exchange building site. The royal party then went up to the Castle esplanade where they were greeted by about a thousand children from various youth organisations. There followed a reception at the Castle hosted by the Hereditary Keeper, the Earl of Mar and Kellie.

The Round Britain Air Race of May 1911, in which Stirling was the return point for competitors. This picture of a Bleriot monoplane on the King's Park is believed to be that of a French pilot called Monsieur Hamil.
Photo: The Collections of the Smith Art Gallery and Museum, Stirling.

Less than a month later the First World War began and that same Castle, headquarters of the Argyll and Sutherland Highlanders, became a scene of very different activity. The 1st Battalion was in India when war broke out. Although brought back to France for the defence of Ypres in 1917, it was thereafter sent to Greece and missed most of the big battles. The 2nd Battalion, on the other hand, was in regular action in France all through the war—indeed, its men were among the very first to land with the British Expeditionary Force in August 1914. They fought mostly around the Belgian frontier in battles at Mons, Le Cateau, Loos, Ypres, the Somme, Arras and Cambrai. In addition to the two regular battalions, the regiment was swollen by the creation of two 'special reserve' battalions, plus five territorial battalions (the 5th and 6th from Renfrewshire, the 7th from Stirlingshire, the 8th from Argyll and the 9th from Dunbartonshire). In due course six more battalions of volunteers and conscripts were formed, so that the regiment eventually consisted of fifteen battalions. Of these men, a total of 431 officers and 6475 other ranks from the regiment died before the Armistice of November 1918 eventually brought the killing to an end. Five VCs were also won by members of the regiment during the war, but it was a costly chapter in the story of the Argylls.

This photograph, believed to date from 1913, shows an unidentified Suffragette in Stirling. In spite of the town's long tradition of support for political reform, she does not seem to have a very sympathetic audience. At Bannockburn, Suffragettes threw pepper at Prime Minister Asquith, on a visit in 1913.
Photo: The Collections of the Smith Art Gallery and Museum, Stirling.

If anything fine can be written of war, then in the case of the Argylls it must be of their heroism and determination. Too often, the ordinary soldiers were exposed to heavy fire by poor leadership but as in previous disasters (notably at New Orleans in 1813 when '524 officers, NCOs and men of the 93rd fell . . . holding their ground because they had received no orders to withdraw'), they did not crumble or panic. When faced with a similar situation at Polygon Wood during the battle of Passchendaele in 1917, their morale and fighting spirit remained high, thanks to the dogged determination of the ordinary men. One history of the regiment in the First World War particularly notes the 8th (Argyllshire) Battalion, as 'the most genuinely Highland of all, which distinguished itself even within the 51st Highland Division which the Germans listed as one of the most formidable fighting formations in the Allied Army'.

For the first time in almost two centuries, Stirling itself was caught up in war. During the first few months, before the horrors of trench warfare were realised, the talk was all about enlisting and war news. On 13th August 1914 the *Stirling Journal* wrote: 'The war has now entered upon its second week . . . The war is practically the sole topic of conversation and as the evenings advance the streets are thronged with citizens earnestly discussing the situation and eagerly buying up the late newspaper "specials" which are rushed through from Glasgow and Edinburgh'.

Almost immediately local members of the army reserve were called up. They constituted the 3rd and 4th Battalions of the Argylls; when the 3rd Battalion (the old Stirlingshire Militia) left, the Stirling Burgh Band, escorted by a company of torch bearers, played them down to the railway station to see the soldiers off. Meanwhile Territorial units were also being called up and sent off with 'confusing rapidity'. Up at Stirling Castle volunteer recruits, responding to Lord Kitchener's appeal for a hundred thousand men, enlisted in the Argylls and were taken off for training. Of course, not everyone chose the Argylls; of the eighty-one men listed on Bridge of Allan's war memorial, for example, nineteen were Argylls, but there were also seven Gordon Highlanders, nine Black Watch, seven from the Canadian army, and some from the Middlesex Regiment, the Lancashire Fusiliers, the Seaforth Highlanders, the Cameronians, the Cameron Highlanders, the Australian army, the RAF, the Royal Navy—even the Camel Corps and the African Rifles.

There were other immediate signs of war. All 'aliens' were detained, for example; within a week numerous Germans, mostly the crews of ships which happened to be at local ports when war began were brought to the Military Detention Barracks for internment. Stirling Castle was closed to visitors and tourists, and became instead a depot for equipping reservists—over 1200 men passed through in the first few days of war. Local newspapers shrank in size as paper became scarce. Throughout the war newspapers varied from week to week in size, depending on how much paper was available. Some local factories, including the Caledonian Carpet Company, went onto short-time work. Excursion trains were cancelled, there was an immediate rush to stock up with food, and so on.

Eventually the excitement died down and Stirling learned to cope with being at war. Army camps and depots sprang up around the town, at Forthside, Back o' Hill, Cornton and elsewhere. Almost every local hall and large house was also commandeered for war use; the Smith Museum, for example, became a cavalry store (the horses were billeted on the King's Park). St Ninian's Public School was taken over by the Royal Army Medical Corps in December 1914, which forced the children to attend the Craigs School in a 'double-shift' arrangement of four hours a day; infant classes were accommodated in two local church halls. Keir House became a VAD hospital. Bridge of Allan became 'one gigantic recruiting and training camp', with the first troops arriving within a week of the war starting—almost overnight the village lost its church halls, schools, Royal Hotel and Museum Hall to the army.

As everywhere else, women took over the jobs left by army volunteers. In May 1915 the first two postwomen began work at Stirling Post Office, and by the end of the war there were tram conductresses, women in local mines, female teachers at Stirling High School and so on. Meanwhile local newspapers increasingly carried the names and often the photographs of local men killed, missing or wounded in action, or decorated for gallantry. By 1917, almost every page of the *Stirling Observer* contained several such announcements. It was a sad business, and a constant reminder of the hardships being endured by local men far away.

There were shortages and hardships at home too, but they were really very trivial. Postal deliveries were cut to just two a day. Railway timetables were cut, particularly for evening and weekend trains. Horse-drawn tram services (by now extended to St Ninians) were affected when most of the company's horses and men were conscripted into the army; as a result the ageing rolling stock could not be maintained and there were numerous derailments and breakdowns. On the roads, only the most vital repair work was authorised and many quieter roads were seriously neglected. Air-raid blackout regulations drastically reduced the number of street lights and so caused most folk to stay indoors at night. Shops, churches and houses all had to shade their lights to avoid helping enemy bombers—in fact, though Edinburgh was bombed by a Zeppelin in 1916, the Stirling area was never attacked.

People could follow great world events in newspapers but there were only occasional ripples of reaction in the town. Events like the great sea-battle of Jutland or the huge attacks in France were mentioned only in passing by the local press. The entire front page was always reserved for adverts, which pushed even the most important headline news onto inside pages. The 1916 Easter Rebellion in Dublin caused greater local comment; local Irish organisations condemned the British army's actions and for a time there was protest in the air—but it died down. Within a few weeks the papers were again full of local cricket matches, school prizegivings, bargains in the shops, comments on the farmers' crop prospects, and the names of those being killed in that summer's battle on the Somme.

In 1916 compulsory conscription was introduced for all men over eighteen and not in vital wartime occupations. Many local employers bitterly objected when their workmen were conscripted, and these complaints were then heard by a Military Tribunal; their decisions appeared each week in the local press. The last week of May 1917 is just a typical example. Twelve men from the local Co-operative Society were called up, but a representative complained that these were his most experienced workers and could the army not select others instead? In the end six were called up. Next came an appeal for seven men from a local ironmonger; two ironmongers, a blacksmith and a clerk were sent back to work. A local butcher then successfully managed to keep his last remaining worker but a local plumber lost his only brass finisher to the army. And so it went on; a local butcher lost his appeal, as did a piano tuner, while a local dairyman convinced the appeal court that the supply of local milk would drop if his son was called up. Bannockburn's only remaining plumber was let off, but made to join the Volunteers instead. In 1917 two more Stirling doctors were enlisted amidst cries of complaint even from the town council, for it left only six doctors in a town of over 21,000 people.

More strikingly, a Royal Flying Corps fighter squadron (number 43) was formed at Stirling in April 1916, followed by 63 Squadron in August that year. Surviving photographs suggest that they flew BE2C aircraft, but by 1916 these were becoming obsolete in battle and were probably only used for training the pilots around Stirling before they moved on to more modern fighters in France. The flat carseland made an ideal training area, with the Wallace Monument and Stirling Castle obvious navigation aids for novice pilots. The planes flew from Falleninch Farm (just west of Stirling Castle), requisitioned like so many other local buildings for war purposes. 43 Squadron has remained in continuous service since 1916; since the Second World War it has been based at RAF Leuchars as an interceptor squadron.

As elsewhere, food shortages eventually affected Stirling. From the start of war prices rose steadily, and announcements often appeared in the local press detailing a penny on this and a ha'penny on that. A Food Economy Campaign urged people not to waste with slogans like 'SAVE FOOD and beat the Germans'. Allotments appeared, where people grew more food for themselves. Amidst a great outcry the King's Park was eventually ploughed up in March 1917 (in spite of complaints from the neighbouring golf club that the line of the first hole would be affected). Local farmers were also ordered to plough up more land for crops and some were prosecuted for not doing so. Eventually, however, shortages of some foods, especially sugar and meat, began to appear. In January 1918 the *Stirling Journal* reported crisis conditions at local livestock marts where butchers were receiving only a sixth of their normal supply. Soon rationing was introduced, and now the local papers began to report the court cases of those who cheated the system—the old man who used someone else's ration card to get more sugar, or the woman who had two cards.

Throughout the war there were also regular flag days, patriotic carnivals, and appeals for all kinds of donations to the war effort. The money went to causes like the Armenian Red Cross, local prisoners of war in Germany, or hospitals established by Scottish women in France and Serbia. In early 1917 the Stirling Co-operative Women's Guild sent boxes of warm knitted woollens to the 14th Battalion of the Argylls—later gratefully acknowledged by the commanding officer. One spring flag day consisted of selling snowdrops donated by local landowners; this alone raised over £90 for the Argylls' Comfort Fund.

Weapons Weeks were also held periodically—in March 1918, for example, Stirling was urged to raise enough for fifteen tanks, while Falkirk aimed for an entire destroyer for the navy. The Dunblane area paid for a Sopwith Camel fighter plane which, in recognition of its sponsors, was called 'Sheriffmuir'. In 1918 the *Glasgow Herald* published a list of lowland Scottish towns and the value of War Bonds bought; Stirling's total of £384,706 was similar to that for Motherwell, Falkirk, Alloa and Hamilton. In another 'league table' for War Bonds and Savings Certificates bought during the final year of war, Stirling's contribution worked out at £29 per head, which placed it a very creditable seventh. Falkirk's average was £23, but Alloa's total of £63 per head was second only to Edinburgh.

By November 1918 everyone knew that the war was nearly over. A false rumour on November 7th caused a premature outbreak of joy in Stirling, but this soon died down when people realised their mistake. As a result, however, the burgh was much more cautious when peace really did begin on November 11th. While other towns rejoiced on the stroke of eleven o'clock, definite confirmation of a ceasefire did not reach Stirling until 12.40—but then the town erupted in celebration. Bells chimed, crowds poured out into the streets and there was an immediate run on anything alcoholic from every available shop. As the *Stirling Observer* said, 'flags and streamers appeared as if by magic in every thoroughfare, and in a short time the town was a blaze of colour'. Soon the Boys' Band of the Argyll and Sutherland Highlanders marched out of the Castle and through the town playing patriotic tunes. During the afternoon, services of thanksgiving were held at the East Church of the Holy Rude, the North Church, and the Albert Hall. That evening lighting restrictions were waived and the town looked brighter than it had done for the entire war, as people danced and cheered. Only later did people count the cost; the war memorial erected in 1922 records that 692 of Stirling's men fell in the Great War. Bannockburn's war memorial lists another ninety-four, Cambusbarron's another thirty-seven, Bridge of Allan's another eighty-one, Causewayhead's another forty-five.

With the coming of peace, Prime Minister Lloyd George spoke of building 'homes fit for heroes'. They were certainly needed in Stirling. In 1900 the 'top of the town' was little more than a huge slum. This became worse after 1904 when new coal mines opened at Bandeath and Polmaise; with no housing provided by the coal companies, mining families came into town looking for cheap accommodation. Old town buildings were progressively subdivided by landlords into hundreds of one and two-room dwellings. By 1908 the burgh's average population density was 14 persons per acre—Broad Street's was 290 per acre. With overcrowding came disease; Stirling's average death rate for 1908 was 19.5 per thousand people (compared to Glasgow's 18.8 and Falkirk's 15.0) but within that, Broad Street's rate was 24.3 per thousand. It was a shocking statistical indictment of the town council. Poverty haunted the old town, and the Salvation Army had its local citadel there. The fact that town councillors actually owned much of the property at the top of the town made the matter little short of a scandal.

Today it is hard to imagine the uninviting closes and dingy back stairs of Baker Street or Broad Street, with their dripping, peeling walls, rickety windows, crowded doorways and draped-out washing. St Mary's Wynd was a very narrow, overcrowded lane, darkened by tall, looming buildings on all sides. Much of Spittal Street, once home to Stirling's gentry, was a derelict remnant of once-fine buildings decayed to near-ruin. In the opinion of the county's Medical Officer, at least one quarter of these slums were unfit for human habitation—but people lived there. As one local miner wrote, why couldn't the council 'knock down some of these old houses . . . widen out the streets and let the poorer class have a mouthful of fresh air and perhaps a little sunshine'.

Of course there were some who cared, including the Medical Officer himself, local newspapers such as the *Stirling Sentinel*, local members of the new Labour Party, the Trades Council and, eventually (when convinced by the statistics), the burgh's Public Health committee. Unfortunately they faced a town council reluctant to spend ratepayers' money on housing (although, under the Housing, Town Planning etc Act of 1909, it could have borrowed two-thirds of the cash required). Instead it appointed a Sanitary Inspector to check for overcrowding and a Lady Health Visitor to attend infants—easing the symptoms rather than tackling the cause. The council also demanded that local coal companies provide housing for their workers—233 families were eventually rehoused at Millhall and Fallin, but the problem of substandard miners' houses persisted at Plean, Bannockburn and elsewhere for years.

A more novel solution was the Homesteads scheme. This was a rather idealistic plan to provide 'garden suburb' housing, with small plots of land, for those willing to work in a co-operative scheme at Stirling. It was rather like the Chartists' 'Land Plan' of the 1840s—a scheme to take folk away from industry and unemployment back to smallholding and a quieter life. Land was eventually acquired in a secluded nook behind the King's Park near Falleninch Farm, and by 1911 ten houses and a farm had been built to high living standards. Unfortunately there were few serious tenants, in spite of adverts in socialist newspapers and the Glasgow press. As an interesting social experiment it remains a curiosity, but it did little to alleviate the town's housing problem at the time. Now traffic on the M9 motorway rushes heedless past the little knot of houses, and new homes have swallowed up the agricultural plots.

The war showed up great deficiencies in the health of army recruits, and much of this was blamed on Stirling's dreadful social conditions at the top of the town. But this was also a national picture, and in 1919 the government produced a housing act. This allowed the construction of subsidised council houses by charging local ratepayers four-fifths of a penny in the pound and claiming the rest from the government. Town councils everywhere rushed to take advantage; £22,000,000 was paid by the government in just three years, forcing it to increase the proportion paid by towns themselves. During the next few years council houses appeared at Riverside, Lower Castlehill, Bannockburn Road and especially at Raploch where the Coronation Building is a particularly eye-catching example of imaginative design. Between 1919 and 1938 a total of 2148 new council houses were constructed in Stirling and went some way towards relieving the chronic need for workers' housing.

As people were moved out of Broad Street and into the Raploch, so the council began to demolish the old town's crumbling buildings. Much of St Mary's Wynd, Bow and the north side of Broad Street was pulled down. This caused an outcry from those who wanted to retain Stirling's historic character, and in December 1928 the Thistle Property Trust was formed. This organisation (the first of its type in Scotland) sought to buy sound but derelict old buildings and restore them to modern standards, rather than have them demolished. Although financed on a shoestring budget, its work was similar to restoration undertaken during the 1930s at Dunkeld and Culross by the National Trust for Scotland. As the noted artist Sir David Young Cameron said in 1933, 'Public bodies only want to sweep away and rebuild in order that they make a wonderful report to Parliament . . . The Trust want to reconstruct. They want to retain the features which made Stirling famous. There are old houses in Stirling which should not be destroyed. Reconstructed and refurbished they should be homes for people for generations to come, long after houses erected by public bodies have become new slums or are in dust and ashes'.

As a result parts of St John Street and St Mary's Wynd were saved in a campaign which would be applauded today but was opposed by the council at the time. In 1952 the town council finally

New housing under construction at Shiphaugh (Riverside) during 1919–20. This was a vast improvement on the insanitary slums of the top of the town. *Photo:* Central Region Archives Department.

Work on Raploch housing in the Drip Road began in 1927, but the Coronation Building of 1936 is the most interesting and eye-catching. *Photo:* Craig Mair.

The Duke and Duchess of York (later King George VI and Queen Elizabeth) plant a tree to mark the opening of the new Stirling Royal Infirmary on 10 August 1928.
Photo: Central Region Archives Department.

compulsorily purchased all the trust's properties and demolished them anyway. The present 'old town' is mostly a post-Second World War reconstruction—in some sympathy with the old burgh's style, but not what it could have been had more old buildings been preserved.

Private house building also went on, but not in large 'schemes' such as the council house developments at Riverside or the Rap-loch. The largest private developments were around Williamfield and Livilands near the present Infirmary (which opened in 1928 at a cost of £108,000), at Causewayhead, St Ninians and Bridge of Allan. Most of these bungalows and villas still stand, some looking rather dated now in a way which the old town's vernacular architecture never did.

This is, of course, only one side of Stirling's life between the two world wars. Unlike some communities badly hit by the years of inter-war depression and slump, Stirling itself was not seriously affected—it did not depend on the major heavy industries which took the brunt of unemployment. Bannockburn's last weaving mills closed in 1924 but the mills at Cambusbarron, shut in 1895 but reopened in 1909, survived this lean period and did not close. Local newspapers were full of moneylenders' adverts and offers to buy cast-off clothes suggesting some poverty, but the crime rate, for example, was not high; in 1928 the number of crimes reported to Stirling police was 687, which actually *fell* to 538 in 1929. Surrounding mining communities were affected—Cowie's pit workforce fell from around 1200 men before the war to just 284 miners in 1934, for example—but there was little trouble or violence, even during the high emotions of the General Strike in 1926.

On that occasion 6000 local miners were involved but it was hardly a militant strike and it began to crumble in a week. The *Stirling Observer* reported: 'In the early days of the strike pickets were very active in the district. On all the roads leading into the Burgh, and at some points within the town, pickets were stationed, stopping motor cars, motor lorries and other vehicles, demanding the production of the strikers' "Permit", and endeavouring to persuade the drivers to cease work. In a few cases in the first days of the strike they were successful, but there was "nothing doing" later on, particularly when the police took a grip of the situation'. Local railway and bus services were briefly stopped, but with police guarding key bridges and dispersing groups of pickets (who were allowed to do little more than shout and boo), transport services reappeared in a few days. Glasgow commuters and cattle trucks coming to market were soon back on the railways. The town's May Fair went ahead uninterrupted, with local farmers and their staff coming into town by cart or bicycle.

The records for Stirling's Poorhouse in Union Street show a sudden huge increase in the number of people seeking outdoor relief during the strike—mostly mining families, or workers locked out or laid off by the disruption. There was never a 'normal' year during the 1920s (applications for Poorhouse relief rose and fell from around 100 to peaks of about 450 seasonally or when work was unavailable). The trend in springtime was normally an increase in applications, but 1926 showed an exceptional leap from 199 in April to 653 in May (and back to 225 in June by which time the strike was mostly over). Strikers' wives were given ten shillings a week, and children received three shillings and sixpence a week to a family maximum of twenty-five shillings; this was in food tokens for local shops, rather than in cash. Strikers themselves received no assistance. Even the local Co-operative Society refused to give the striking workers tick or credit, being still owed over £2000 from the miners' strike of 1921. And yet, despite eventual failure of their cause, few local strikers resorted to violence.

The fact is that Stirling was not the sort of heavy manufacturing town where strikers could expect much support. Its industries were generally small-scale family businesses, with many other people employed in retailing, offices, domestic service and other non-industrial work. Only once in the first eighty years of the century did Stirling people vote Conservative (in 1931), but most people were Liberal rather than strongly Socialist.

Most people had at least some money to spend, and some leisure time to enjoy themselves. The *Stirling Observer* carried dozens of reports each week of bowling clubs, staff dinners, whist drives, local choirs, the rifle club, golf clubs, the local canine club, the local billiards league, football matches, horse shows, ploughing matches, reviews of films at local cinemas, and a host of other activities followed by the population. There were also periodic special attractions like the two spectacular air shows held at Stirling in 1933 which thousands attended—if the event was attractive enough, people could usually find the time and money to go.

A look at the papers offers another picture of local life. Just as today, there were hundreds of adverts for sales, bargains and consumer goods; you could buy a frock for less than £1, a gent's suit for fifty shillings, a newspaper for 1½d, a ticket to the cinema for 4d, or a permanent wave at the hairdresser's for twenty-five shillings. A Raleigh bicycle, complete with Dunlop tyres and three-speed gear, was around £7. A Morris Oxford car was around £285 but you could buy a second-hand car for less than £50. Electrical goods were expensive—a radio could cost over £20, but there were still many adverts (and customers) for such things. As summer approached, holiday adverts appeared, ranging from bus tours to the Trossachs for six shillings to twenty-two day cruises to the Canary Islands for thirty guineas and holidays in Norway by White Star steamer for £21. A working man earned around £2–£4 a week, so a motor car or foreign holiday was completely beyond him. But the proliferation of adverts does not convey a picture of Stirling racked by depression and poverty.

One of the most popular activities (in the days before television) was going to the cinema. Stirling's first was the Electric Theatre, which opened in 1912, in the Craigs. By the 1930s there were six 'picture-houses' in Stirling (not including the Alhambra Theatre, the Olympic roller-skating rink and the Miners' Welfare, where films were also shown regularly). The present Allan Park cinema opened in 1938 with a staff of no less than twenty-four people. And if folk didn't like the films on offer, they could always watch the local King's Park football team in action at Forthbank—the team played in the Second Division (there was no Premier League then) along with teams like Dunfermline, Morton, Brechin City, Dundee United, Edinburgh City, St Bernards, and Leith Athletic.

Over the span of twenty inter-war years Stirling's face did, of course, change. In 1935 the two congregations of the Holy Rude church finally reunited; the building itself was restored and the dividing wall came down in 1940 to return the church to something more like its original medieval appearance. The Poorhouse, replaced by Public Assistance Boards and the 'dole', was closed by government legislation in April 1930; all reference to 'poorhouse' or 'paupers' ended and the building became the Orchard House hospital for elderly people. In the centre of town little shops began to give way to large department stores, dislocating the scale and 'streetscape' of Murray Place, King Street and Port Street. Local firms like Graham and Morton, McLaughlan and Brown, McCulloch and Young, and Gavins appeared. So did national chain stores like Woolworths (in 1924) and Marks and Spencer.

Traffic also increased; although animals were still brought to market in herds through the streets, the number of motor vehicles steadily rose. By the 1920s there were five garages in Stirling, while a traffic census in 1931 estimated over 6000 vehicles a day used Stirling's streets. Stirling's local road surfaces, of whin setts, were considered very good in the 1920s, but when thirteen miles of main streets were laid with asphalt in 1921 (the first in Scotland), the difference was immediately noticeable. As Bob McCutcheon writes: '. . . the reduced noise level [from iron shod cart wheels] meant that shopkeepers along the main streets could actually speak to their customers'.

The last antiquated trams disappeared in 1920, victims of competition from motor buses. The Stirling Horse Tramway Company's line from St Ninians to Bridge of Allan was never electrified, and although it did acquire a second-hand petrol-driven tram in 1913 to supplement the horse-drawn vehicles, rival motor

One of the Stirling Horse Tramway Company's vehicles, standing near the Bridge of Allan terminus at Well Road. The conductress suggests a First World War picture because men were previously employed. *Photo:* Dr W.H. Welsh Educational and Historical Trust.

buses were already in service and only the outbreak of war saved the trams from an earlier end. Scotland's last horse tram pulled into its Causewayhead depot on 5th February 1920 and the petrol tram stopped on 20th May that year. In August the rails were lifted and thereafter only trains (to Causewayhead station, for example), or bus companies like Walter Alexander, operated in the area.

As with the passing of Stirling's trams, the harbour dwindled almost to extinction. Shipbuilding reached a peak during the 1850s when a 500-ton clipper called the *Stirling* was launched at James Johnstone's yard in 1852, followed by the *William Mitchell* of 1000 tons launched in 1856, but no more significant ships were built thereafter. By 1914 railways had captured much of the freight market and cargo traffic was virtually dead. Pleasure steamers still bustled down the Forth to Granton, usually calling at Alloa, Dunmore, Kincardine, Bo'ness, Crombie Point, Charleston and Queensferry, but these were suspended by the war and never revived. During the 1920s and '30s only a handful of small freight ships made the awkward voyage up the windings and over the Forth's shallow fords to Stirling. When the Second World War broke out this meagre traffic finally ended. In 1936 even the

The opening of a concrete foot-bridge from Cambuskenneth to Riverside came on 23 October 1935. The construction provided some work during the Depression of the 1930s but ended an age-old tradition of ferries at Cambuskenneth.
Photo: The Collections of the Smith Art Gallery and Museum, Stirling.

historic Cambuskenneth ferry disappeared with the opening of a concrete footbridge between Riverside and the old Abbey village.

The coming of war in 1939 did not catch people by surprise, as it did in 1914. Events and tensions in Europe built up gradually and by 1st September, when Hitler's Germany invaded Poland, many preparations had already been made in Britain—Stirling folk already had gas masks, for example. Unlike 1914 when the troops marched off expecting to be 'home by Christmas', people spoke of a three-year conflict at least. Britain declared war on Sunday 3rd September and, for the first time, most Stirling folk heard it on BBC radio rather than by a public announcement in the town. Within hours the trans-Atlantic liner *Athenia*, on its way to Canada with 1700 passengers on board, was torpedoed by a German U-boat; several Stirling people were among the victims.

There was, of course, an immediate flurry of activity in the town. Public buildings were requisitioned—Allan's School became a recruiting office, for example, while Annfield House was used as a surgical supply depot and Airthrey Castle became an evacuee centre and maternity hospital. St Mary's School in Raploch and Westerton House in Bridge of Allan even became prisoner-of-war camps for a time. Air-raid sirens were tested and shops began to advertise the blackout material and sticky window tape needed for air raids. Blackout times and reminders about carrying gas masks were printed in local papers. Advice appeared in the papers about what to do with pets during attacks, and how to immobilise vehicles if the Germans arrived. The ringing of church bells was stopped; from then on the sound of bells would signal only a German invasion. Petrol was rationed and people were warned not to hoard food. As in the First World War, 'aliens' were again rounded up and interned; Stirling's Italian community, some of whom had lived for generations in the area, became the target for occasional anti-Fascist criticism, but several locals with Italian names fought in the British army and most comments were undeserved.

Calls went out for first-aid volunteers, air-raid wardens, mobile canteen drivers, blood donors and auxiliary firemen. Youth organisations like the Boys' Brigade, the Boy Scouts and the Girl Guides asked how they could help; Girl Guides wanted to wear uniform at all times, even to school, so that they would be recognised as helpers in emergencies.

Many joined the Local Defence Volunteers, later renamed the Home Guard. They were formed into platoons, drilled, trained, given armbands and then uniforms, and eventually armed; Stirling's LDV were affiliated to the Argylls as the local county regiment, and wore the Argylls' badge on their caps. Their image today, an impression of keen but incompetent squads of inexperienced youths and old men, is very unfair. At least once, on the night of 7th September 1940 when church bells were sounded in a false invasion alarm, they unhesitatingly turned out in the belief that they really were going to fight the Germans in battle. But even on more routine duties their work was vital and released proper soldiers for fighting service. The Stirling-Bridge of Allan area, with its many military camps and depots (the entire REME depot for Scotland was at Forthside, for example) was a 'restricted area' from which unauthorised people were excluded, so the LDV guarded crossroads and strategic installations, set up Identity Card checkpoints at road blocks, railway stations and bus stops (very unpopular after Saturday night dances), and guarded bridges, telephone exchanges and so on. Sometimes they did particular work, such as erecting poles all over the local carseland to prevent invasion gliders from landing.

As a small, non-industrial, provincial town Stirling actually saw very little of the war. There was great excitement when, early in the war, German bombers were shot down around Edinburgh—for a time Stirling people who had witnessed this were almost local press celebrities. Only two landmine bombs actually hit Stirling when, on Saturday 20th July 1940, a German raider being chased away from the Glasgow area dropped its bombs over the town. One fell harmlessly in a field but the other hit the King's Park's football ground at Forthbank, causing serious damage to the stand, turnstiles and surrounding houses, and even breaking shop windows a quarter of a mile away. Nine people were rescued from the debris by ARP men; Mr Hugh McColl, a Mrs Tetstall and a young boy were taken with injuries to hospital. Such was the novelty of this bomb in quiet Stirling that even the family goldfish (whose tail was blown off by the bomb, though the fish lived) got a mention in the papers.

From the outset the area was regarded by the government as a safe place for Glasgow evacuees—175 actually arrived on September 1st before war had even been declared, and within a week hundreds more came by train from Glasgow. There was an immediate shock as local householders encountered Glasgow inner-city deprivation for the first time; as one town councillor said, 'It has lifted the veil on the lives of thousands of the populace, disclosing squalor, disease, dirt and ignorance of the elementary laws of health and decent living that has appalled those of us who have had to cope with it . . .' As a result there was an outbreak of delousing (much of it at Orchard House) and scrubbing with soap and water until local housewives and nurses were satisfied that the new arrivals were clean. For a time the influx also caused some tension; Glasgow mothers were accused of not helping their new hosts, and of not disciplining their children (who, in the recollection of numerous local people, were certainly very difficult). Local schools were overcrowded and there were fights between local and incoming children, but it all settled down eventually.

When it became apparent that Glasgow was not going to be bombed immediately, many evacuees went home; by October 1939 there were only 110 left in Bridge of Allan and the nineteen Glasgow teachers assigned to the village were complaining that they had not enough to do. Unfortunately for Glasgow the heaviest bombing did not come until after the fall of Norway in 1940; over 1000 people were killed during the worst blitz of 11th–13th March 1941. Stirling people could only stand and watch the terrible orange glow of fires in the night sky over Glasgow, and wonder if the children they had briefly known were still alive. In the morning only eight Clydebank houses remained undamaged—in Stirling barely eight houses were even scratched during the entire war.

It is difficult now to imagine Stirling completely darkened every night, but for many the blackout was a symbol of the town's part in Britain's war effort. Streets, shops, houses, cafes, the railway station—*everything* was completely blacked out. Vehicles crept along with dark paper gummed over the headlights and only a tiny slit of light permitted; many people could not tell what bus was coming until it passed them. Police and wardens patrolled streets with hooded torches, on the look-out for any house showing even a chink of light—the theory was that if a German pilot could not find his target, he would bomb any visible light in the hope of killing someone. Blackout offenders faced fines and imprisonment for showing a light. Of course there were complaints, as in this letter to the *Stirling Observer*: 'Sir, A writer in your correspondence columns the other week pulled a dirty crack about the poor people in the Raploch showing lights. Has he ever watched the "toffs" in the Terraces? From people who should know better and who have bags of money to spend on blackout arrangements the example they show is very discreditable. Of course, some of this class think they are a law unto themselves, and all they have to say when challenged is "I am so-and-so, don't you know?" '

Another enduring symbol of Stirling's war effort was the voluntary service which so many people gave. Many houses still show the stumps of railings cut down and donated in response to the government's call for metal; the first Stirling people to offer their railings were Mrs Wilson of Melville Terrace, Dr Baird Ross of Victoria Square, Dr Cuthbert of Melville Terrace, Mrs Dewar of Craigdhu, and the Episcopal Church in Dumbarton Road. But if only a few were praised in the newspapers, there were thousands more who were Women's Voluntary Service members, who made cups of tea for soldiers, or helped collect scrap rubber, or organised fundraising fetes and concerts—someone persuaded the great entertainer Sir Harry Lauder to perform at Bridge of Allan, not once but twice, in 1943 and 1945. As in the First World War, local people raised enough money for a fighter aeroplane—a Spitfire called 'Stirling Rock' (which was eventually shot down over France).

One noticeable difference from the First World War was the number of Allied troops who appeared in the area. As various countries fell to the Nazis, men in strange uniforms escaped to Britain to continue the fight. At least a fifth of RAF pilots in the Battle of Britain were Poles, for example, but there were also Free French, Dutch, Czechs, Norwegians and many others. They were further reinforced by Empire troops from Canada, Australia or New Zealand and, after the Japanese attack on Pearl Harbor in December 1941, by the Americans ('over-paid, over-sexed, and over here'). Central Scotland became especially a Polish area. Polish troops, with their cheerful personalities, unpronouncable language, distinctive square caps and Continental heel-clicking, hand-kissing, polite-bowing, charmladen manners became a common sight in Bridge of Allan especially. They were billeted in almost every house, and the tanks of their cavalry regiment often lined the streets. Many Poles later married and settled locally; some changed their names to easier Scottish alternatives and were absorbed into Stirling's postwar life. The Polish ex-combatants' club and Polish-speaking Roman Catholic church at Falkirk still continue at time of writing.

While Poles trained in their jeeps or bren-gun carriers for their part in D-Day and the liberation of Europe, the Argylls fought abroad to save their homeland from similar defeat. The 1st Battalion had a comparatively quiet war; badly mauled in the defence of Crete in 1941 (when they lost half their men), they saw little action again until the battle for Monte Cassino in 1943, after which they assisted in the gradual Allied push up through Italy until victory in 1945. The 2nd Battalion fought in the jungles of Malaya but was caught by the rapid Japanese advance of January 1941 and forced to retreat south. They were the last to retire across the causeway bridge into Singapore, which they did, as one history puts it, 'marching in stately open order, their two surviving pipers in front playing "A Hundred Pipers" and "Hielan' Laddie", with Drummer Hardy at the rear, alone, unhurried, and heedless of the shouts of sappers anxious to blow the necessary gaps in the causeway'. With the fall of Singapore the battalion's fifty survivors became prisoners of Japan and the battalion ceased to exist.

In 1942 the 15th Battalion (the most junior conscript battalion in the regiment) was unexpectedly re-formed as the 2nd, with all the responsibilities to uphold that battalion's tradition of gallantry and courage. As part of the 15th Scottish Division it fought in Normandy after D-Day, particularly in the 'bocage' fighting of the Scottish sector. The Battalion's proving time came at the village of Gavrus near Caen where, having been pushed forward from the general Scottish advance, the 600 riflemen were engaged by overwhelming numbers of tanks and heavy infantry; like their predecessors at New Orleans or Balaklava, they did not crack but held on until relieved.

Other Argyll battalions fought in various theatres of war. Though destroyed with the 51st Highland Division in the 1940 collapse of France, the 7th and 8th Battalions were re-formed after the evacuation at Dunkirk and were eventually sent to North Africa, where two VCs were won. Thereafter they fought up through Italy; by the end of the war the 7th Battalion, recruited mostly from Stirlingshire men, is said by William McElwee to have 'seen more active service than any other British battalion'. By a pre-war re-organisation of units, other Argyll battalions were incorporated into different regiments; the 5th and 6th became anti-tank gunners (mostly in North Africa) and the 9th became anti-aircraft gunners. But as McElwee puts it, 'they all, to the exasperated fury of the High Command, obstinately refused to be properly incorporated into the Royal Regiment of Artillery. The 5th and 6th became the 91st and 93rd Anti-Tank Regiment, Argyll and Sutherland Highlanders . . .', complete with pipe band, kilts, Balmoral bonnets and Argyll badges.

On 8th May 1945 the Germans surrendered and part of the war was over. In spite of rainy weather 'the staid people of Stirling' (as the *Stirling Journal* put it) celebrated Victory in Europe Day with 'flags, fairy lights, bonfires and floodlighting', especially at the Black Boy fountain. While police chased revellers for stealing beer-bottles from a delivery lorry at Goosecroft, impromptu street dances and organised celebrations at the Albert Hall, the British Legion Hall, and Burghmuir Hall went on into the small hours. It was a moment of relief before a return to the reality of rationing, travel restrictions, and the war against Japan.

In July there was a General Election. The country turned against its wartime Conservative leader Winston Churchill and voted for Clement Attlee and Labour's promises of improved post-war living

Presentation of the freedom of the burgh to the Argyll and Sutherland Highlanders and their commander-in-chief H.R.H. Princess Elizabeth (now the Queen) on Saturday 20 September 1947. The Second Battalion are formed up with their colours on the Castle esplanade. *Photo:* Museum of the Argyll and Sutherland Highlanders, Stirling Castle.

conditions. Stirling people felt the same and returned the sitting Labour MP, J.C. Westwood, with an increased majority. A footnote to this election was the defeat of the Scottish Nationalist candidate at Motherwell—this was Dr Robert McIntyre, a Stirling man who, in an April 1945 by-election, became the first-ever Scottish Nationalist member of parliament. McIntyre lost at Motherwell by a big majority in July, but for a time he carried the Scottish Nationalist banner—another Stirling man, like generations before him, turning against the British political establishment. Later he became one of Stirling's best-known and best-respected provosts.

Then at last, at midnight on 14th August 1945, came the news over BBC radio that Japan had surrendered and the Second World War was over. As soon as the broadcast ended there was, according to the *Stirling Journal*, 'a rush for the streets. Crowds began to gather, bells to ring, fireworks to crackle . . . Bonfires were hastily lit in open spaces in many of the suburbs of the town, and singing and dancing round these continued until an early hour . . .' By the following evening 'the carnival spirit was in full evidence. The Municipal Buildings in Corn Exchange and the Old Burgh Buildings and Steeple in King Street were floodlit. The Black Boy Fountain was also brilliantly lighted and the water in the fountain playing. Gaily-coloured lights hung from the trees and the sight was one resembling fairyland . . .' Later there was dancing in the Albert Hall, and soon there were services of thanksgiving in the Holy Rude church and others around the town.

There was cheering again when the Argylls finally came home, but it did not last long. By 1947 they were in Palestine, suffering casualties in the British peacekeeping operation there. Then in 1950 they went to Korea, little knowing that on Hill 282 Major Kenneth Muir would win a posthumous VC but they would lose an entire company in the battle. The century had opened with the Argylls fighting in South Africa. Fifty years and two world wars later the Argylls were still fighting abroad.

As late as 1967 the regiment again hit the headlines when, with Colonel Colin Mitchell ('Mad Mitch') and pipers to the fore, it marched into the sniper-infested crater district of Aden to subdue a terrorist uprising in the Protectorate. Five men were killed during that five-month operation, but the Argylls became a household name to a new generation of Britons. Just a year later the Ministry of Defence tried to disband the regiment but over one million people signed a successful petition organised by the Duchess of Argyll and the War Department was forced by popular opinion to back down. The regiment still goes on, serving in Germany, Cyprus, Hong Kong, Northern Ireland, the Falkland Islands and wherever else may lie ahead.

CHAPTER 14

Into the Future

It is probably true to say that Stirling has seen greater change since 1950 than during any comparable period of its history. The town has seen daily living patterns change completely, it has found a prosperity for almost everyone undreamt of by past generations, it has gained a university—and yet it has ceased to exist as a Royal Burgh.

In many ways the town council of 1950 was little changed from that of 1850. It was still run by enthusiastic but amateurish independent councillors who decided everything from siting waste-paper bins to the line of vital by-pass roads according to the town's finances. Costs were certainly rising, for education, housing, health and roads especially, but wider concerns for the quality of life, the preservation of heritage, or the provision of leisure facilities, tended to be neglected by these guardians of Stirling's money coffers. Sometimes the council consulted experts, but that did not mean that it followed their advice—when faced in 1954, for example, with a letter from expert consultants recommending that old houses in Bow Street should be restored rather than demolished, six councillors called it humbug and voted against. More important to many councillors was *cost*—how much would it add to the rates? The days of Victorian philanthropists who would give money for public buildings or parks were gone, but long-established local families or businesses had no wish to shoulder higher rates just to pay for amenities. Provost MacIntosh voted against proposals for a swimming pool, for example, because it would mean a 2½d increase on the rates—meanwhile Grangemouth, Falkirk and Alloa had swimming pools decades before one finally opened at Stirling in 1974 (Grangemouth even had a sports stadium, opened in 1966).

Faced with a pre-war picture of overcrowding and dilapidation, the council demolished some of the worst old slum dwellings at the top of the town during the 1920s and '30s. The problem was that, by doing so, it also destroyed part of Stirling's history and there were protests. In the original development plan by Sir Frank Mears, the intention was to preserve the best of Stirling's historic or structurally sound buildings, but to demolish the others—these would be replaced with modern equivalents, complete with old-looking features like crow-stepped gables and little windows, but also proper sanitation and running water. For a time the Thistle Property Trust tried to rescue some buildings from the bulldozers, but its finances could support little more than a modest rearguard action. Much of Broad Street and St Mary's Wynd therefore disappeared, replaced by 'old-looking' but better-quality housing. The coming of war meant that many old buildings still survived in 1945, but by then they had deteriorated still further and it was more difficult to justify their retention when peace came.

After the war there was a general desire in Britain to make a fresh start with almost everything. With the new Health Service and nationalised industries came new fashions, new styles, new music—and new attitudes. People wanted to sweep away the past, and an obvious start could be made with housing. Stirling was hardly touched by bombs, but nationally one third of all houses were either damaged or destroyed so that a rebuilding programme was required anyway—new building became all the rage. Evacuation also highlighted inner-city deprivation and the housing germ grew to become 'comprehensive redevelopment'. Continental cities, bombed flat and now cleared away, began to build clean new shopping centres, pedestrian precincts, apartment blocks and ring roads. So did Coventry, London, Birmingham, and the fashion caught on. To Stirling's council, with its slum clearance programme interrupted by war, 'comprehensive redevelopment' must have seemed like the answer.

The pre-war plan was modified. Everything at the top of the town would be demolished and replaced with modern, but old-looking, substitutes. An important attraction for many town councillors was that new building would be cheaper than restoration, while any passing qualms about destroying history were soothed by the reassurance that replacement houses would incorporate the old styles of earlier buildings. Given the scale of dilapidation and poverty which the council was, above all, trying to alleviate, it was perhaps an attractive solution. The skills of restoration were also less developed than they are today, when apparent miracles can be achieved with almost any old building. Nevertheless, the fact that town councillors were willing to erase centuries of Stirling's history at the stroke of a pen cannot be ignored.

By 1951 the demolition men were at work, tearing down Baker Street, Bow and Broad Street until the area looked like a bomb site—indeed, one foreign visitor mentioned in the press 'expressed regret that historic Stirling had been so badly bombed'. For years the top of the town was a scene of gaping houses, piles of stones, and roads cleared for the rubble lorries to cart away the ruins—250 tons were carried off every working day for over seven years.

As the work progressed and familiar landmarks came down, new views opened up of buildings once hidden streets away—but it was a painful sight. The *Stirling Observer* carried regular photographs of the work and today they seem very poignant and melancholy, almost terrible, like the post-war streets of Warsaw or Berlin, or the clearance of the Gorbals in Glasgow. Many buildings could not even come down quickly; their death was slow, and painful for those who cared for Stirling's history. Ancient stone walls, often four feet thick, took time to demolish. Many stones had to be levered and crowbarred out by hand for re-use in later buildings—at least an attempt to retain something of the old town's stonework. Many houses were also tottering in a dangerous state and had to be dismantled very carefully—one vehicle fell into unsuspected cellars as they opened up under its wheels.

There was, of course, a cry of protest at this wholesale destruction. In 1948 Ian Lindsay and Ronald Cant produced *Old Stirling*, an influential booklet describing the burgh's architectural riches, which helped to open eyes and stir an appreciation of the town's history. But even 1948 was too late to save everything, as the authors already knew: 'the survival of Old Stirling is imperfect and precarious—a mere shadow of what it might have been. Too much has gone, too much that remains has been mutilated or allowed to fall into decay. It may be that, even now, the value of this remarkable architectural inheritance is insufficiently appreciated'. As demolition work then progressed anyway, the *Stirling Observer* used headlines like 'Stirling's Heritage Vanishes', or 'Shovelling Away History', or 'Bow Street No More' to stir up protest over the relentless eating away of the old burgh, but it was to no avail.

One who did show concern was Burgh Architect Walter Gillespie. With grant aid from the Historic Buildings Council and

An ugly gap at the bottom of Broad Street as demolition of Bow Street begins in 1951. Darnley's House on the left was rescued just in time, but was already damaged.
Photo: Central Region Archives Department.

other groups who offered seventy-five per cent of renovation costs, Gillespie belatedly tried to save what important buildings still survived, and to ensure that post-war austerity programmes did not water down the plans for the old-looking buildings to replace those already lost. Even so, every step was another battle; one councillor described restoration as a waste of public money; another declared that money was being wasted on sentiment. As a result of Gillespie's efforts, however, Darnley's House, though damaged already by demolition, was restored. So was Norrie's House, Spittal's House, the Tolbooth and a few others, but it was too little and too late. The real things were gone and the new houses, though sincerely intended as vernacular replacements to preserve the character of the old town, were no substitute.

Old photographs show clearly that there is simply *no* similarity between the present artificial 'old town' and the real top of the town as it was for centuries. The street scene and skyline have a superficial seventeenth-century look about them, but even the most casual passer-by would never imagine that they are the real thing. The streets are wider, the closes are mostly gone, the buildings are regular, fresh-looking and sanitised. Above all, no-one could replace generations of living—the faded street signs, the graffiti, the accumulated bumps and bulletholes, the half-torn posters and worn doorsteps. The old atmosphere—and, admittedly, the poverty, disease and overcrowding—is gone, because it was cheaper to demolish than to restore.

Today such civic vandalism is less likely to occur. People have a greater appreciation of Stirling's layers of history and the burgh's gradual evolution; if nothing else, they realise that visitors attracted to the old town and its castle are a vital part of the area's economy. But even in the later 1950s there were those who could already see what irretrievable damage had been done. Actor and broadcaster Moultrie Kelsall wrote in 1957 of '. . . new buildings, with only here and there an old one, mute witness of what might have been . . . Down the years the protests are heard. Lord Cockburn, writing in his *Memorials* (1845) of destruction in Stirling cries—"Anything is credible!" George Scott Moncrieff in *The Lowlands of Scotland* (1939) says, also of Stirling, "It could happen in no other country". Today it still goes on; soon there will be little left to destroy'. It was a time in the burgh's history much to be regretted.

Having 'redeveloped' the top of the town, the town council

turned its attention to other parts of Stirling. During the 1950s housing remained the most pressing problem. Some 'pre-fabs' were built to solve the immediate post-war demand, but these were designed as short-life dwellings and eventually had to be replaced. Council-house schemes therefore appeared at Broomridge, Torbrex and Cornton, and the Raploch scheme was extended. Unfortunately post-war council housing was not of the same pre-war quality; rooms were made smaller, and buildings were standardised to monotonous regular designs like rows of shoeboxes. Nevertheless, with tenants also moving back into the new top of the town, the worst of the housing shortage was solved. There was, of course, a price to pay—neighbouring communities began to disappear, swallowed up into 'greater Stirling'. By 1970 there was an almost continuous sprawl of housing from Bannockburn to Bridge of Allan, and Cambuskenneth to Cambusbarron. Victorians from 1870, then just beginning to build in Snowdon Place, would have been amazed at the town's extraordinary spread.

After housing came the centre of the town. Even by the 1950s it was dreadfully congested with motor cars; just as medieval carts were once obliged to go by the Barras Yett, up Baker Street and down St Mary's Wynd to the old bridge, modern traffic now had to enter by Port Street and snake through the town by Murray Place and Wallace Street before crossing the new bridge. And yet this was the A9, Scotland's main route north to Perth, Aberdeen and Inverness. With business centred on the county town, shoppers attracted there by chain stores, and even cattle still plodding through the streets to market at Wallace Street, traffic hold-ups and bottlenecks were embarrassingly frequent. Something had to be done.

Several important changes reshaped the town centre during the 1970s. Firstly, the livestock market moved from Wallace Street to a new site at Kildean, on the fringe of Stirling. That opened up the centre of town for a bypass road, which was built in two stages from St Ninians to Goosecroft at the bottom of the Craigs, and then in 1970 on to the end of the 'new' bridge. People could now avoid the town almost completely on their way to Perth; in one fell swoop the emphasis of traffic moved even further away from the old burgh at the top of the town. Congestion was further relieved when the Pirnhall to Keir section of the M9 motorway opened on 28th December 1973, enabling traffic to whizz past Stirling almost without a second glance.

The back of Darnley's House, a mixture of old buildings (right) and new replacements (left), but no substitute for the real old town, much of which was swept away.
Photo: Craig Mair.

Housing in St John Street, built in traditional style with crow steps and little windows, but too new and clean to pass for the worn old houses of the past. *Photo:* Craig Mair.

Many shopkeepers thought that a bypassed Stirling would ruin them, but with every step to relieve the congestion in town, traffic has simply increased to absorb the additional space and the town is as busy as ever. Planners have added a new distributor road and bridge from Manor Powis to Bannockburn, a new road through the Craigs and Wellgreen part of the burgh, a one-way traffic flow through the town centre, and a pedestrianised area in Port Street, but the traffic problem, with its attendant nightmare of parking, has remained apparently insoluble.

The main concourse of the Thistle Centre, with part of an interesting frieze of medieval crafts. People now travel from far and wide to shop at Stirling.
Photo: Whyler Photos for the Stirling Observer.

The second key step came with the decision to build a shopping precinct in the middle of town. The eventual result was the Thistle Centre, a monolithic shopping mall facing Murray Place and begun in 1975. For many people this is a boon, housing most of the town's largest stores under one roof, and allowing all-weather shopping with comfort and convenience including car parking, toilets and restaurants. For others the centre is an architectural monstrosity which destroyed an interesting segment of the Victorian town, including Kinross's famous coach works, and now ruins the scale of old Stirling.

In fact, the Thistle Centre could have been *much* worse. Plans survive from the 1960s period of 'comprehensive redevelopment' which would have swept away much more than actually disappeared, and would have blighted the town with hideous architecture, without the slightest concern for history or atmosphere. Throughout Britain the 1960s are now regarded as a period of dreadful building, which has not dated well and is now often either falling down or being pulled down. Stirling was, fortunately, spared the worst of this. The Thistle Centre did, for example, preserve part of the old burgh wall, including an almost unique bastion tower and bottle dungeon, in the service area underneath the shops; this can be visited by a spiral stair from the shopping area. The centre also preserved the flavour of the burgh's old crafts and merchants with an illustrative frieze and display of banners in the main concourse. And, perhaps more importantly, many of the older shops facing Murray Place were retained so that the centre is barely noticeable except from the rear where the bypass road lies.

By the 1950s many local and national stores, still popular today, were already established in Stirling. In 1959 you could buy a two-piece man's suit at Henderson's in Friars Street for about £19. A pair of nylons ('Moonbeams ultra-fine for glamour') cost 7s 11d at Gavin's. Axminster carpets were from £1 11s 6d a yard at Behar, while a three-piece lounge suite at Grant's might cost only £50. You could buy an Austin A40 car at Menzies Motors for £676 7s, while second-hand cars at Morrisons ranged from around £270 to £550. A pram at Graham and Morton's cost about £18, while a washing machine (with electric wringer) cost 59 guineas (that's £61 19s) at Clydesdale's. A permanent wave (whole head) at Green's the hairdresser cost £2 5s. Half a pound of Bluebell margarine cost 10½d at the Co-op, while a pound of Cheddar cheese cost 3s 4d at William Low. Finally, the *Stirling Observer* (from whose adverts these prices were obtained) cost 3d.

As the pattern of settlement changed to one of inner-town shopping and suburban housing, the town evolved to keep pace. New primary schools opened at Raploch, Cornton, Bannockburn and elsewhere to cater for new housing areas. Meanwhile two older town-centre schools closed. These were the Territorial School at the foot of Upper Bridge Street (which became the Cowane Centre), and the Craigs School—closed instead of Allan's School in Spittal Street following a campaign by parents in the King's Park area. New secondary schools also opened. By the 1960s Stirling had a population of over 27,000 and yet (with the exception of St Modan's High School, attended by Roman Catholic pupils from a wide local area), the High School was the only 'senior secondary' school; a 'junior secondary' school at Riverside catered for less academic pupils, but both were over-full.

In 1962 a new Stirling High School was built on a greenfield site at Torbrex. On 25th April that year there occurred the 'long march' when all the High School classes, escorted by their teachers, walked through the town from Spittal Street to their new school and a new era. The school was officially opened on 14th June 1962. This was followed by the nationwide introduction of 'comprehensive' education in 1971, a governmental decision which involved the merging of senior and junior secondaries into mixed-ability schools. As a result Riverside became a primary school, and the former junior secondary was replaced in August 1971 by Wallace High School, built on a greenfield site at Causewayhead. This school was officially opened on 4th March 1972.

These changes caused some stir in the town, but it was nothing compared to the impact of Stirling University, which opened in September 1967 on the Airthrey estate—now widely accepted as the most beautiful campus in Britain. Lord Robbins was the first Chancellor, while the first Principal (who actually had day-to-day dealings with staff and students) was Tom Cottrell. The arrival of the first 160 students locally provoked some anxiety, especially in quiet, leafy, rather faded-old-spa, Bridge of Allan. But fears of a 'hippy' invasion, with all its imagined horrors of drinks and drugs and orgies, were dispelled by the first students, who did little more than rattle collecting tins at people during their annual charities' Rag Week.

Slowly a fair amount of goodwill developed between Stirling and its university population, but at least once this was seriously tested. In 1972 the Queen was regrettably insulted by a few students while on a visit to the campus; this received widespread publicity and seriously damaged the university's image and the goodwill of sponsors. The impression today is that this was the work of the original students—that from the outset Stirling was bedevilled by unruly louts. In fact the original batch of students graduated in 1971 and were long gone by 1972.

The original Pathfoot building was soon augmented by student residences, followed by the Cottrell Building and MacRobert Arts Centre, begun in 1968 and opened in phases, which included teaching blocks, a theatre, art gallery, restaurant, library and shopping complex. Since then people from all around Stirling have mixed at many functions with students from all around the world. Many students come from Arab, African and far-Eastern countries but Stirling has become used to their presence. As with the Irish, the Italians or the Poles, the town has absorbed the change.

If the coming of the university caused change to the town, a more drastic change came in 1975 when 'regionalisation' began. This involved the abolition of Scotland's old counties and burghs, and the creation of regions and districts. As a result the police burgh of Bridge of Allan and the royal burgh of Stirling both disappeared into Stirling District, an area stretching from Bannockburn to Loch Lomond. With their passing went centuries of history—Stirling's burgh charters, generations of provosts and town councils, centuries of struggle to retain the burgh's lands and privileges, generations of delegates to the Convention of Royal Burghs, over eight hundred years of pride in a *town*—something definite, surrounded by a wall and populated by folk who all knew each other and shared the same heritage. Somehow, 'Stirling District' and, even worse, 'Central Region', does not have the same attraction.

The new Central Region headquarters were established at Viewforth in Stirling, previously the County Buildings. Viewforth was originally acquired during the 1880s, and was extended progressively in 1927, 1937 and 1962. Eventually the County Council decided to demolish most of this and build a completely new headquarters in the grounds of Viewforth and neighbouring Langgarth. The new Viewforth building opened on Tuesday 29th February 1972—better designed and built than Falkirk's new burgh buildings, so that when regionalisation was introduced in 1974–5, Stirling was favoured as Central Region's capital. But for the quality of its administrative offices, Stirling might not have been an automatic choice.

The conversion from county and town councils to regional and district administrations was phased over one year, ending on 15th May 1975—next morning was the first day of the new system. As a result, outgoing local councils had a chance to implement last-minute decisions before they disappeared for ever. The Thistle Centre's foundation stone was laid by Provost Robert McIntyre on 2nd May 1975, just two weeks before the council which he headed was ended. Another example was the Provost Pool, opened at last in 1974.

The new District Council, very Labour in its political outlook, took a different view of local life. One of its first acts was to abolish

Stirling has been welcoming royalty for many centuries. Happy faces at Annfield during the Queen's visit in 1977.
Photo: Central Region Archives Department.

Queen Elizabeth and Prince Philip visited Stirling in 1977 and were welcomed by enthusiastic crowds at Annfield Park, the home of Stirling Albion F.C.
Photo: Central Region Archives Department.

the ancient office of Provost and to replace it with that of Convener—sacrilege to many folk, but actually just as Scottish, and a title often used in old Stirling, provided it is spelled conven*er*. Even the Provost Pool was renamed a 'leisure centre', though some folk still call it by the old 'Provost' name. Thereafter the District and Regional Councils went on to develop many more local amenities, neglected or never provided by the old town council. More leisure and community centres sprang up at Bridge of Allan, Causewayhead, St Ninians and elsewhere. Children's creches were provided to help shoppers. The Smith Museum, closed by dampness in 1974, partially re-opened with help from local authority funding in 1977 and has gone on from strength to strength. A host of leisure interests, ranging from a local youth orchestra and choir to writers' workshops and badminton classes, were started at centres all over the area. Council housing was improved and updated with double glazing or loft insulation. It was a tremendous programme of renewal.

The cost was high—by the 1980s Stirling District Council was almost perpetually at loggerheads with the Conservative government over the size of its local rates. The District was even 'punished' for imposing what the government thought were excessive rates increases by having its rates support grant 'clawed back' or reduced by central government. As a result, local spending was cut back, with effects on everything from local education to provision for old folk. This was exacerbated by a long-running feud between local Conservative MP Michael Forsyth and the Labour-controlled District Council (which hardly endeared itself to the government by declaring itself a 'nuclear-free zone' in 1982 and supporting the miners' strike of 1984, for example). In 1983 local constituency boundaries were changed, as a result of which Stirling area's tendency to vote traditionally Liberal or Labour was counterbalanced by a strongly Conservative farming hinterland. For only the second time in over 150 years, Stirling's constituency returned a Conservative member of parliament in 1983; indeed Mr Forsyth won again in 1987, increasing his majority while the overall Conservative representation in Scotland fell to just ten MPs out of seventy-one. Nevertheless, continuous dispute between a hardline Conservative MP and a committed Socialist local authority was regrettable.

In 1963 the Argyll and Sutherland Highlanders gave up Stirling

Castle as their barracks and went to a new training base at Bridge of Don. The regimental headquarters remained, with some administrative offices and the magnificent regimental museum, but in day-to-day practice the Castle was abandoned. This included the Argyll Lodging, previously used as a military hospital, and various other buildings at the top of the town. Immediately, new opportunities opened for improved tourism at the Castle, and overnight Stirling's fortunes rose. Except for Edinburgh, no other fortress in Scotland is so dramatic or steeped in history as Stirling Castle.

The redevelopment of Stirling Castle took time. In being adapted for nineteenth century military use, the Castle was necessarily mutilated. The Great Hall was converted to a four-storey barrack block and the medieval windows, fireplaces and stairways were ripped out. The Palace Block was stripped bare, the Stirling Heads were discarded and the royal chambers were converted to mess rooms and officers' quarters. So the Castle was in a sorry state when returned to civilian use. Restoration work by the Scottish Development Department began in 1964 and at time of writing is still going on, but with every year the old castle has increasingly re-emerged and visitors have come in ever greater numbers. Stirling Castle is now the second-most-visited ancient monument in Scotland.

One worry was that tourists would visit only the Castle, arriving by bus or car at the esplanade and leaving again with little impact on the town. During the 1980s the District Council countered this with a series of imaginative ideas, including 'medieval markets' in Broad Street, complete with singers, jugglers, stalls selling wares, and local craftsmen such as coopers and stonemasons at work. There were also open-topped bus tours to local historic places including the field of Bannockburn and the Wallace Monument. Nowadays minibuses are also provided to ferry people from the spruced-up railway station to the Castle, and on the way visitors have a chance to meet famous characters from Stirling's history—locals dressed as Mary Queen of Scots, Damian the flying monk, Tommy Chalmers the Bellman, Baird and Hardie, Agnes the girl who had John Cowane's child, John Knox at the Holy Rude church, and so on.

These are colourful ploys to entertain local visitors and help them enjoy the burgh as much as the castle. Much more controversial, however, have been the District Council's more grandiose

Summer visitors to Stirling may now meet characters from the burgh's colourful past, such as these standing outside the Guildhall: left to right, the judge who sentenced Allan Mair to Stirling's last public hanging in 1843, John Cowane the great merchant who died in 1633, Jenny McBain and her husband, a stonemason working on the construction of Mar's Wark in 1570, and John Knox pointing at the Holy Rude kirk where he brought the Reformation to Stirling in 1559 and attended the Protestant coronation of King James VI in 1567.

schemes to 'develop' the Castle and old burgh area. During the early 1980s, for example, 'Futureworld' was launched. This was a plan to revive the top of the town by encouraging craft enterprises and pavement cafes in Broad Street, developing the potential of underused buildings like the Military Prison and the Tolbooth and—far more controversially—to construct plastic tunnels into the Castle area, with a walkway to a plastic-domed interpretation centre on the Gowan Hill. Outrage spread, and the most discordant parts of the plan were dropped. Then followed an alternative scheme to construct funicular railways up the castle rock from a car park and terminus in the Haining, close to the King's Knot. Outrage greeted this plan too, and at time of writing the latest idea is to provide fleets of buses to shuttle visitors from an interpretation centre at Riverside up through the town to the Castle. This plan

Stirling County rugby club have climbed from the seventh to the first national league and now draw larger crowds than Stirling Albion football club. Here they score against mighty Hawick in a match which 'county' won by 16–15 at Bridgehaugh.
Photo: Whyler Photos for the Stirling Observer.

may also founder, but Stirling is at least trying to exploit the history which it has inherited from past generations.

Today the town of Stirling is very different from the burgh of 1950. Widespread car ownership has transformed daily life; 'mystery' bus trips (invariably to Crieff) have declined; band concerts in the King's Park have disappeared; only one cinema has survived competition from television; Sunday afternoon walks to Cambuskenneth or Cambusbarron have dwindled; shopping has spread from the town centre to more peripheral superstores like Tesco and Safeway where almost anything can be bought under one roof; industries have changed from the textile mills and agricultural firms of the past to electronics and service industries today.

Leisure interests have also changed. Several famous international sportsmen such as Billy Bremner (football), Willie Carson (horse-racing) and Kenny Logan (rugby) have emerged from Stirling, for example. In 1945 Stirling Albion FC was born from the remains of King's Park FC (whose ground was bombed). For a time

Yet another royal visit. Watched by Robert the Bruce, Prince Edward chats at the Castle esplanade to local children in October 1989 and thereby maintains a tradition of royalty at Stirling going back for over a thousand years.
Photo: Whyler Photos for the Stirling Observer.

'the Albion' see-sawed between the First and Second Divisions (for which it was nicknamed the yo-yo team), enjoying a record attendance at Annfield Park of 26,410 in a 1959 cup-tie against Celtic. Today the club plays at its new Forthbank Stadium on the Springkerse outskirts of town, but crowds are smaller and don't often exceed 1000. However, Stirling County Rugby Football Club does attract good crowds; in 1989 the team won promotion to the national first division and in 1994–5 went on to win the first division championship, to scenes of great celebration at its Bridgehaugh ground. 'County' are now one of the established top clubs in Scottish rugby, with several internationalists in the team.

Fortunately, rugby and football have not crowded out other interests. Cricket, tennis, golf, skating, swimming, cycling, gymnastics, table-tennis and curling still thrive along with newer arrivals such as squash, archery and pony-trotting (which attracts enthusiasts to its special stadium at Corbiewood, near Bannockburn). The MacRobert Theatre at the university continues to offer a wide choice of cultural events, from orchestral concerts to drama, films and jazz (although the only performances certain to have week-long full houses are the local operatic club's musicals, and the local Scouts and Guide 'Gang Shows'!) Sport and recreation in the town have never thrived so much as now, in these days of more leisure time and better incomes.

The future does not look so bad. Stirling still has the feel of a small town, in a beautiful setting, comparatively unspoiled, and surely more prosperous than it ever was before. Common sense usually restrains excessive change, and the town is still an enjoyable place in which to live and work. If the ghosts of Stirling past are watching, it is, we hope, with a smile of approval.

Further Reading

This list does not include books of a general nature which give only short or passing references to Stirling, e.g., biographies of royalty, works on Scottish castles or religious buildings, descriptions of Scottish burgh life, accounts of travel in Scotland, collections of letters etc. Other than this work, there is no broad history of the burgh of Stirling; the nearest is perhaps Duncan McNaughton's *A History of Old Stirling* (1980), but it is very patchy. Many of the titles listed here are now out of print and can only be obtained through libraries or at the Central Region Archives Department. Others on this list are little more than booklets and pamphlets, sometimes very informative and useful but rather short.

General Area

History of Stirlingshire (2 vols): William Nimmo, 3rd edn, 1880

A History of Stirling: author anonymous, published by C. Randall, 1812

The Stirling Region: Edited by Duncan Timms, published by the British Association for a conference at Stirling University in 1974

Stirlingshire: An Inventory of the Ancient Monuments (2 vols): Royal Commission on the Ancient and Historical Monuments of Scotland, 1964

Stirling and the Trossachs: an architectural guide by Charles McKean, 1985

Statistical Account of Scotland vol 9: Dunbartonshire, Stirlingshire and Clackmannanshire (includes parishes of Stirling, St Ninians, Logie etc.), 1793

New Statistical Account of Scotland, vol 8: Dumbarton, Stirling and Clackmannan, 1845

Central Scotland: land – wildlife – people: various authors and editors, published by the Forth Naturalist and Historian, 1993

Transactions: Stirling Natural History and Archaeological Society, 1878–1939

Education in Stirlingshire from the Reformation to the Act of 1872: Andrew Bain, published by the University of London Press, 1965

Historical Sources for Central Scotland series: general editor B.J. Elliott and published by Central Regional Council in cooperation with Stirling University.

No 1: *World War One:* Susan Hobbs and Lynda Wright, 1977
No 2: *The Coal Industry (17th–20th centuries):* Lynda Wright, 1978
No 3: *World War Two:* Susan Hobbs, 1979
No 4: *Transport (18th–20th centuries):* Lynda Wright, 1980
No 5: *Law, Crime and Punishment:* Lynda Blair, 1982
No 6: *Housing, Health and Welfare:* Susan Hobbs, 1982

Stirling Castle and Local Battles

Stirling Castle: Its Place in Scottish History: Eric Stair-Kerr, 2nd edn. 1928

Stirling Castle: Official guide, HMSO 3rd edn. 1978

Stirling Castle: a popular guide by HMSO 1983

Tales of Stirling Castle and the Battle of Bannockburn: Rennie McOwan, published by Lang Syne (no date)

The Stirling Heads: HMSO 1975

Baptism of Prince Henry 1594: first printed 1809, revised by Sir Walter Scott, and reprinted by Bob McCutcheon and Stirling District Council, 1984

William Wallace: Andrew Fisher (chapter on the Battle of Stirling Bridge), published by John Donald, 1986

The Battlefields Around Stirling: John E Shearer, 1913

The Battle of Bannockburn: W. Mackay Mackenzie, 1913, republished by the Strong Oak Press, 1989

Bannockburn: booklet by the National Trust for Scotland, 1987 (and which contains a further specialised reading list)

Rob Roy MacGregor: Hist Life and Times: WH Murray, (chapter on the Battle of Sheriffmuir) republished by Canongate, 1993

The Jacobites in Stirlingshire: Lewis Lawson, 1971

Argyll and Sutherland Highlanders: William McElwee, published by Osprey (Men-at-Arms series), 1972 and reprinted three times to 1988

Stirling's Burgh History

Historic Stirling: The Archaeological Implications of Development: Robert Gourlay and Anne Turner. Published by the University of Glasgow for the Scottish Burgh Survey, 1978

Stirling: Historical and Descriptive: R.S. Shearer, 1897

A History of Old Stirling: Duncan McNaughton, published by C.R.C. Educational Resources Unit, 1980

Old Stirling: a Guide to the Castle and Town: David Hayes, 1973

The Making of Modern Stirling: Tom Lannon, published by Forth Naturalist and Historian, 1983

Stirling's Road to Mass Culture: Tom Lannon (no date)

Scottish Urban History: G. Gordon and B. Dicks (Chapter 3, by R.C. Fox, deals with Stirling 1550–1700), published Aberdeen 1983

Scottish Historical Review LVII I: contains a paper by F. McKichan on Stirling's urban growth 1780–1880

The Stirling Merchant Guild and the Life of John Cowane: David B. Morris, 1919

The Guildry of Stirling: Harold Whitbread, 1966

Stirling Observer 1836–1936: Centenary number

Stirling Observer 150 years on: Bob McCutcheon, 1986

Old Faces, Old Places, and Old Stories of Stirling (2 vols): W. Drysdale, 1898 and 1899

Stirling and the Trossachs: Life in Days Gone By: Lang Syne publishers, 1975

Pictures from the Past: Bob McCutcheon, 1984

The Tramways of Stirling: Alan W. Brotchie, 1976

Five Bob a Week: Stirling Women's Work 1900–1950: Edited by Jayne Stephenson and produced by the Stirling Women's Oral History Project, 1988

Duncan and Jamieson's Directory 1868–69: reprinted by Stirling District Libraries, 1988

Stirling Races: Gillian Sloan, published as a Community Heritage Booklet, 1986

Worthies: Curious Characters of Old Stirling: G. Craig Robertson, published as a Community Heritage Booklet, 1987

Singular Occurrences: Anecdotes from the Stirling Observers: a Community Heritage Booklet, 1987

Ballengeich to Barras Yett: the Origins of Stirling Street Names: Michael J. Melville, published as a Community Heritage Booklet, 1987

Stirling Old Town: a heritage walk guide booklet, 1989

Queen Victoria's Visit to Stirling 1842: extract from *Memorial of the Royal Progress in Scotland* by Sir Thomas Dick Lauder published in 1843 and reprinted by Bob McCutcheon, 1983

Stirling Presbytery Records 1581–1587: edited by James Kirk Ph.D., published by the Scottish Record Society, 1981

Stirling Burgess List 1600–1699: John Harrison, published by the Central Scotland Family History Society, 1991

Stirling Burgess List 1700–1799: edited by J Lockhart Whiteford, published by the Central Scotland Family History Society, 1992

Early Gravestones in Holy Rude Kirkyard, Stirling: John Harrison, offprint published in booklet form by the Forth Naturalist and Historian, no date

Allan Mair, the last person to be executed in Stirling: Craig Mair, offprint published in booklet form by the Forth Naturalist and Historian, 1994

Old Stirling Clockmakers: Charles Allan, published by the author 1990

Jeely Pieces and Clootie Dumplings: Stirling Childhoods in the 1920s and 30s: Jayne Stephenson, published by Stirling District Libraries, 1992

The Home Front: Stirling 1939–1945: Jayne Stephenson, published by Stirling District Libraries, 1991

Pictures from the Past – Auld Stirling: Bob McCutcheon, 1990

Buildings in the Burgh

Old Stirling: Ronald Cant and Ian Lindsay, 1948

Auld Biggins of Stirling: W. Drysdale, 1904

The Old Ludgings of Stirling: J.S. Fleming, 1897

Old Nooks of Stirling: J.S. Fleming, 1898, reprinted 1974

Ancient Castles and Mansions of the Stirling Nobility: J.S. Fleming, 1902

Landmarks of Old Stirling: J. Ronald, 1899

The Earl of Mar's Lodging: J. Ronald, 1895

The Story of the Argyle Lodging: J. Ronald, 1906

Kings Park: R. Aitken, C. Cunningham and R. McCutcheon, 1984

The Homesteads: Stirling's Garden Suburb: R. Aitken, C. Cunningham and R. McCutcheon, 1984

The Parish Church of Stirling: David B. Morris, 1911

The Church of the Holy Rude, Stirling: History and Guide Book: W. Douglas Simpson, published by the Society of Friends of the Church of the Holy Rude, 1967

Ebenezer Erskine, the Secession of 1733, and the Churches of Stirling: Kenneth B. Scott, published by Viewfield Church, 1983

A Kirk and a College in the Craigs of Stirling: D.D. Ormond, 1897

Cambuskenneth Abbey: Leaflet guide by Stewart Cruden, HMSO, 1978

History of the High School of Stirling: A.F. Hutchison, 1904

Old Boys: Their Stories of the High School of Stirling: J.L. Graham, 1900

From Castle Rock to Torbrex: Essays on the High School of Stirling: Jessie M. Thomson and Charles Strachan, 1962

The Guildry of Stirling: The Guildry Window 1993: published by the Stirling Guildry 1993

Holy Trinity Episcopal Church, Stirling – 1878–1978: Miss C E Saunders, 1978

Neighbouring Communities

Stirling's 'Neebour' Villages: Bob McCutcheon, 1985

A Week at Bridge of Allan: Charles Roger, 1851 and 1852, reprinted by Heritage Press, 1980

Bridge of Allan: the Rise of a Village: Ella Maclean, 1971

By Allan Water: Katherine Steuart (no date)

R.L. Stevenson and the Bridge of Allan: J.A. MacCulloch, 1927

Airthrey and Bridge of Allan: a guided walk: booklet published by the *Forth Naturalist and Historian*, 1986

Bridge of Allan in Old Photographs: J. Malcolm Allan, published jointly by the Dr W.H. Welsh Educational and Historical Trust and Stirling District Libraries 1989

Bridge of Allan's Activities in the Great War 1914–1919: John J. McKay, 1925

Cowie: A Mining Village: Jayne Stephenson, published as a Community Heritage Booklet, 1986

Bygone Days in Cambusbarron: P.J. Paterson, published by Cambusbarron Community Council, 1981

Bridge of Allan: a heritage of music and its Museum Hall: Gavin Millar and George McVicar, offprint published in booklet form by the Forth Naturalist and Historian, 1994

Lecropt Kirk and Parish 1827–1977: J Graeme B Young, published by the church 1977

The Wilson Mills of Bannockburn: J R Ritchie, published by Bannockburn Heritage Group, 1990

The Wilson Letters: Yarns from a Bannockburn Weaving Firm: J R Ritchie, published by Bannockburn Heritage Group, 1991

Cowie, Fallin and Plean in Old Photographs: published by Stirling District Libraries, 1990

Fallin: Tales from a Mining Village: Hugh G Kerr, published by Stirling District Libraries, 1991

Polmaise 3 & 4 Mining Fatalities: Archie Bone, 1994

Polmaise: The Fight for a Pit: John McCormack, published by Index Books, 1989

For Younger Readers

A Young Person's Guide to Stirling Castle: Celine Castelino, published by the National Trust for Scotland, 1985

A Young Person's Guide to Bannockburn: Jan Keen, published by the National Trust for Scotland (1980s but no date)

John of Bannockburn: G Docherty, I Gould and E Melvin, published by John Murray (People of the Past series), 1984

John Cowan—Scottish Burgess: Norman Nichol, published by Oliver and Boyd (Flashbacks series), 1973

Stirling Old Town: a Heritage Walk: A resource book/pack produced by the Smith Art Gallery Education Service and C.R.C. Education Department, 1989

Documentary Sources

The Central Region Archives Department houses innumerable documentary sources concerning Stirling. These could not possibly all be listed here, but they range widely from the minute books of old craft guilds, the minutes and accounts of Cowane's Hospital, Census returns from 1851 onwards, and the Holy Rude kirk session records, to a complete run of past copies of the *Stirling Observer* newspaper. A serious reader's first step would probably be to the burgh records, however, which span from around 1550 onwards. During the 1880s some were extracted, printed and indexed;

1. Charters and Documents Relating to the Royal Burgh of Stirling, 1124–1705
2. Extracts from the Records of the Royal Burgh of Stirling, 1519–1666
3. Extracts from the Records of the Royal Burgh of Stirling, 1667–1752
4. Extracts from the Records of the Stirling Merchant Guild, 1592–1846.

In addition to the bulk of records held by the regional archive, the Scottish Records Office in Edinburgh contains another important collection of documents. This includes valuation rolls, heritor records, Sheriff Court minute books (1633–1957), local railway records, various police, health, tax, banking and other records, local turnpike trust papers and a large assortment of local maps and plans.

Stirling's Central Library holds complete runs of the *Stirling Journal* newspaper. A three- volume index to the *Stirling Journal* has also been produced, covering 1820–1869, 1870–1919, and 1920–1970.

Alan Godfrey's series of 1890s Ordnance Survey Maps, now reprinted and available in many shops, includes Stirling & District (at six inches to the mile), plus larger scale sheets covering Stirling, Stirling North, St Ninians, Bannockburn, Bridge of Allan, Dunblane East, Dunblane West, Alva, Menstrie & Tullibody, etc.

Index